THE WESTERN FRONTIER LIBRARY

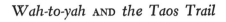

Wah-to-yah AND *the Taos Trail*

WAH-TO-YAH
AND
THE TAOS TRAIL

OR PRAIRIE TRAVEL AND SCALP DANCES, WITH A

LOOK AT LOS RANCHEROS FROM MULEBACK AND

THE ROCKY MOUNTAIN CAMPFIRE

BY LEWIS H. GARRARD

WITH AN INTRODUCTION BY A. B. GUTHRIE, JR.

UNIVERSITY OF OKLAHOMA PRESS
NORMAN

RedRiver books

Library of Congress Catalog Card Number: 55-9623

ISBN: 0–8061–1016–3

Wah-to-Yah and the Taos Trail is Volume 5 in The Western Frontier Library.

New edition copyright © 1955 by the University of Oklahoma Press, Norman, Publishing Division of the University. All rights reserved. Manufactured in the U.S.A.

13   14   15   16   17   18   19   20   21   22   23   24

CONTENTS

MAP

INTRODUCTION
BY A. B. GUTHRIE, JR.

T HE FIRST if not the sole service of an introduction to this volume is to set the immediate experience against the background that the author tended to ignore, either out of absorption with affairs at hand or on the assumption of a general acquaintance with the larger scene. For the rest, the book speaks so well for itself that only a little in the way of examination, comparison, and additional information about the author seems appropriate. To praise it is only to second the reader's sentiments. Any more than a few words of recapitulation appear gratuitous, and so pale by comparison with the original as to be tedious.

Hector Lewis Garrard (alias Lewis H. Garrard) ventured west, then, at the time of the Mexican War, which accounts among other things for his numerous meetings with details of the military. It was the time, too, or shortly was to be, of a brief but bloody uprising at and near Taos, New Mexico, where Pueblo Indians and Mexicans in revolt at American rule killed twenty people, including Charles Bent, New Mexican governor by appointment. A little later Fort Mann came into process of being as a military post of repair near where the trail crossed the Arkansas River. These items of fact, not textually explicit, need expression to save most of us some sense of bewilderment.

Garrard, a Cincinnatian, was just seventeen when he started for St. Louis and the great western regions beyond. Presumably the lack of a stout constitution, about which he says virtually nothing, was a factor in his parents' decision to let him go. From St. Louis he traveled by water and land to Westport Landing, since swallowed up by Kansas City, and joined one of the caravans that made ready there for the long journeys to the wild trading and trapping country penetrated by the Santa Fé and Oregon trails. His luck was good: the leader of the expedition happened to be the experienced and well-known frontiersman, Céran St. Vrain, member of the trading firm of Bent and St. Vrain, which wasn't noted for sending out ill-equipped trains, and the destination naturally was famous Bent's Fort, located on an alternate branch of the Santa Fé Trail in the southeastern part of present-day Colorado.

For a couple of months he lived at the fort and, as companion to venturesome traders, in the lodges of the Cheyenne Indians, apparently enjoying both as completely as a man can enjoy any life. But with the arrival of 1847 came the news of the killings at Taos. Garrard joined a little company of volunteers recruited by William Bent, chief of the fort and brother of the slain governor, and set out for the scene, committed to "kill and scalp every Mexican to be found . . . ." Distance and weather delayed their arrival until after the end of hostilities, but there remained for their eyes and ears the procedures of the frontier court and the hangings of the rebels brought to bar.

Back at Bent's Fort in the spring Garrard concluded regretfully that he had had enough of frontier life and so took the opportunity to travel east with a military train.

His conclusion was short-lived. He got as far as Fort Mann and there enlisted in the scanty garrison. The reason? He'd never been in an Indian fight and wanted that experience and its excitement. He stayed one dangerous month and then resumed the journey east, arriving at Fort Leavenworth a few weeks afterwards.

In the next few years, between fits of "abominable chills and fever," he filled in "the scanty pencilings" of his ten months in the West. His book came out in 1850.

Not much remains to be said of the man, in contrast to what may be said of his work. Though he wrote a couple of volumes later, neither attained any renown. The years after his great adventure were years of comparative obscurity no matter if of local importance. He returned to Cincinnati. He studied medicine and maybe law. He ventured into the interior Northwest, into Minnesota, and was one of the early settlers and one of the namers of the small town of Frontenac. He moved to Lake City. At one place or the other he was county supervisor, township chairman, state representative, bank founder, and mayor. He moved back to Cincinnati. At fifty-eight he was dead. A full enough life, busy, responsible, important parochially. It is his book, his first book, that makes it anti-climax.

Other narratives inevitably are brought to mind by this one. Gregg's *Commerce of the Prairies* and Chittenden's *History of the American Fur Trade of the Far West* are two, though both are more extensive and ambitious. George Frederick Ruxton is closer with his *Adventures in Mexico and the Rocky Mountains* and *Life in the Far West*. But first in thought come Francis Parkman and *The Oregon Trail*, not so much through similarity of work as coincidence of circumstance. Both Parkman and Garrard were young men in 1846, Parkman being about five years

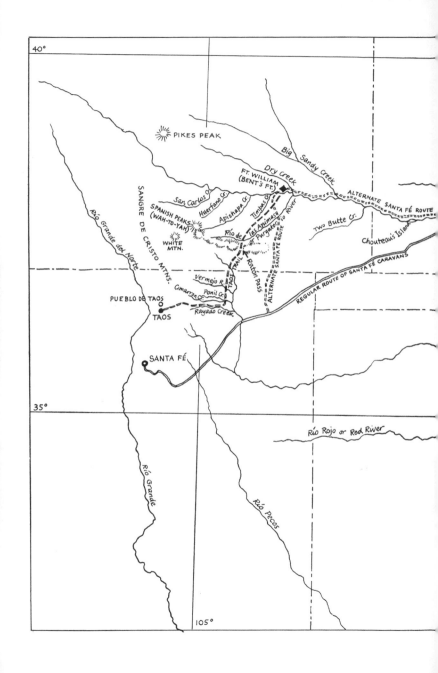

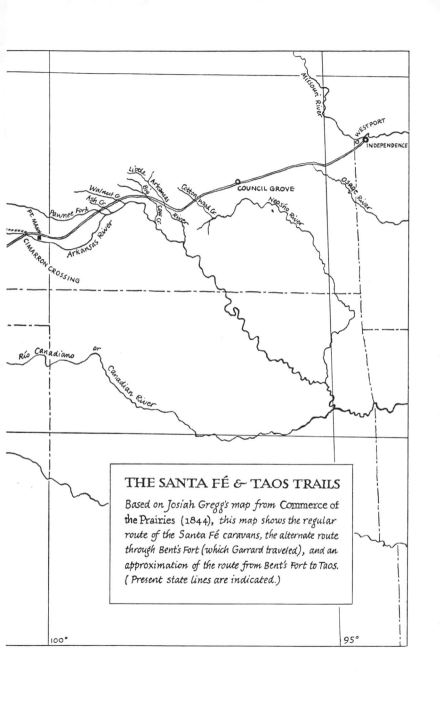

THE SANTA FÉ & TAOS TRAILS

Based on Josiah Gregg's map from Commerce of the Prairies (1844), this map shows the regular route of the Santa Fé caravans, the alternate route through Bent's Fort (which Garrard traveled), and an approximation of the route from Bent's Fort to Taos. (Present state lines are indicated.)

the senior. Both traveled west that season, one along the Oregon Trail to Fort Laramie and the Sioux, the other along the Santa Fé to Bent's Fort and the Cheyennes. Both were less than rugged physically. Both were brave, enduring, curious, observant. Both took notes, and both wrote books.

Here end the parallels, except for one. Garrard's book got a good reception and fell from sight, not to be rescued for three-quarters of a century and then in an emasculated edition. Parkman's got a good reception, was often reprinted, and won recognition as a classic.

It's difficult, or impossible, to understand their different fortunes. Allow for the fact that Parkman followed with other and noteworthy books and so enhanced the reputation of his first. Credit *The Oregon Trail* with every rightful excellence. Neither later career nor admitted excellence explains the contrast. *Wah-to-yah and the Taos Trail* bears comparison with Parkman's masterpiece and in some ways is the better—the fresher, the more revealing, the more engaging, the less labored. It is remindful of Parkman's rather recently published notes, which had on-the-spot bits of vigor and spark and naturalness that the author was too "literary" to let stand when he returned to his study.

A further reason for Garrard's points of superiority suggests itself. He not only liked the rude and unfettered life of the frontier; he liked his companions, the traders, the mountain men, the bucks and squaws and papooses. Occasionally, as if in duty bound, he made contrasts between outpost and settlement, between red life and white, and deplored the barbarity and ignorance of the Indian, but hardly had he set down such sentiments than he hurried on to report good hours with the Cheyennes, good tales from the mountain men, good times all around while the cup or the pipe passed and a stew fretted over the fire. One feels that in criticism he was bowing to convention or perhaps reminding himself of rightnesses taught earlier and now grown unconscionably dim. In any case he liked people. Parkman didn't, save precious few. To his judgments he brought the attitudes of mind associated with Boston. No wonder, then, that one book seems warmer and closer to life.

Another author, traveling the mountains and plains in that 1846–47 season, needs additional mention, if here only because he and Garrard preserved for today the affected, effective, peculiar speech of the fur hunter. That man was Ruxton, whom Garrard met in his travels. But for the two, both of whom had ears and appetites for the lingo, we would have lost or thought altogether preposterous such habits of tongue as:

"Well, hos! I'll dock off buffler, and then if thar's any meat that 'runs' that can take the shine outen 'dog,' you can slide."

Or:

"Hatch, old hos! Hyar's the coon as would like to hear tell of the time you seed the old gentleman. You's the one as savvys all 'bout them diggin's."

The quotations can be translated:

"Well, friend, I'll except buffalo, and then if there's any meat afoot that surpasses dog, you're crazy."

"Hatch, old boy, I'd like to hear of the time you saw the devil. You understand all about his place."

But what of this book, really? What gives it quality? What sets it apart and above? Why has it been rediscovered, and reprinted now for the third time?

Some of the answers have been suggested or given, but more as effects or extensions or incidental collaterals of the prime element. Others, though of the same kind, demand at least mention. Garrard's story of the trials and hangings at Taos is the only eyewitness account. To the fund of knowledge about mountain men, not by any means rich, he deposited sums special to some of the greatest—Céran St. Vrain, William Bent, Lucien B. Maxwell, Kit Carson, Jim Beckwourth, John L. Hatcher. Lonely men out of loneliness tend to become great tall-story tellers, and nowhere is one likely to find more convincing and humorous evidence than in Garrard's version of Hatcher's report of his visit to hell. It is a little aside but remarkable nevertheless that a narrative like this one should have come from a teen-ager, as it is aside but remarkable, too, that no writing of consequence was done by him afterwards. To the point is the over-all fact that in these pages, to the satisfaction of the general reader and the delight of the researcher, is the genuine article—the Indian, the trader, the mountain man, their dress and behavior and speech and the country and climate they lived in.

But while values like these help explain the rank of the book, what explains them? In a kernel it is that Garrard saw with a fresh eye and wrote with a free and innocent confidence that what interested him would interest others. By some happy accident he possessed at seventeen the combination of eye and spirit that recovers life in words.

The end of his own introduction is end enough now. Mark it well! After observing, quaintly to present-day ears, that some might think his book gross and the quotations uncalled for, he added:

"I have naught set down in malice, and it is no more my prerogative to exclude than to add."

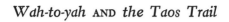

Wah-to-yah AND *the Taos Trail*

INTRODUCTORY

IN OFFERING this little volume to the public, I must, in self-justice, be briefly introduced, so that the obliging peruser, with all the facts before him, may extend a benevolent forbearance, and restrain too severe a criticism on this, my first essay.

In February, 1846, being then in my seventeenth year, I tossed away schoolbooks, and glided down the Mississippi River, and along the Mexican Gulf, to Texas; and, shortly after, back to the Louisiana coast, where I stayed until the middle of May, visiting friends, riding horses, and shooting alligators, duck, and rail, from the bow of a long canoe in the cypress swamps.

Returning home, the glowing pages of Frémont's tour to the Rocky Mountains in 1842–43 were so alluring to my fancy that my parents were persuaded to let me go westward; and they, furnishing letters of credit, cash, a pocket Bible, and rifle, with a few calico shirts, started me to St. Louis, on a low-water steamer, in the hot month of July. The miseries of running "hard aground" on sandbars in the sweltering sun; a surfeit of sleep, and "James's last," with an occasional peep at the leaves of my Testament, were the most striking incidents until reaching the narrow St. Louis wharf—where, amid the din of importunate hotel attachés, I passed my baggage into safe hands, and, threading the busy throng, entered my name on the Planters' House books.

Through the kindness of Colonel A. B. Chambers, of the *Missouri Republican*, I was made acquainted with the firm of Pierre Chouteau, Jr., & Co., to whose numerous forts in the Indian Territory I was given a letter of recommendation. Mr. Kenneth McKenzie, one of the first traders with the Blackfeet Indians, treated me and my many queries with even more lenity than I could reasonably expect. Mr. St. Vrain, of the firm of Bent, St. Vrain & Co., Indian and Mexican traders, was at the Planters' and soon to start for the Rocky Mountains and Santa Fé; on his kindly consenting to accept me in his mess, Colonel Chambers furnished additional letters.

My elder brothers wished me to note the occurring events for their gratification. It was done, though in a desultory style. Abominable chills and fever greeted my return to civilization, and it was through the intervals of study that the scanty pencilings have thus been augmented —and not until the greater portion was written had I the hardihood to think of publishing. Then, the request of friends, coupled with the bidding of a pardonable vanity, produced them in the present form.

I have thought proper to so entitle the work, as my wanderings were in sight of the Spanish Peaks and along the Taos Trail. The accent, in pronouncing *Wah-to-yah*, is on the second syllable. *Taos* is pronounced *Touse*, as in *house*—the Spanish Mexican accent, however, being prolonged on the word, as *Ta-ouse*.

Should any account be deemed either meager or fulsome, I cheerfully apologise with the single remonstrance —it has at least the merit of truthfulness. Imagination plays but a very minor part, and in no instance as to give an improper conception of scene, time, or manner. An accusation of grossness may be raised, and that the characters use seemingly uncalled-for expressions. I have naught set down in malice, and it is no more my prerogative to exclude than to add.

CHAPTER I

THE START

Hᴀᴠɪɴɢ ᴍᴀᴅᴇ all necessary preparations, such as laying in a good store of caps, fine, glazed powder, etc.; and having seen the shot towers, French Town, public and private buildings at the instance of Mr. St. Vrain, our worthy *chef du voyage,* I crammed my purchases, clothes, etc., in my trunk, put it in charge of the porter, and walked to the steamer *Saluda,* bound for Kansas, on the Missouri River, with many kind wishes uttered in my behalf; and, after the third tolling of the bell, and in obedience to the signals of the pilot, we were stemming the uninviting, yellow Mississippi.

I knew no one, and was left to range of thought and a poor "Havana" without interruption; but, amid the "talk" of fellow passengers, who, in armchairs and feet on the boat railing, were twisting their necks to gaze at a very common-looking man in a check-linen coat and trowsers; I learned that their "center of attraction" was Mr. Edwards, the governor *regnant* of Missouri. On scrutiny, the countenance of Mr. Edwards indicated considerable shrewdness; but, altogether, he fell below my ideas of a governor.

At the mouth of the Missouri River, the mingling of the waters was no less novel than curious. A volume of water from the muddy and rapid Missouri, sent by the force of the under current far out in the transparent Mississippi, would boil up to the surface, contrasting oddly enough.

We had a pleasant trip to Kansas, but the turbid stream and mud bluff banks destroy the pleasing effects generally attendant on northern rivers. Colonel Chick, the principal man at Kansas, treated me kindly during my stay, and with his clever sons, the horse ferry, skiffs, and duck shooting, afforded entertainment.

To my surprise, Mr. T. B. Drinker, formerly an editor of a paper in Cincinnati, advanced toward me, after looking at the name on my trunk, and introduced himself. We were together much of the time while waiting for Mr. St. Vrain and company to arrive from St. Louis, with whom we expected to traverse the prairie as far as Bent's Fort.

The Wyandotte is the nearest Indian tribe to Kansas; and, one afternoon, Mr. Drinker and myself visited the agent, Doctor Hewitt. A walk of a mile, through woods on the river bank, brought us to the mouth of the Kansas, or Kaw River, a stream ferried by a tall, good specimen of a full-blood Wyandotte, who received the toll with a look as if to say, "Your money's no account, and I've a mind to toss you in the river for offering it"; our attempts at conversation failed.

Mr. Walker, with whom we had previously become acquainted, is one of the first men of the tribe, once editor of the *Wyandotte Advocate*. Mr. Armstrong is also an intelligent gentleman; he has a *white* wife, a good farm, and (the year I saw him) was to receive ten thousand dollars improvement money for his farm in Ohio, which state he, with the rest of the nation, were forced to vacate three years previous.

Returning from our visit, Mr. Drinker walked on out

of sight, while I shot repeatedly and ineffectually at a woodpecker. On the third discharge of my rifle, a heavy hand was laid on my shoulder, accompanied by a firm grip. I jumped around, to confront a drunken Indian, whose face was red with paint and blood; and, holding in his free hand a broken bottle, he said,

"You bad, you shoot, you scare me," and he tightened his grasp on my collar.

"No, I didn't, *sir*,—I didn't mean to scare *you*, sir," replied I in a tremuolus voice; but, seeing that would not do, I changed tack, and edged in, "Don't you want a 'bit' to buy liquor?" and, as he held out his hand, I left in a hurry.

Drinker and I, hiring horses, rode through the town of Westport and galloped over the undulating prairie, studded with plum bushes and small oak. Emerging into the bare plain, we saw a group of men busied in loading a wagon, of which there were some twenty or more drawn up in the form of a pen. Mr. Bransford, the gentleman in charge, received my "letters" with the prairie welcome of, "Won't you make camp?"

We were invited to stay until Mr. St. Vrain would arrive; and in two days our trunks were there. Every morning we rode to Westport and saw the different Indians, in fanciful dresses, riding in to trade and look around (on their handsome ponies). Some of the squaws were possessed of good features, though gross forms; and both men and women were debased by liquor. The laws are not stringent enough on this point. The unsophisticated Indian, too much exposed to the seductive language of the unprincipled trader in liquor, soon barters away all his valuables and annuity money.

Heretofore we had been sleeping under a tent made of

wagon sheets, but the freight had arrived at Kansas, the sheets taken from us, and the wagons sent to be loaded; from that time we reposed in the open air, which, at first, was refreshing, invigorating, life-inspiring. I used to lay admiring the bright stars until overpowered by sleep.

There were eighteen or twenty Canadian Frenchmen (principally from St. Louis) composing part of our company, as drivers of the teams. As I have ever been a lover of sweet, simple music, their beautiful and piquant songs, in the original language, fell most harmoniously on the ear as we lay wrapped in our blankets.

On the first of September, Mr. St. Vrain's arrival infused some life into our proceedings, but nothing more worthy of note occurred, except riding and looking at horses, of which Drinker and I were in need; one of which, Frank De Lisle, *"le maître de wagon"* sold me for fifty dollars, whom, from his fanciful color, brown and white spots, and white eyes, was designated, by the descriptive though not euphonious name of *"Paint."* He was a noted buffalo chaser, and I anticipated much excitement through his services.

The way the mules were broken to wagon harness would have astonished the "full-blooded" animals of Kentucky and other horse-raising states exceedingly. It is a treatment none but hardy Mexican or scrub mules could survive. They first had to be lassoed by our expert Mexican, Blas, their heads drawn up to a wagon wheel, with scarce two inches of spare rope to relax the tight noose on their necks, and starved for twenty-four hours to subdue their fiery tempers; then harnessed to a heavy wagon, lashed unmercifully when they did not pull, whipped still harder when they ran into still faster speed, until, after an hour's bewilderment and plunging and kicking, they became tractable and broken down—a labor-saving operation, with the unflinching motto of "kill or cure."

In the afternoon of the 12th of September, the train rolled out—the heavily laden, high before and behind, Pennsylvania wains careening from side to side in the ruts, the shouts of the drivers to the newly-yoked teams, and the "*vaya, hu-a, caraho,*" of Blas and his two fellow-Mexican herders, and the *caballada*[1] imparted a freshness and added vigor to our movements; horsemen going to and fro for things forgotten and missing, Mr. St. Vrain and De Lisle, passing and re-passing from one end of the train to examine the strength and capabilities of the weaker wagons; and ourselves, with *new* companions, talking and chirruping to our horses, slowly bringing up the rear, gave an appearance of efficiency and progress. Amid the bustle the foremost teams and ourselves reached the "Delaware Spring" after dark, and the whips and shouts applied to the sluggish oxen of the lagging teams did not cease until far in the night. Our horses were turned out to graze, the blankets unstrapped from the saddles, and we laid down supperless.

This was a most desirable spot for camping, as wood, grass, and a running, limpid stream were close at hand. It is generally the first day's drive. On the 16th we encamped at the "Lone Elm," in the midst of a hard rain which poured on us the entire day; and, the wagons being full of goods and we without tents, a cheerless, chilling, soaking, wet night was the consequence. As the water penetrated, successively, my blankets, coat, and shirt, and made its way down my back, a cold shudder came over me; in the gray, foggy morning a more pitiable set of hungry, shaking wretches were never seen. Oh! but it was hard on the poor greenhorns!

The Start

On the 18th (we still at the "Lone Elm"), a Shawnee Indian rode into camp from out of the high bottom grass to the south, informing us that another Indian had three oxen marked with the company's brand, ")–B," upon which intelligence, Messrs. St. Vrain and Bransford started in pursuit, returning with fifteen yoke. On the 19th, the train was started along the heavy road; dense fogs dampened our clothing and spirits, and but for brandy, and other liquors, fever and ague would have predominated; as it was, Blas and Pierre shook, for which "*cholagogue,*" "quinine," and pills were administered by the "doctor," as I was styled. Beauvais and I made quite a detour through the prairie, during which we saw two deer, several prairie chickens, and obtained fine views of the adjacent country. That night we encamped on "Bull Creek," and, on the 29th, at a most delightfully gushing fountain, Big John Spring, flowing from the hillside, all stopped and drank.

As we are all collected, it would be well to state the size and intention of the company. It was commanded by St. Vrain, an old mountaineer of the firm of Bent, St. Vrain & Co., Indian and Mexican traders. The firm is rich, and owner of several forts, of which Bent's or Fort William, on the Arkansas River, is the principal. Mr. St. Vrain was a gentleman in the true sense of the term, his French descent imparting an exquisite, indefinable degree of politeness, and, combined with the frankness of an ingenuous mountain man, made him an amiable fellow traveler. His kindness and respect toward me I shall always gratefully remember. Mr. Folger, another of our company, was a gentleman, so wedded to a roving prairie life that he has accompanied Mr. St. Vrain for several years in pure love of adventure. His mule, "David," was a comical, anti-

[1] Herd of horses and mules.

quated animal; the study of the expression of his grizzled phiz was truly laughable; and much merriment was caused by the master's *sensible* and affectionate advice and consolation to David.

Mr. Beauvais was a Frenchman, employed to trade with the Sioux Indians; Frank De Lisle, a clever fellow, the wagon master, or director—an officer of trust; Bransford was clerk to the company; and General Lee, of St. Louis, Beaubien, of New Mexico, and Drinker and myself, of Cincinnati, constituted *our* mess. There were, besides, twenty-three teamsters, and the same number of wagons; every man armed, equipped, and ready (if forced upon us) for a fight with the "yellow skins."

On the 30th of September, we arrived at Council "Grove"—considered the best camping spot on the road. On the west skirt of the belt of timber, under the wide-spreading protection of a huge oak, was a diminutive blacksmith's shop, sustained by the government for the purpose of repairing wagons *en route* to the army at Santa Fé.

We remained for two days at the "Grove," to recruit the oxen after the heavy pulling from Westport, and as this is the last place (traveling westward) where *hard* timber can be procured, the men were busy felling hickories and oaks for spare axletrees, and swinging the rough-hewn pieces under their wagons. I took my rifle in search of a flock of turkeys, whose tantalizing piping was easily heard from camp, and in the evening, Beauvais and I washed our shirts—my first essay—in the clear brook; succeeding tolerably, *only*.

What a pleasing appearance have the dark-green fringes of timber, standing far out in the prairie, lit up and variegated by the early tints of fall. I have been extremely delighted, since setting out, with the lovely scenery—a too vivid picture of which cannot be portrayed.

On leaving Council Grove, the verdure and scenery change; the grass is much shorter, partaking of none of the luxuriant growth of the herbage a few days back; wooded creeks become scarce, and timbered principally with sweet cottonwood.

The maneuvers of the Mexicans of our company are really astonishing in lassoing unruly mules and horses; dodge as they may, or run about, the lariat noose is sure to fall on their unwilling necks; a loop thrown over the nose, the gagging Spanish bit forced into the mouth, the saddle clapped on, and the rider firmly in that, with galling spurs tickles the side ribs, and flies and curvettes on the plain in less time than it can be written. But it does confound an animal to have a Mexican horse furniture and rider strapped on to him!

Mr. St. Vrain started in advance of the train, with three or four persons, for Bent's Fort, but meeting a return government train, who reported the Indians troublesome, he waited for us to come up, preferring slow travel and a large company to a small party and uncertain possession of his scalp. Toward eleven o'clock in the morning, we arrived at Cottonwood Fork—a small stream, so called from the number of cottonwoods growing on its banks. One of the wagons overturned while crossing, breaking two boxes of claret. Those around had a treat most unexpectedly. A government train crossed soon after; and, at sundown, Captain Thompson, U. S. Dragoons, and lieutenant colonel of the Mormon Battalion, arrived with three light wagons and an escort of ten dragoons. He gave us the latest news.

In the morning, he was off early, in a gallop; his wagons, with clean, tightly drawn sheets and four fast mules attached, showed well, coursing up the hill at a rapid rate.

We could not leave camp that day. De Lisle was under a wagon containing forty-five hundred-weight of freight, making some repairs, one wheel being off and propped up by a board, when the support gave way, and the wagon fell, confining him to the earth. His cries drew the men together, and while the wagon was lifted off him, he was drawn from under, almost dead. He was so far recovered that the next day we traveled.

So soon as a faint streak of light appears in the east, the cry *"turn out"* is given by De Lisle; all rise, and, in half an hour, the oxen are yoked, hitched, and started. For the purpose of bringing everything within a small compass, the wagons are *corralled*, that is, arranged in the form of a pen, when camp is made; and as no animals in that country are caught without a lasso, they are much easier noosed if driven in the corral. There, no dependence must be placed in anyone but one's self; and the sooner he rises when the cry is given, the easier can he get his horse.

Like all persons on the first trip, I was *green* in the use of the lasso, and *Paint* was given to all sorts of malicious dodging; perhaps I have worked myself into a profuse perspiration with vexation a hundred and one times in vain attempts to trap him.

Not being able to catch my horse this morning, I hung my saddle on a wagon and walked, talking to the loquacious Canadians, whose songs and stories were most acceptable. They are a queer mixture anyhow, these Canadians; rain or shine, hungry or satisfied, they are the same garrulous, careless fellows; generally carolling in honor of some brunette Vide Poche or St. Louis Creole beauty, or lauding, in the words of their ancestry, the soft skies and grateful wine of La Belle France; occasionally uttering a "*sacré*," or "*enfant de garce*," but suffering no cloud of ill humor to overshadow them but for a moment. While walking with a languid step, cheering up their slow oxen, a song would burst out from one end of the train to the other, producing a most charming effect.

On the 6th of October, we met a government train from Santa Fé, which reported buffalo in plenty ten miles ahead; and, about four o'clock in the afternoon, Edmond Paul, near whom I was walking, shouted "*bison!*" pointing with his whip to the westward, where were several running and soon disappearing in the *mirage*, which transformed them into huge, shapeless masses.

The first time I ever witnessed the *mirage* was in Texas. The friend with whom I was riding pointed toward the illusion, with the remark: "What a beautiful *lake*"; and it was not until we found it to be receding at our approach that we were undeceived.

We encamped on a slope, using "*bois de vache*" (dried buffalo excrement) for want of better fuel. We, on horses, selected the camp before the wagons came up; Mr. St. Vrain and I, Folger and Chadwick, and Drinker and Bransford, each pair taking an *apishiamore* (saddle blanket), would collect our blankets full of the fuel (for the "wood" lies in all directions), bring up to the intended fire, and off again, until a pile several feet high would be collected. It burns well and freely, catching the steelsparks like tinder; but, being light, is soon fanned into a hot coal, and turns immediately to ashes. Wind prevails to such an extent on the prairie that no ashes are ever seen about a camp a day or two after the fire is made; nothing but black spots on the ground mark the site.

Mr. St. Vrain and companions brought in the choice parts of a buffalo, and every person was busied in cooking on their "own hook" and swallowing the tender meat. For the first night or two after entering the buffalo region, we were serenaded by the Coyote wolf, a species of *music* much like a commingled bark, whine, yelp, and occasionally a spasmodic laugh, now tenor, now basso; then one would take a treble solo, and, after an ear-piercing prelude, all would join in chorus, making an indescribable discord.

In the morning the train started as usual; Mr. St. Vrain, Drinker, Bransford, Folger, and I left the trail for a buffalo hunt, intending to make a large circuit before meeting the wagons. I had a shot at a large white wolf—the first we had seen. He was loping around camp when my shrill whistle brought him to a stand still; at the sharp crack of my rifle, the keen-faced stranger took to the plain. Their presence indicates the vicinity of buffalo.

All were on the *qui vive* for the new game, and Mr. St. Vrain, who was in the lead, "motioned," with his hand, for us to lean forward on our horses, so as to keep the buffalo from seeing us. In a little while we dismounted in a hollow, and all but Bransford and I, who were left in charge of the horses, "approached" a band of bulls. At the report of the guns we led the animals toward them. "No meat," was the answer to our queries. The whole country was cut up with innumerable buffalo paths, intersecting one another at all possible angles.

Mr. St. Vrain on my horse, and Drinker on his own, started in pursuit of a band, and their movements were most exciting. Being without a horse, I waited on the prairie, looking at the flying buffalo, ten or twelve of whom came tearing toward me as I lay in the grass, but they looked so frightful when within thirty yards, I jumped up and fired, without any perceptible effect, as they slightly turned and lumbered on.

We never eat but twice a day, *very* often but once in twenty-four hours, at which scarcity of food, of course, there was grumbling. Bransford, who disliked it very much, said, after having concealed his feelings some length of time, "Darn this way of living, anyhow; a feller starves a whole day like a mean 'coyote,' and when he *does* eat, he stuffs himself like a snake that's swallowed a frog, and is no account for an hour after." It was about the truth, for our ravenous appetites scarcely knew bounds.

More buffalo in sight the third day than heretofore— the plain literally covered. We crossed "Big Cow Creek," but no cows were seen, and thinking best to secure meat, such as it was, while an opportunity presented, our worthy leader approached a band of bulls and fired, bringing down one. It is with difficulty that buffalo can be approached, it requiring a skillful person who will not permit the keen-scented animal to get to his leeward, or in sight; for they run when a person is in view as far as a mile, and from the scent still further; so we waited, with suppressed breathing, for the report of the rifle. There lay a fine, fat, young male —ere long he was on his knees (for the hump prevents his being placed on his back) and the hide off. The men ate the liver raw, with a slight dash of *gall* by way of zest, which served *à la Indian*, was not very tempting to cloyed appetites; but to hungry men, not at all squeamish, raw, warm liver, with raw marrow, was quite palatable. Before the buffalo range was half traversed, I liked the novel dish pretty well.

It would not do for small hunting parties to build fires to cook with; for in this hostile Indian country a smoke would bring *inquiring friends*. Speaking of hostile Indians reminds me of a question related by one of our men: At a party, in a Missouri frontier settlement, a lady asked a mountaineer, fresh from the Platte, "if the *hos*tile Indians are as savage as those who serve on foot!"

Returning to camp, the prairie was black with the herds; and, a good chance presenting itself, I struck spurs into Paint, directing him toward fourteen or fifteen of the nearest, distant eight or nine hundred yards. We (Paint and I) soon neared them, giving me a flying view of their unwieldy proportions, and, when within fifteen feet of the nearest, I raised my rifle halfway to the face and fired. Reloading, still in hot pursuit (tough work to load on a full run), I followed, though without catching up. One feels a delightfully wild sensation when in pursuit of a band of buffalo, on a fleet horse, with a good rifle, and without a hat, the winds playing around the flushed brow, when with hair streaming, the rider nears the frightened herd and, with a shout of exultation, discharges his rifle. I returned to the party highly gratified with my first, though unsuccessful, chase; but Mr. St. Vrain put a slight damper on my ardor, by simply remarking—

"The next time you 'run meat,' don't let the horse go in a trot, and yourself in a gallop" (I had, in my eagerness, leaned forward in the saddle, and a stumble of the horse would have pitched me over his head); by which well-timed and laconic advice I afterward profited.

We encamped on "Cow Creek"; the buffalo around us in every direction; now lost in the *mirage,* now appearing, some herds wending slowing to an overflowing *slue* near camp, and others (the males) who, strutting in all the pomp of conscious dignity and supremacy, until a whiff of wind from camp is wafted to them, would lift their tails on high, scud before the wind, up and down, like a ship in short seas. Two staid old fellows came to the pond; after a half hour's crawling on our knees (Chadwick, Tibeau, and I), drawing our guns after us; then, when the buffaloes' backs were turned, running a few steps, then stopping and crawling again, all the time closely watching the sagacious animals, who would stop short every little while to give a side glance around them, we fired, bringing one to his knees.

In the afternoon, I borrowed General Lee's double-barreled shot gun, and sallied out again for the slues, returning with five ducks, killed on the wing in seven shots. We picked them, in anticipation of a feast—something new. He (the General) had a saying, "rather tight on the American people"; and, when we were eating but once in twenty-four hours, his "rather tight" always elicited laughter, which, however, was "rather tight" on an empty stomach.

The morning following our stay at Cow Creek, we were on the hunt for the all-engrossing game, and the General accompanied us for the first time, mounted on a large gray, fit for a charger, who, scenting the buffalo, was so unmanageable he was sent back to the train. Mr. Chadwick (of St. Louis, on his first trip, like several of us, for pleasure) seeing a partially blind bull, concluded to "make meat" of him; crawling up close, the buffalo scented him and pitched about every way, too blind to travel straight or fast. Chad fired; the mad animal, directed by the rifle report, charged. How they did "lick it" over the ground! He pursued, yelling, half in excitement, half in fear, till they were close to the wagons, where the pursuer changed tack, only to be shot by one of the teamsters with a nor'-west fusil.

We led a horse with us the next hunt; a band of cows

were seen; St. Vrain approached, and fired; Lupton gave chase on the led horse; following him for three miles as fast as our horse and mule flesh would permit, we gave it up. Lupton returned unsuccessful.

We reached the Grand Arkansas for noon camp; here quite broad, with two feet of water, sandy bottom, and high *sand buttes* on either bank, as bare and cheerless as any misanthrope could wish.

Toward four o'clock in the afternoon's travel, I took a pair of holster pistols for a chase. I rode behind a sand butte, and on emerging from it, a "band" was tearing over the ground three hundred yards distant; and giving Paint the rein, we soon neared them, but, as none were cows, I merely kept alongside, taking sight with my pistol, for practice, until the thoughts of Camanches flashed across my mind, and turning Paint's head, I regained the party. To look at a buffalo, one would think that they could not run with such rapidity; but, let him try to follow with an ordinary horse, and he is soon undeceived.

The next day, while riding among the hollows, far off the road, we found a mule. In order to secure it, we rode around several times, on each circuit gradually nearing, so as not to frighten by too sudden an approach; and, when within thirty feet, a lasso was thrown over its neck. Mr. St. Vrain and a Mexican ran their horses after a band of cows; they were soon out of sight, scaring the buffalo for miles around, from us, who returned to the wagons, then crossing Walnut Creek.

We rode through two prairie-dog villages in the course of the day. Generally, as I have ascertained through inquiry and observation the ground selected for the village, is a level, gravelly, sandy soil. The spot constituting the village is dug full of holes a few steps apart, two feet or more in depth, and six or eight inches in diameter at the top, lessening toward the bottom. Underneath the ground, the burrows communicate, forming subterranean chambers, the whole of which, in some instances, covering many acres of ground. The excavated earth is thrown out at these holes, forming cones a foot or more in height, which can be seen some distance before reaching the village, and also serve to keep the rain from draining in and drowning the inmates.

The prairie dog (a species of marmot) is somewhat larger than the Norway rat; a scanty covering of rusty brown or sandy hair renders the similarity the more striking. Their heads are short, bearing some resemblance to that of a young bulldog.

It was quite amusing to watch their movements on top of the cones; on our approach, they barked, their short tails nervously fluttering, and receiving a new impetus from the short, quick, and sharp tiny yelp, which they constantly uttered; when they thought themselves in danger, with an incredibly quick motion, they threw themselves back in the holes, and immediately reappeared with an impertinent, daring bark, as if to say, "You can't get *me*." Others slowly "crawfished," hiding, by their singular way of crouching the back, until nothing but their heads and tails could be seen—these latter shaking tremulously. Succeeding a silence of a few minutes, after scaring in the "dogs," we could see, by lying flat on the ground, so as to get the tops of the cones between the sky and our eyes, with the closest scrutiny, the head, here and there, of a dog almost imperceptibly moving, and with a cautious reconnoiter to see if the coast be clear, he would show himself, and then, with a knowing yelp, apprise his neighbors of the result of his investigations.

The snake and prairie owl hold companionship with these dogs; and not infrequently their "pups" become victims to the vipers nestled in their bosoms. These villages are frequent; often we came across them several miles from water; but whether they abstain from it totally is a question not solvable by any mountain men with us. Very little or no dew falls in this region, so these strange animals do not depend upon this source to quench their thirst. They live on grass; as the season advances, for some distance around the villages the ground is bare.

The grass in this region is short, early, and highly nutritious. It has a withered, brown appearance even early in the spring, and is designated as "buffalo grass," from the fact that it grows in the present buffalo range and forms their principal food. Mr. St. Vrain came in without meat, and we fared poorly on bread and coffee.

The day was unusually warm and clear; so that the vertical sunbeams beat down on us with almost scorching intensity; no water was near, and long before night we suffered with thirst. We endeavored until nine or later at night to reach water, but the rapidly failing oxen compelled us to stop without it. Having no water to prepare our food, we made a small *bois de vache* fire, by which we lit and smoked our pipes in sullen silence. The oxen were turned out to shift for themselves; and several of the thirsty men struck a "bee line" for the river, four or five miles distant. I was too tired to go, and concluded to bear the torment until morning, when I heard Petout's voice (one of the Canadians) calling me. He came and whispered a few words in my ear, and, thereupon, we went to a wagon, where my friend produced a gallon keg of water from the front part. We drank without speaking, and never did water taste sweeter than that long draught. Petout stole the keg from a brother Creole; and, after slaking our thirst, we acted honorably, returning the keg and contents to its place, saying nothing about it.

It was two o'clock in the afternoon of the 13th of October that we arrived at "Pawnee Rock": a point of friable sandstone jutting out from the rising ground to our right. It is thirty-five or forty feet in height, and its accessible front is cut with the names of ambitious travelers who wish future generations to know that they in such a year journeyed along the Santa Fé Trail.

On the top of the rock, near the edge, was a deposit of earth, where the remains of some poor fellow had been placed. To die anywhere seems hard, but to heave the last breath among strangers, on the burning, desolate prairie, with no kind mother or sister to pay those soothing attentions which divest the bed of sickness of many of its pangs, is hard indeed. How must we pity the invalid, who, after being jolted in a wagon under the scorching rays of a summer's sun for days, until nature yields, is put into a mere hole, with his blanket for coffin and shroud, without a prayer or tear! Yet such is a frequent fate on the Santa Fé Trail.

We encamped on Ash Creek; and, up to that time, we had been two days without meat, and, as Lupton said, we were getting "grease hungry."

In consultation, next morning, we became desperate for something more substantial than short rations of bread and coffee. Bransford had a gun of which we entertained a poor opinion; he determined before starting from camp to bring in "cow meat," at which we all laughed. He started by himself in the direction of Pawnee Forks—at great risk, however, as the neighborhood was infested with hostile Indians. I joined a party of two, who deviated to the right of the trace. Toward twelve o'clock we saw a large band of buffalo, among them a number of cows, making their way, leisurely, to a small, intervening stream of water. Mr. St. Vrain dismounting, took his rifle, and soon was on the "approach," leaving us *cached*[2] behind a rise of the ground to wait the gun report. We laid down with our blankets, which we always carried strapped to the saddle, and, with backs to the wind, talked in a low tone until hearing Mr. St. Vrain's gun, when we remounted. Again and again the rifle was heard, in hasty succession, and hastening to him, we found a fat cow stretched, and a wounded male limping slowly off. The animals were tied to the horns of our cow; and, with butcher knives, we divested the body of its fine coat; but, finding myself a "green hand," at least not an adept, in the mysteries of prairie butchering, I mounted Paint for the wounded fellow, who had settled himself, with his fore legs doubled under him, three hundred yards from us. Mine was a high-pommeled, Mexican saddle, with wooden stirrups; and, when once seated, it was no easy matter to be dislodged. Paint went up within twenty yards of the growling, wounded, gore-covered bull, and there stood trembling and imparting some of his fear to myself.

With long, shaggy, dirt-matted, and tangled locks falling over his glaring, diabolical eyes, blood streaming from nose and mouth, he made the most ferocious looking object it is possible to conceive; and, if nurses could portray to obstinate children, in true colors, the description of a mad buffalo bull, the oft-repeated "bugaboo" would soon be an obsolete idea.

While looking with considerable trepidation on the vanquished monarch of the Pawnee plains, he started to

2 *Cached*—from the French *"cacher"*—to hide.

his feet; and, with a jump, materially lessened the distance between us, which so scared Paint that he reared backward, nearly sliding myself and gun over his tail; and, before the bridle rein could be tightened, ran some rods; but, turning his head and setting the rowels of my spurs in his flanks, I dashed up within thirty feet of the bull; and, at the crack of the gun, the "poor buffler" dropped his head, his skin convulsively shook, his dark eyes, no longer fired with malignancy, rolled back in the sockets, and his spirit departed for the region of perpetual verdure and running waters, beyond the reach of white man's rifle, or the keen lance of the prairie warrior.

Loading our animals with choice pieces of the tender cow, we left for the trail, much to the apparent satisfaction of some wolves, loping and howling or sitting on their haunches, seemingly resolved to bide their time. Looking back, after we left a short distance, we saw them fighting, with their tails whisking about quite lively, in the struggle for "spoils."

Ravens took the place of the crows after leaving Walnut Creek, who seem to be limited to a few days' journey of the frontier cornfields. From the somber hue of the ravens, we are continually reminded of evil spirits, as they slowly flap their black wings overhead; and we felt almost the same reverence for them as do the superstitious mariners for the wild, screaming, darting Mother Carey's chickens.

We were going slowly, by reason of our heavy loads of meat—the wagons were far away, stretched along the level trace, with their dazzling white sheets, while the oxen seemed mere pigmies wending a snail-like pace. To the south were several hundred buffalo, confused by the sight of the wagons and us; as we drew near, their bewilderment increased, and they scattered, a few within a hundred yards. We hurriedly dismounted, not holding our animals, and fired, while off with the clattering herd galloped Chadwick's horse and Paint, the meat flapping their sides, accelerating their speed at every jump. I did not shout "my kingdom for a horse" to pursue the runaway Paint, but felt like sending a rifle ball as a check, though, fortunately, my gun was unloaded. Blas, our Mexican, seeing the mishap, came from the wagons with lasso in hand, and soon returned with the fugitive, after a chase of two miles, for which service I gave him *dos pesos* (two dollars) and *muy gracias* (many thanks).

Bransford was waiting for us at Pawnee Fork—a bold, limpid stream, with waters of a refreshingly cool sparkle—by his saddle the fattest "cow" that had "gone under" that trip. Nothing more was said in disparagement of his gun, skill, or bravery. The immense herds feeding and running near camp enticed the men to many a "crawl" that evening, and more than one greenhorn took his first trembling and unsuccessful shot. Close was the grave of one of Bent and St. Vrain's men, who, imprudently going too far in advance of the train last spring, was charged upon and scalped by the Pawnees, in sight of his companions. Two others of the company had to run for it—just escaping.

Good humor reigned triumphant throughout camp. Canadian songs of mirth filled the air; and, at every mess fire, pieces of meat were cooking *en appolas*; that is, on a stick sharpened, with alternate fat and lean meat, making a delicious roast. Among others, *boudins*[3] were roasting without any previous culinary operation but the tying of both ends, to prevent the fat, as it was liquified, from wasting; and when pronounced "good" by the hungry, im-

[3] *Boudins*, the intestine in which is contained the chyme.

patient judges, it was taken off the hot coals, puffed up with the heat and fat, the steam escaping from little punctures, and coiled on the ground or a not particularly clean saddle blanket, looking for all the world like a dead snake.

The fortunate owner shouts, "Hyar's the doins, and hyar's the coon as *savvys* 'poor bull' from 'fat cow;' freeze into it, boys!" And all fall to with ready knives, cutting off savory pieces of this exquisitely appetizing prairie production.

At our mess fire there was a whole side of ribs roasted. When browned thoroughly, we handled the long bones, and as the generous fat dripped on our clothes, we heeded it not, our minds wrapped up with the one absorbing thought of satisfying our relentless appetites; progressing in the work of demolition, our eyes closed with ineffable bliss. Talk of an emperor's table—why, they could imagine nothing half so good! The meal ended, the pipe lent its aid to complete our happiness; and, at night, we retired to the comfortable blankets, wanting nothing, caring for nothing. One remarkable peculiarity is there about buffalo meat—one can eat beyond plenitude without experiencing any ill effects.

CHAPTER II

THE TRAIL

W E AWOKE on the morning of the 16th with a *Norther* penetrating our blankets. The river Arkansas, almost dry, and on whose north bank we were encamped, was covered with floating particles of thin ice. Drinker had but two blankets, and, on awakening, we found him lying near the remains of the *bois de vache* fire, the light ashes of which, on his clothing, gave the appearance of snow. We wore extra clothing during the morning's ride, and Drinker looked badly, from the effect of last night's wakefulness. We rode in silence for a time, somewhat in advance of the party, in vain attempts to encourage conversation. At length, after a long pause, he said: "St. Vrain and Folger sleep together, Chad and Bransford do too, hadn't we better?" I acquiesced with pleasure. With saddles and overcoats, we had good pillows—the other clothing remained on us. Wherever camp was made, a place was selected by each *couple* for sleeping before dismounting (mountaineer custom); and, ere dark, the pallet of robes, etc., was always spread. We huddled around the miserable "cow wood" fires, chilled by the cold winds.

We nooned the next day near a United States mule train—the one from which the man was killed at Pawnee Fork by the Indians, who slipped up as they were at supper.

The captain of the train also received an arrow through his coat collar.

On the 19th, we made a late start—encamping several hours after dark. The weather grew much cooler, and the river valleys became much narrower than toward the States, and the prairie was at an elevation of twenty-five or thirty feet above the bottom. Bleak hills of drifted sand met the eye on the opposite side of the river, giving shelter from the icy blasts to the different game, and too often to the unfriendly savage, who watches from his secure position and waits for fit opportunity to pounce upon, rob, and scalp weak parties of pale-faced enemies from the east. About four o'clock, Bransford killed, with his *popgun*, four buffalo out of a band of five; the nearest at fifty yards, and, as they retreated, the other three, the last at 250 yards. Another evidence of his gun's little worthlessness!

If, when buffalo are shot at, one is brought to the ground and bleeds freely, and if the hunter is not discovered, by sight or scent, the surviving buffalo will smell the blood and stop—often permitting themselves to be killed without running.

Two deer were brought in, in the course of the evening hunt; and, buffalo and venison being before the campfires at the same time, the superiority of "fat cow" was fairly tested and acknowledged. While riding leisurely along, shortly after Bransford's inimitable shots, our attention was drawn to a band of buffalo running across our path, a half-mile to the rear, and two hundred or more large wolves, who, with outstretched necks and uplifted sharp heads, were in sure, noiseless, though swift pursuit. It was a magnificent sight to watch them dashing along—the poor buffalo straining their utmost to elude the sharp fangs of their persecutors—the wolves gaining at every stride. On they went, now out of sight, now in the river, where the buffalo had the advantage; a cool swim invigorated the pursuers, who, loping with dripping hair, howled, as they pressed on to victory.

On the 23d, we came to the "Cimarone" crossing of the Arkansas River—the shortest of the two routes to Santa Fé, which here diverge—one over the sand desert, void of water; and, in the severe *jornadas*, the oxen often drop with thirst—the other, following the river bank to Bent's Fort, crosses a spur of the Rocky Mountains—a longer, but safer and easier road.

The river, at the "crossing," was wide and but a few inches in depth—a good ford. Seeing some men on the opposite side, I crossed on Paint to learn the *news*—something seldom found and eagerly sought for on the plains. Captain Murphy (volunteer service), Roubideau, and two others composed the party. They were the government express to the States. Roubideau wished to buy Paint, offering me a fine bay horse, and, finally, ten dollars "to boot"; but I felt, or fancied I felt, like the Arabian, and I thought of the long weary miles I had been carried—the exciting buffalo chases, with the accompanying feeling of true liberty, while coursing over the bare plains on his back; so, grasping my rifle, I turned his head without a reply, and, with a shout, urged him away in a gallop, loving him more than ever.

In the afternoon, I went out with the hunters. The day was warm; the transition from the bottom to the upland was rendered agreeable by a gentle breeze, which kept us in a proper state of coolness.

The *mirage* threw its optical illusion around everything; a buffalo seemed a shapeless mass, and, browsing or running, its side or front turned to us, it would, at times, dwindle to a transparent shadow, or stalk forth in magnified proportions. The heat glimmering up from the parched ground dazzled the eye, and we rode as if on the ocean—so shut up were we by the plain stretching away on all sides, no object to break the monotonous view except a stray bison or antelope.

Here, for the first time, we noticed the cactus—the same as the most common of the species in the States, only this had a ruddier, healthier color, probably owing to the continued, exposed action of the sun. We regained the trace before dark and waited for the train.

On the 24th, we passed "Pawnee Forts"; a grove of timber in which a war party of Pawnees, some years before, fortified themselves when besieged by a hostile tribe. Nothing now remains but a few crumbling logs to mark the site of this Indian bulwark.

At noon camp two Indians came in—runners for the grand war party of the Cheyennes—the first wild Indians I had seen. They were innocent of clothing, with the exception of a cloth around the loins, a pair of moccasins, and a robe which was drawn around while walking; but, on sitting down, it was permitted to fall off, leaving nude the body from the waist upward. Frank De Lisle talked by signs with them; and, after they ate and smoked, we learned that a party, numbering 122 warriors, were encamped up the river, on a scalp and horse-stealing expedition in the Pawnee Nation, with whom they are at war. The runners left us when their curiosity and appetites were satisfied.

In the morning, at ten o'clock, we were at the camp of the Indian braves. Many of the younger and more ardent met us; as they dashed by on their handsome horses, I thought, with envy, of the free and happy life they were leading on the untamed plains, with fat buffalo for food, fine horses to ride, living and dying in a state of blissful ignorance. To them, who know no other joys than those of the untaught savage, *such* a life must be the acme of happiness; for what more invigorating, enlivening pleasure is there than traversing the grand prairies, admiring the beauties of unkempt, wild, and lovely nature, and chasing the fleet-footed buffalo—to send the death-abiding arrows, with the musical twang of the bowstring—then partaking of the choice parts, cooked by themselves, by their own fires; and, afterward, lying down to enjoy such sweet sleep as is within the comprehension of those only who have traveled and hunted on the lordly parks of the Far West.

Shaking hands, we (Messrs. St. Vrain, Folger, Chadwick, Drinker, and myself) dismounted, and sat in a row with several of the principal warriors. The pipe of red marble, four inches in length, the bowl three in height, with a stem two feet in length, was passed around, containing a mixture of tobacco and the bark of the red willow or swamp dogwood. First, one chief took the pipe, and after presenting its mouth to the sky and to the ground, he drew four whiffs—blowing one toward the heavens, one to the earth, one to the east, and the other to the west. Each Indian did the same. Some must have the pipe presented to them stem downward; others with the bowl resting on the ground; and others, again, with the stem upward. All have their peculiar *medicine* or religion, and they are as punctillious in this matter as ever was a Hidalgo in politeness.

The smoke was inhaled by the Indians, who, after filling their lungs with repeated whiffs, blew it out in a continuous stream from nostrils and mouth, in three distinct lines. I tried the same process; but coughing slightly in the attempt, the chiefs looked so solemn and stern, I felt almost afraid to try further, and contented myself with the usual way. The pipe was passed from right to left, then back from hand to hand, without smoking, to the first one, and the same round was repeated, until exhausted of its contents.

Being in want of a rope, I went with a piece of tobacco to an Indian, and by pointing to a neatly-platted rawhide rope and holding out the tobacco, we made an exchange. Mr. St. Vrain made the party, through the chiefs, a present of tobacco and ammunition—not through love of the guttural-toned warriors, but to influence them in his favor; for they belong to the Cheyenne Nation, with whom the firm of Bent, St. Vrain & Co. trade largely for robes.

A number of Indians went with us to "noon camp," in expectation of a *feast*, where they sat in a circle outside of the corral. A kettle of coffee, of which they are extravagantly fond, with a pile of bread, was placed in their midst —two officious Indians helped each one to a portion of bread, and one cup served several. They appeared to enjoy the luxury.

Before I could distinguish the men from the women in attendance, I asked Beauvais:

"Is that the way all the squaws dress?"

"Which squaws?" said he.

"Why, those yonder," replied I, pointing to some Indians whom I mistook for women. Often afterward, my *compagnons de voyage* had many a hearty laugh at *my* "*squaws.*"

Hitherto I had been wearing shoes, but for some powder and ball an Indian gave me a pair of moccasins, which I wore, discarding the shoes. The grass here is dry, by reason of absence of dews; consequently the slippery sole of the shoe makes walking unpleasant and laborious—like taking two steps forward and slipping back one—but, with a pliant, neatly-fitting moccasin, one can catch hold with his toes on the ground, thereby aiding himself considerably.

On my neck was a black silk handkerchief; for this several Indians offered moccasins, but I refused to part with it. At last, one huge fellow caught me in his arms and hugged me very tight, at the same time grunting desperately, as if in pain; but one of the traders who understood savage customs said that he was professing great love for me. Who could withstand such *pressing* appeals? So pulling off the object of his love I gave it to him; though, be it said, the grunt of a porker in the last stages of obesity would have been quite as intelligible and acceptable.

On the morning of the 26th, we came to "Chouteau's Island," taking its name from a trader who was here long and hotly besieged by a war party of Pawnees. Our wagon wheels needed repairing, and we stopped for the day to set tire, which had become loose by reason of the long drought.

The wagons started the morning of the 27th, and I went with the hunters; but, after breasting the wind for six or eight miles, we struck the trace, so as to meet the wagons; and, by looking at the road, we saw they had not passed. We went back a mile and found the men cooking, and Frank De Lisle, assisted by two Canadians, shoeing the barefooted oxen. The legs of the ox are entangled in a rope to throw him down, and drawn up to prevent his kicking, while a partly circular piece of iron, made to fit but the outside division of the hoof, is nailed on in the same manner, and with like nails, as a horse is shod.

In beating through a bottom for game, overgrown with

high weeds, grass, and covered with fallen trees, Drinker, who was a short distance from the rest of us, shouted, "Here is a porcupine." The porcupine gave unmistakable evidence to our nasal organs of its being a "polecat,"[1] and "David" (Mr. Folger's mule) carried from the field of sanguinary conflict that which rendered his proximity anything but agreeable—even the rider did not escape scatheless, much to the amusement and feigned abhorrence of the jovially-inclined camp.

We passed by a *medicine* lodge of the Cheyenne Indians about twelve o'clock on the morning of the 28th—now abandoned, as a new one is erected whenever it is deemed necessary by their priests. It was made of cottonwood poles, from four to five inches in diameter and eight to fifteen in length. In form, the *tout ensemble* approximated more to a hexagonal than a circular form, though strictly neither. Its altitude was twenty by twenty-five feet in diameter; and the poles composing the sides were planted perpendicularly, from the top of which, other smaller poles, composing the roof, were fastened, converging to the center perpendicular post. Among the roof poles, or rafters, boughs of trees were rudely interwoven, to exclude the sun's rays. Near the apex, on the inside, was pendant an untanned, long-haired buffalo bull's head, with the lower lip attached, by strips of skin, painted on the one side red, the other black. The poles were daubed in the same manner. In a well-trodden, clean spot of ground within the lodge were two oblong holes, a few inches wide and about two feet in length; around and in them were a number of small sticks, painted the two colors.

A few steps from the outside was a *sweat* lodge, so called by the mountaineers, in which the medicine men

[1] Skunk.

enter before performing their sacred duties. It is nearly or quite four feet in height, and five in breadth at its base; the general contour is not unlike an inverted round basket. In the center is dug a hole, similar in shape to a cogwheel, where are placed heated stones, on which water is poured to generate steam and cause perspiration. After this, they plunge, reeking with sweat, in the river. In the Indian village, I have seen them jump from their *hot* lodges in the water when the margin of the stream was ice-bound. I thought the shock too severe, but, on inquiry, ascertained that no ill effects ever ensue.

To those fond of speculating on the origin and probability of the North American Indians belonging to the lost tribes of Israel, I would here say that these Indians *purify* themselves before entering upon the performance of their religious duties.

The evening following the visit to the lodge, we encamped near the banks of the Arkansas, where a creek, fringed with timber, made a graceful curve, emptying its modicum of water into the main stream. The pleasing position and grouping of the trees render this spot picturesque, and it is well known to travelers as the "Pretty Encampment."

Before the break of gray dawn, Messrs. St. Vrain, Folger, and Chadwick left us for the Fort, some eighty miles distant.

Early the morning of the 30th, we awoke with our bedding, selves, the firewood, and ground wet with rain. All rode sulkily along, having had an unsatisfactory breakfast. The oxen slipped on the muddy trail, the drivers uttering "*sacrés*" and "*avances*," with more than the usual emphasis. Now and then, a Canadian ditty would break forth, but it was no use attempting songs; the charm for the nonce was broken, and it died away, as if choked by the damp atmosphere. Riding in a wet saddle, in rain-saturated clothes, and inhaling the steam from our clammy, unpleasant animals caused feelings most undesirable.

We reached the "Salt Bottom" in the morning, so called from the salt marshes and saline efflorescence appearing in spots, as if flour had been sprinkled on the ground.

We traveled long after dark by the bright moon, which cast a shade, or lit up the crawling train, as it alternately appeared and disappeared behind the fleeting clouds. We crowded together, listening with much interest to tales of western life; amid the silent intervals, songs and shouts of the drivers were heard far in the rear. Our mules outwalked the oxen, and we often were too far in advance for safety; then, stopping for the slow train, we would dismount, light our pipes, and chat away with much satisfaction, for the rain had early ceased and the sun had dried our clothes. We were, however, living meanly on the flesh of worked-down oxen, too poor to travel, with about as much masticable flesh on them as in the cottonwoods lining the river bank.

On October 31st, we crossed "Big Sand Creek," a large bed of sand, one hundred yards in width, covered with water during very rainy seasons, but then dry. The Indians camp upon it a half-day's journey from its mouth, where there is much water. Below that point the sand absorbs it. Our teams had to be coupled to get the wagons through the sinking mouth.

Three of us, riding up the creek for antelope, saw, on the horizontal limbs of a cottonwood, two Indian graves, thirty feet or more from the ground. Short poles were tied transversely, from one limb to another, and the deceased, wrapped in many folds of robes with a few ornaments, was tied on this scaffolding with thongs of rawhide. This mode of burial is preferred to interment in the ground, as the wolves would scratch the bodies up again; and, besides, the Indians have no implements for digging the compact gravel. There may be some superstition connected with the present form of burial—be that as it may, it has always been the custom to put the bodies in trees. The wind had blown to the ground some of the robes and blankets from the corpses, and they were torn in tatters by the wolves.

We nooned at the roots of a fallen cottonwood, called "Dead Indian." The lower jawbone of a woman was picked up by Bransford. The teeth were sound and regular; I put it in my bullet pouch for safe-keeping.

There is much that is singular about the antelope, it being a most inquisitive creature; their curiosity, like Eve's, often results in their downfall. While hunting, before reaching camp, a band came running past. Bewildered and fascinated, they described two complete circles around us, during which we gave them several shots, though their motions were too swift for sure aim. A handkerchief on a gun rod will cause them, now advancing, now retreating, to approach until within rifle range.

The mountaineers spin long yarns of their exploits in hunting and *toling* game; and they say that standing on the head and shaking the legs in air is a successful and favorite mode. Marcellus St. Vrain, brother to our leader, is noted in coming this dodge over them.

At night, the rain fell and the wind blew, driving the smoke in our faces: all went to bed early, leaving me sitting by the fire. It was my favorite pastime to take a blanket and lie on the ground with it wrapped around me, with back to the wind, apart from the noisy camp, to read, or scrawl a few words in a blank book of the events of the day, or think of friends far away; or, perchance, nodding, and, in a dreamy state, with the warm sun beaming on me, build castles in the air. Many object to this idle run of thought, as it exerts, say they, a pernicious influence on the mind; that it drives away rational, sober thought, and distracts the mind from business; but what satisfaction it is, especially on the prairie, where there is no mental occupation, to think of things not in our power to possess; for, during the brief moments we indulge in this train, we are as much gratified and happy as if in actual possession; and why deprive one of this *poor* luxury? With myself it was like the two-mile heats in races—"once around and repeat;" for, on every opportunity, I endeavored to resume the thread of the last reverie, and dream away, sometimes in a conflict with the Indians, or rescuing a fair maiden from the hands of ruthless savages; or, again, chasing buffalo and feasting of the fat of the land. Anyone, in the Far West, is romantically inclined.

We awoke in the morning, again drenched, cold, and uncomfortable, with saturated clothes hanging on us. A kettle of beans was on the fire cooking when the men went to bed; and, while I was punching the savages in imagination, I had punched the fire too much. The consequence was a mess of burnt beans; some tough, stringy, old steer meat, emitting such an unpleasant smell, which to eat seemed almost a sin. Maybe the fellows didn't swear at me! Tell it not in Gath! but I laughed until their woe-begone faces relaxed into good-humored smiles.

The pelting rain enlivened the scene; and Drinker, General Lee, and I started for the fort, nearly forty miles distant. The sorry breakfast sat uneasily on our craving stomachs, and we spurred our animals over the ground for miles without speaking, with rain falling just enough to penetrate our clothing and cause suicidal feeling. Our ideas of the beautiful had fled; and, after a weary day's trot, we arrived in sight of the fort, where our animals were soon unsaddled, and turned out at the gate, to wander in quest of grass. Going in, we found Mr. St. Vrain, who introduced us to William Bent, a partner, Doctor Hempstead, and several traders. We sat down to a table, for the first time in fifty days, and ate with knives, forks, and plates.

A room was given us, in company with several government teamsters, in which to sleep; had our inclination been consulted, the open air would have been preferred to the unpleasant sensation of oppression felt in being shut up within four walls; but, *n'importe*, we didn't have to guard against Indians.

I arose early in the morning, and going on top of the fort, had a good view of the "Spanish Peaks" to the northwest, apparently fifteen miles distant—in reality *one hundred and twenty*. They were of a dull gray color; while a lower range were dazzling white, all perpetually covered with snow. To the northeast, a faint outline of a mountain was descried—James's or Pike's Peak!

William Bent and Marcellus St. Vrain (the former a partner and the latter a trader in the company's employ) have Indian wives. In the fort was a *mélange* of traders and employers, government officers and subordinates, Indians, Frenchmen, and hunters.

The fort is a quadrangular structure, formed of *adobes*, or sun-dried brick. It is thirty feet in height, and one hundred feet square; at the northeast corner, and its corresponding diagonal, are bastions of a hexagonal form, in which are a few cannon. The fort walls serve as the back

walls to the rooms, which front inward on a courtyard. In
the center of the court is the "robe press"; and lying on the
ground was a small brass cannon, burst in saluting General
Kearney.

The roofs of the houses are made of poles and a layer
of mud a foot or more thick, with a slight inclination, to
run off the water. There was a billiard table in a small
house on top of the fort, where the *bourgeoise* and visitors
amused themselves; and, in the clerk's office, contiguous, a
first-rate spyglass, with which I viewed the *caballada* coming from the grazing ground, seven miles up the river. In
the belfry, two eagles, of the American bald species, looked
from their prison. They were two years old, but their heads
do not become bald until attaining the age of three. Antelope and other fresh meats were scarce, and the eagles had
to starve two days. One evening they were let loose; one
escaped unharmed, the other flew a short distance, and a
Cheyenne shot him for the feathers, to adorn his own ugly
head. "*Enfant de garce!*" muttered I. How I wanted to
retaliate on the savage.

On the evening of the 3d of November, three men
arrived from the direction of the "States," on express, from
a government train of 28 wagons and 160 mules, which
had been robbed by the Pawnees; one man killed, several
wounded, a wagon burnt, all the mules but 7 taken; and,
to use their euphonic language, "the devil to pay"—Uncle
Sam, we suppose.

One of the express came forward and shook hands with
me; he was a lieutenant of Captain Holt's company of
Missouri volunteers. The regiment had been ordered out,
but disbanded. Buchanan (the lieutenant) was not to be
deprived of a visit to "*Nueva Méjico*"; so, doffing his
clothes of the military cut, he left Fort Leavenworth as

wagonmaster of the train just robbed. Buck (as he was familiarly called by way of abbreviation) was full of fun, and he related the circumstance with as much *sang froid* as if he had done nothing else all his life but fight Indians.

CHAPTER III

THE VILLAGE

O<small>N THE</small> evening of the 8th of November, I started for the Indian village with John Smith. Yes! John Smith! the veritable John Smith! After leaving cities, towns, steamboats, and the civilized world, and traversing the almost boundless plains, here, at the base of the Rocky Mountains, among buffalo, wild Indians, traders, and Spanish mules, have I found a John Smith. And, probably, for fear the name might become extinct, he has named his little half-breed boy John, whom we called Jack, for brevity's sake.

Pierre, a good Canadian, drove the four-mule wagon, in which was our bedding, a little provision, and an outfit for mule trading. Smith's squaw, a woman of thirty years or about, with prominent cheek bones and other Indian peculiarities, rode astride of a high-pommeled Indian saddle. The horse was decked out with a saddle cover of blue cloth, worked according to fancy, with many-colored beads, and tin pellets pendant from the fringed edges, covering him from wethers to rump. Little Jack, three or four years of age, clung behind his mother, plainly showing in his complexion and features the mingling of American and Indian blood. His gray eyes were continually centered on me; but I could say nothing intelligible to him, as he spoke only the Cheyenne tongue. A boy, ten years

45

old, son of Smith's squaw (a full-blood), cantered along on a pony.

We went down the river bank to the mouth of *Río las Animas*[1] or *Purgatoire,* and stopped in a grove of young cottonwood. Hard by, in a marshy spot, grew many rushes, on which our small *caballada* fared well. Ours was a nice little camp. The sun, in setting, cast long shadows through the trees on the gray grass so calm and solemn; the smoke curled upward in a continuous blue line, losing itself high in the open space; and the air was cool enough to be bracing, and to render the fire agreeable. On an outspread robe, at one side of the fire, sat Jack and his mother, Smith sharing the seat with them; myself, cross-legged, looked around with silent satisfaction and admiration; and Pierre, a short distance off, was gathering wood for the night.

The squaw lifted the coffeepot from the coals, and we unstrapped our tin cups from the saddles; with dried, pounded buffalo meat and the *sine qua non* of the mountaineer—the pipe—we did well, talking and smoking until the fire grew dim, when we separated. Wrapping up in my blankets and covering my nose from the frost, I watched the stars in the clear, blue vault above and listened to the distant howl of the coyote, until I unconsciously fell asleep.

> *The wolves have preyed; and, look, the gentle day,*
> *Before the wheels of Phoebus, round about,*
> *Dapples the east with spots of drowsy gray.*

Shortly after sunrise we were once more in the saddle. Our animals, with rush-distended stomachs, gave prospect of doing good service. The route was the same over which

[1] A Spanish-Mexican term, signifying *River of Souls.*

46

The Village

Lee, Drinker, and myself passed the day we started in advance of the train. We were then too wet to enjoy anything.

The soap plant (*Amole* or *Yucca augustifolia*) dotted the prairie, here and there, in the strange-looking garb of green. Its root is much used by the New Mexicans in washing clothes—more especially the finer goods—it not possessing alkaline properties in so great a degree as the common soap of wood ashes. The plant is an evergreen, not dissimilar in general appearance to the palmetto of Louisiana and Texas.

We had much to speak of: Smith of the States; and, to my many inquiries of the Indians, he expatiated at length on their customs, food, and easy life. Of the viands, he lauded *dog's* flesh to the very skies; on my expressions of abhorrence at the bare thought, he said:

"I bet I'll make you eat dog meat in the village, and you'll say it's good, and the best you ever hid in your 'meat-bag'" (stomach).

"No you will not," rejoined I; "the mere idea is enough to sicken one—slimy pup meat! ugh! not enough of the carnivorous in me for that; besides buffalo meat, in my opinion, cannot be surpassed for delicacy of flavor in this or any other country."

"Well, hos! I'll dock off buffler, and then if thar's any meat that 'runs' can take the shine outen 'dog,' you can slide."

I still persisted that there was no convincing me; and, though firmly believing that "dog" could not pass, yet, in this country, circumstances bring us down to many things which before seem impossible; and no one can tell but that a piece of *old mule* would be quite acceptable, ere passing through the fiery ordeal of a year in the Far West.

Indeed, we had already eaten the next thing to mule and nothing—broken-down steer meat. Oh grief! my jaws ache to think of the sobby *dejeuners,* in the soaking rain, of old steer; or, as the Canadians termed it, "*sacré boeuf.*"

In a narrow bottom, well sheltered by abrupt hills in the background, we made our stay for the night. Turning out our animals and fixing things rightly, Smith and I waded the river, where, among the underbrush and tall marshgrass, we had a few shots at a band of white-tailed deer.

At twelve o'clock the next day, we came to three Indian lodges, where we found William Bent's squaw and her mother on their way to the fort. We were invited to the back part of the lodge, where dried, pounded cherries, mixed with buffalo marrow, and a root, eaten raw, resembling in taste and appearance the *Jerusalem artichoke,* were set before us. Whiffing the long pipe with the clever inmates, we remounted.

Toward evening, Smith pointed to some objects, inquiring of me what they were, but I could not guess aright. "That's the village," said he. Mountain men can distinguish objects which to a novice in prairie ken have no tangible form or size. By sundown we were at the lodges, whose conical shape and dusky yellow hue looked oddly but welcome to our tired eyes and limbs.

It is Indian rule that the first lodge a stranger enters on visiting a village is his home during his stay—whether invited or not, it is all the same—and, as we wished to be at the "Lean Chief's," we inquired for him. Without saying a word or going in the lodge first, we unsaddled in front of it, putting our "possibles" in the back part, the most honored and pleasant place, for there is no passing by or other annoyance.

The owner occupies the back of the lodge, which is given up for a guest; and the Lean Chief's squaw and daughters removed his robes, etc., to one side. The women and children crowded around us while unsaddling; the strange dress and appearance of the boys attracted my attention; which latter, from their infancy to the age of six and seven, go without a particle of clothing, *dans costume à l'Adam*—a string of beads around the neck. The girls are clothed from the earliest hour.

The white man is always welcome with the Cheyenne, as he generally has *mok-ta-bo-mah-pe*—coffee. We went in the lodge; the grave-looking head, V*ip-po-nah*, or the Lean Chief, and his two solemn coadjutors shook hands with us, with the salutation of, *"Hook-ah-hay! num-whit!"*—equivalent to *"Welcome, how do you do"*; and then they relapsed into silence. Water was handed us to drink, as they suppose a traveler must be thirsty after riding; then meat was set before us, as they think a tired man needs refreshment. When we had finished, the pipe was passed around, during which soothing pastime the news were asked.

There is much to admire in this praiseworthy forbearance; and, although the Indians are as curious as any people, yet, through their consideration, the cravings of hunger and thirst are first satisfied; then, under the communicative influence of the long pipe, the topics of the season are discussed.

A lodge, generally, is composed of seventeen or more slender poles of pine, three inches in diameter at the butts, finely tapering to the small ends, and eighteen to twenty-three or four feet in length. These poles are tied together a few inches from the small ends, with the butts resting on the ground, so that the frame resembles a cone, over which a covering of buffalo skin is neatly fitted, divested of hair

49

and rendered pliant by means of the *dubber*—an adze-shaped piece of iron fitted to an angular section of elk's horn—which chips off pieces of the hard skin until it is reduced to the requisite thinness. Brains are then rubbed on it, making it still softer. The skins are then cut and sewed together with awl and sinew, so that they fit neatly the pole frame. By rolling up the lower edge of this covering, it makes a commodious, airy habitation in summer, and, by closing all the apertures, a warm shelter in winter. At the apex an opening is left, through which the ends of the poles protrude and by which the smoke finds its way out. The fire is built in the center; and, to prevent the smoke being driven back by the wind, there are two flaps or continuations of the upper skins, with poles attached on the outside. These flaps they shut, shift, or extend, as occasion requires.

We made known our business, and immediately a "crier" was sent out. Throwing back the skin-door of the lodge, he protruded his head and then his whole body, and uttered in a stentorian voice something similar to the following, "*Hibbolo, hibbolo! Po-ome, ho-o-o, nah wah-he, se-ne-mone, nah tah-ti-ve woh-pshe-o-nun, nah mod-ta-bo woh-pshe-o-nun, nah woh-pi woh-pshe-o-nun, nah mo-tah-ke, nah o-ne-ah-wokst*"; meaning, in regular succcession, that "Blackfoot [Smith] had come for mules; and all who wished, to come and trade; that we had tobacco, blue blankets, black [deep blue] blankets, white blankets, knives, and beads."

It is contrary to Indian *medicine* or religion, to pass between the landlord (owner of the lodge) and the fire, for, they say, it dissolves friendship, and any infringement of this custom is looked upon with displeasure.

We were very comfortably situated; the lodge was large

enough to admit our lying with feet to the fire—made true
Indian fashion in a small space, and heaped continually in
a rounding, compact form. As the night waned apace, we
were visited by the prominent men; who, in a dignified
manner, shook hands with us, and sat with crossed legs,
propounding questions: *ad interim*, passing the pipe. As
each Indian appeared at the lodge entrance, *"Hook-ah-
hay"* or *"num-whit"* (the mode of congratulation) escaped
his lips; to which a like response was given by the landlord or us.

We sat in our places at the back part, and the Indians,
according to rank, took seats to our left, on mother earth
or their own robes. To the right was our host; and, if a man
entitled to notice by right of seniority or daring deeds of
valor entered, those inferior in honors gave place next the
white man (us). Sometimes Indians of equal rank were in
the lodge at the same time, and then a *sotto voce* dispute
as to the "upper seat" would be carried on with much
gesticulatory motion.

Their dusky faces, viewed by the yellow blaze, together
with the unintelligible jargon, filled me with new and
strange thoughts; and, when the old crones swung the
seething black pot of meat from the fire of dried sticks, I
could not but think of the gipsy tribes, who possess many
traits resembling theirs, and who, in common with them,
have an unconquerable love for roaming.

One by one the grave councilors took their leave.
When the fire grew low, all had retired to bed but myself,
puffing, slowly, a pipe, uninterruptedly thinking of all the
analogies written (that I had read) between the Indians,
Hebrews, and Gipsies; but, presently, through the wreaths
of white smoke, the sleeping face of our host's daughter,
just visible in the expiring light, intercepted the delivery of

a grave dissertation, in imagination, to an intelligent audience. Then, I mused of her awhile, until the neglected pipe, dropping out of my hand, roused me from a doze; so, reaching around for the blankets, and cutting a piece of dried "buffler" to "chew," I folded my hands over my breast, and traced, with my eye, the lodgepoles, running way up to a center, which, in the vacillating, dying flame, were alternately revealed and hidden, until I thought I was dead and sentenced, forever, to run backward up and down seventeen lodgepoles for the amusement of a merry set of laughing devils, and in that state I fell asleep, undisturbed but by the occasional baying of a village dog or the dismal howl of a coyote.

Early in the morning we sat around the fire, waiting for the host's meat to cook, to which we contributed the coffee—the most important and rare addition.

The Indians talked of moving to the "Big Timber," a few miles above, and soon the village was in commotion, the young men driving up their different bands of horses, the squaws catching them. Some took down the lodges, and tying the poles in two bundles, fastened them on either side of a mule or horse, like the shafts of a dray—the lower ends dragging the ground; and, behind the horse, a tray-shaped basket or hoop, latticed with hide thongs, was tied on these poles, in which were put the children too young to ride alone, and other things not easily carried on a horse. Some of the mules were saddled, and on each side were slung square bags, of thick buffalo hide divested of hair, in which stone hammers, dubbers, wooden bowls, horn spoons, etc., were thrown.

The skin of which these convenient hampers are made is called *par flêche*—a French term Anglicised, as are many other foreign words in the mountains, by general usage. Its literal meaning is, *"arrow fender,"* or *"warder"*; for, from it, the prairie Indians construct their almost impenetrable shields. Moccasin soles is the principal use, for which purpose it is admirably suited, it being pliant to the foot, while it serves as a protection from the cactus growing so prolifically in this country. Without care, one in walking will stumble over these, and the long, slender thorns, penetrating with ease, cause an acute, stinging pain, worse even than nettles. Being without socks most of the time (and none to be had), often, while hunting, a hole would wear in the toe of my moccasin, and unavoidably, the thorns would stick most painfully. My "big toe" looked like a lady's[2] finger punctured in sewing.

The village was, ere long, in motion. Looking back to the old site, we saw nothing but eighteen thin pillars of smoke finding their way to the upper air, marking where had been the lodges; pieces of old, cast-off robes, and the usual *debris* of a deserted Indian camp; which, with a few snarling coyotes and large gray wolves, were all the signs of life remaining of the noisy, bustling town.

We crossed a large bottom, where we had a fine opportunity of seeing the moving village to great advantage. First went four or five lodges; and, following after, our wagon, with fifteen or twenty Indians talking to *Po-ome*, or "signing" with me. Young men were scattered in every direction, galloping to and fro, chasing stray animals, or coursing over the prairie for amusement.

Each lodge had its own band of horses, which presented a strange appearance; eighteen or more bands close to each other, walking along but not mixing; each band following a favorite mare, or, perchance, a woebegone, scrawny mule, not worth the powder and ball to kill it. It

[2] I hope the ladies will pardon the simile.

is a strange and general fact that *caballadas* are mostly led by a no-account mare or mule—the greatest devil in the drove. They follow their erratic leader everywhere, like sheep, whether jumping, running, or grazing.

The animals with the lodgepole *travéés* jogged along, no care being taken of them, while the fat little inmates laughed, or, with "wond'ring eyes," stared at us silently.

The young squaws take much care of their dress and horse equipments; they dashed furiously past on wild steeds, astride of the high-pommeled saddles. A fancifully colored cover, worked with beads or porcupine quills, making a flashy, striking appearance, extended from wethers to rump of the horse, while the riders evinced an admirable daring, worthy of Amazons. Their dresses were made of buckskin, high at the neck, short sleeves, or rather none at all, fitting loosely, and reaching obliquely to the knee, giving a relieved, Diana look to the costume; the edges scalloped, worked with beads, and fringed. From the knee downward, the limb was encased in a tightly fitting leggin, terminating in a neat moccasin—both handsomely worked with beads. On the arms were bracelets of brass, which glittered and reflected in the radiant morning sun, adding much to their attractions. In their pierced ears, shells from the Pacific shore were pendant; and, to complete the picture of *savage* taste and profusion, their fine complexions were eclipsed by a coat of flaming vermillion.

Altogether it was a pleasing and desirable change from the sight of the pinched waists and constrained motions of the women of the States, to see these daughters of the prairie dressed loosely—free to act, unconfined by the ligatures of fashion; but I do not wish to be understood that I prefer seeing our women dressed *à la Cheyenne,* as it is a costume forbidden by modesty, the ornaments gaudy and common and altogether unfit for a civilized woman to wear; but here, where novelty constitutes the charm, 'twas indeed a relief to the eye.

Many of the largest dogs were packed with a small quantity of meat, or something not easily injured. They looked queerly, trotting industriously under their burdens; and, judging from a small stock of canine physiological information, not a little of the wolf was in their composition. These dogs are extremely muscular, and are compactly built.

We crossed the river on our way to the new camp; the alarm manifested by the *ki-kun*—children—in the lodge-pole drays, as they dipped in the water, was amusing; the little fellows, holding their breaths, not daring to cry, looked imploringly at their inexorable mothers, and were encouraged by words of aprobation from their stern fathers. Regaining the grassy bottom, we once more went in a fast walk.

The different-colored horses, the young Indian beaux, the bold, bewildering belles, and the newness of the scene was gratifying in the extreme, to my unaccustomed senses. After a ride of two hours, we stopped, and the chiefs, fastening their horses, collected in circles, to smoke the pipe and talk, letting their squaws unpack the animals, pitch the lodges, build fires, arrange the robes, and, when all was ready, these "lords of creation" dispersed to their several homes, to wait until their patient and enduring spouses prepared some food. I was provoked, nay, angry, to see the lazy, overgrown men do nothing to help their wives; and, when the young women pulled off their bracelets and finery to *chop wood*, the cup of my wrath was full to overflowing, and, in a fit of honest indignation, I pronounced them ungallant and savage in the true sense of the word. A wife here is, indeed, a helpmeet.

Once more ensconced in the back part of Vip-po-nah's lodge, we felt at home. A large wooden bowl of meat was set before us, to which, with coffee, we did ample justice.

The horses belonging to an Indian community are numerous; with us, there were nearly or quite two hundred, of different colors and sizes, scattered over the gentle hillsides in picturesque groups.

After two days' entertaining sojourn at the village, we left, with four fine mules, for the fort, which place we reached at the close of the second evening, where we found the employees reloading the wagons for a start to Santa Fé. I learned that Colonel Doniphan's regiment, with which I wished to travel, had left Santa Fé; and, being pleased with Indian life, I returned with Smith and William Bent, with full complements of goods for robe trading. We encamped the first night on an island in the river, with plenty of wood and grass near and sheltered by a patch of high weeds from the winds.

Crossing the clear stream on the firm sandy bottom, we regained the trace early in the morning, and, at night, after a continuous day's jog, we were at the village. William Bent stayed in his own lodge; Smith and I, in Vip-po-nah's, by whom we were welcomed.

The air was much cooler than before; quantities of thin ice floated down the gliding river current. It was right pleasant to get back and be surrounded by Indians.

In Vip-po-nah's lodge was his grandson, a boy of six or seven months old. Every morning, his mother washed him in cold water and sent him out to the air to make him hardy; he would come in, perfectly nude, from his airing, about half-frozen. How he would laugh and brighten up as he felt the warmth of the fire! Being a boy, the parents have great hopes of him as a brave and chief (the acme of Indian greatness); his father dotes upon him, holding him in his arms, singing in a low tone, and in various ways showing his extreme affection.

The girls do not receive much attention from the father; they are reared to implicit obedience, and with a feeling of inferiority to the males. What a happy contrast does the state of society show in enlightened countries, where woman is in her proper sphere, loved and looked up to as an adviser and friend—here, a mere "hewer of wood and drawer of water"—a nonenity, a mere cypher—treated as a slave and unnoticed. It is, indeed, an almost inappreciable blessing that we live in an age of progressive civilization—an age in which true worth is rewarded, irrespective of sex; though there yet is room for improvement.

CHAPTER IV

PECULIARITIES

T HE MORNING came, and we were somewhat occupied in trading, but robes were scarce, the buffalo hair not being in prime order.

We were invited to *Gray Eyes'* lodge, to a feast, early in the day. Sitting down, after shaking hands, a wooden bowl of choice pieces of fat meat was set before us. We used our *own* knives and fingers. Gray Eyes has two wives and twelve children, two of whom—fine-looking boys of fifteen and thirteen summers, respectively—were in the lodge; their father's eye beamed on them fondly when he spoke of their killing buffalo from horseback with bow and arrow. The eldest had an open, frank countenance—the reverse of his father, whose features plainly showed duplicity, and his small gray eyes—hence his cognomen— twinkled replete with rascality, for which he is noted.

It is Indian custom that whatever is set before the guest belongs to him; and he is expected to take that he does not eat home with him; so we stuck our knives in some of Gray Eyes' fat slices when the pipe was finished.

Smith's son Jack took a crying fit one cold night, much to the annoyance of four or five chiefs, who had come to our lodge to talk and smoke. In vain did the mother shake and scold him with the severest Cheyenne words, until Smith, provoked beyond endurance, took the squalling

58

youngster in hands; he "shu-ed," and shouted, and swore, but Jack had gone too far to be easily pacified. He then sent for a bucket of water from the river, and poured cupful after cupful on Jack, who stamped, and screamed, and bit, in his puny rage. Notwithstanding the icy stream slowly descended until the bucket was emptied, another was sent for, and again and again the cup was replenished and emptied on the blubbering youth. At last, exhausted with exertion and completely cooled down, he received the remaining water in silence, and, with a few words of admonition, was delivered over to his mother, in whose arms he stifled his sobs, until his heart-breaking grief and cares were drowned in sleep. What a devilish mixture Indian and American blood is!

The Indians never chastise a boy, as they think his spirit would be broken and *cowed* down, and, instead of a warrior, he would be a *squaw*—a harsh epithet, indicative of cowardice—and they resort to any method but infliction of blows to subdue a refractory scion.

Jack has three names: that of Jack, so called by the whites, and two Indian ones—*Wo-pe-kon-ne* and *O-toz-vout-si*—the former meaning "White Eyes"—a nickname —the latter, his proper title—"Buck Deer."

For pastime, I began a glossary of the Cheyenne tongue, to facilitate its acquirement; the visitors, thinking me a queer customer (*mah-son-ne*—"a fool"—as they were pleased to denominate me and my vocabularic efforts), replied willingly to my inquiries of "*Ten-o-wast?*"—"What is it?"—at the same time pointing to any object whose name I wished to know. I wrote their answers according to the pronunciation. The squaws of our lodge gave me words, purposely, not easily articulated or written; my attempts at correct enunciation were greeted with lively sallies of laughter. Our conversation was carried on in broken, very broken, sentences; and, I must say, the part that they too ably sustained was not of the most refined character. No person so young as myself had ever visited the Cheyennes, and the gentle fair seemed glad to meet one divested of the trader's assumed consequence.

The visits of the Indians were divided between Mr. Bent's lodge and our own; but we saw as many as we wished, for our coffee and sugar cost us a dollar a pound. To secure the good will and robes of the sensitive men, we had to offer our dear-bought Java at meal time—the period of the greatest congregation. Still, their company was acceptable, as their manners, conversation, and pipes were agreeable.

So complete and comprehensive is their mode of communication by signs that they can understand each other without a word being said, and with more facility than with the lips.

I had a small box, in which were shirts, tobacco, a backgammon board, and a few books; one of them from Harper's series of the Family Library, on the heavenly bodies. The plates were incomprehensible to the natives; and, with all my efforts, I could but imperfectly make myself understood, even on most commonplace matters. Some of the chiefs, having seen this book, would not be put off without an answer to their queries; and it brought all my ingenuity into play to make suitable similes between the plates and things within their knowledge; consequently, great perversion of Dick's celestial geography took place.

A chief, named *Mah-ke-o-nih*, or the "Big Wolf," professedly took a great liking to me. We went, by his invitation, one day, to a feast, guided by his youngest son, where we found Mah-ke-o-nih in a small lodge. After the customary salutations, we sat down to a bowl of dried stewed pumpkin, with a horn spoon sticking in it, from which we partook by turns. The spoon was a curiosity in its way—manufactured from the horn of a Rocky Mountain sheep and holding at least a pint. The childish hint, "take a spoon pig," would not help the matter much if these kind were in use.

The meaning of *feast* (a term much in vogue with the traders) is anything set before one, by invitation, be it much or little, rare or common.

Mah-ke-o-nih was in mourning for the loss of a near relative; and, to show the outward customary signs of grief, he lived in a small lodge. He is now old; but, in younger days, the name of Mah-ke-o-nih was well known as that of a brave, and, in later years, as a fearless warrior of un-spotted fame. Now he is honored and respected for his Indian virtues.

I gave him a bent piece of hickory, from an ox yoke, with which to make a bow. As hard wood is scarce, and as the chief knew that I had been offered, several times, a robe for it, he was much pleased by my preference; and, in return, gave me his title. After this circumstance I was known among the Cheyennes as *Mah-ke-o-nih*—sometimes as *Veheo-kiss*, or the "Young Whiteman."

In this village were more than a hundred dogs—from the large half-wolf down to the smallest specimen. Often, during the night, they broke forth in a prolonged howl, with the accompanying music of hundreds of prowling wolves making a most dissonant, unearthly noise. And such a fuss! Everyone ceased talking until the Voices of the Night were hushed. In our lodge were three huge curs and four cross fiists; and, whenever the signal for a general bewailing was given by some superannuated mother of many canine generations, out, pellmell, tore our loud-mouthed curs and the snarling squawpets to join the doggish revelry.

The love of gaming seems inherent in our very natures; as a proof of this, it was ever a favorite amusement with the Cheyennes and other Indians long ere they became acquainted with the whites. Their game, however, is simple, though not the less injurious in its effects. It is played by the young men and women; who, sitting in a circle, and with a rocking to-and-fro motion of the body, accompanied by a low, quiet chant, increased in vigor as the game progresses, hold a bit of wood, cherrystone, or anything small in the hand; and after a series of dexterous shiftings, so as to deceive, hold them out, while the singing stops, for the players to bet in which hand is the stone. So soon as they say, the object is shown; the fortunate ones sweep the stakes; the stone is given to the next, in order of rotation, the chant again strikes up—other trinkets are put up, and the betting recommences. They laugh and get much excited over their primitive game; and, often, an unlucky maiden rises from her amusement without the numerous bracelets, rings, and beads with which she came gayly decked to the meeting lodge.

This morning was one of November's most genial days. About ten o'clock, I walked out and sat on a dry cottonwood log to admire the rural and domestic scene. The grass was green in many places—the majestic cottonwoods, not yet entirely robbed of their foliage, upreared their imposing trunks, while the branches gracefully overhung the clean, wind-swept grass.

The yellow, cone-shaped lodges looked like so many pyramids. Near them were industrious squaws; bringing, by dint of constant exertion, buffalo skins down to the required thinness by means of the *dubber*, which, as it struck the hard and dry robe, sounded like the escapement of steam from a small pipe. The valley was partly locked in by a low range of hills, on whose sides numerous bands of gay-colored horses were luxuriating on the fine, nutritious verdure. Around the lodges troops of boys were shooting at marks, with bow and arrow, or tumbling on the grass in childish sport. Dignified chiefs walked with stately step and erect heads to grave council or taciturn smoke.

I sat long—collecting and embodying the thoughts and actions of the past four months, summing up the whole, with a glance at my then present situation. My companions were rough men—used to the hardships of a mountaineer's life—whose manners are blunt, and whose speech is rude—men driven to the western wilds with embittered feelings—with better natures shattered—with hopes blasted—to seek, in the dangers of the warpath, fierce excitement and banishment of care. The winter snow wreaths drift over them unheeded, and the night wind, howling around their lonely camp, is heard with calm indifference. Yet these aliens from society, these strangers to the refinements of civilized life, who will tear off a bloody scalp with even grim smiles of satisfaction, are fine fellows, full of fun, and often kind and obliging.

John Smith was a modified[1] specimen of this character. Ten years before, he left his employer, a tailor, and ran off from St. Louis with a party of traders for the mountains; and so enamored was he with the desultory and exciting life that he chose rather to sit cross-legged, smoking the long Indian pipe, than to cross his legs on his master's board. He first remained a winter with the Blackfeet; but,

[1] The meaning attached to *modified* is that he is not one of the worst characters—rather peaceable than otherwise.

running too great a risk of "losing his hair" (scalp) at the hands of the impetuous, *coup*-anxious braves, he sojourned awhile with the more friendly Sioux; and, subsequently, wended his way, while pursuing the trail of a horse-stealing band of Arapahoes, to the headwaters of the Arkansas; and, in the quiet nooks and warm savannas of the Bayou Salade, took up his abode and a squaw with the Cheyennes, with whom he has ever since remained. At times he lived as they did, with lodge and horses, running buffalo, and depending on it, as did his new-found friends, entirely for subsistence; dressing robes for the trade; taking part in the council; looked up to as a chief, and exercising much authority. He became such an adept in the knowledge of the Cheyenne tongue, and such a favorite with the tribe, that his services as trader were now quite invaluable to his employers. Possessed of a retentive memory, he still spoke the dialects of the three nations just named, and, in addition, French like a native, Spanish very well, and his mother tongue. Though subject to privations of a severe nature, he thought it

Better to reign in hell than serve in Heaven

and nothing could persuade him to lead a different life.

The New Mexicans often came in small parties to his Indian village, their mules packed with dried pumpkin, corn, etc., to trade for robes and meat; and Smith, who knew his power, exacted tribute, which was always paid. One time, however, refusing, Smith harangued the village, and calling the young men together, they resolutely proceeded to the party of cowering Mexicans; and, emptying every sack on the ground, called the women and children to help themselves, which summons was obeyed with alacrity. The poor *pelados* left for El Valle de Taos, poorer by far than when they came: uttering thanks to Heaven for the retention of their scalps. This, and other aggravated cases, so intimidated the New Mexicans and impressed them so deeply with a sense of Smith's supreme potency that ever after, his permission to trade was humbly craved by a special deputation of the parties, accompanied by peace offerings of corn, pumpkin, and *pinole*. Once, as he was journeying by himself, a day's ride from the village, he was met by forty or more corn traders; who, instead of putting speedily out of the way such a bane to their prospects, gravely asked him if they could proceed, and offered him every third robe (a large percentage) to accompany and protect them, which he did. For the proceeds of his three days' protection, he received more than two hundred dollars. Indeed, he became so independent and so regardless of justice in his condescension toward the *Carahos*[2] that the Governor of New Mexico offered five hundred dollars for him, dead or alive; but, so afraid were they of the Cheyennes, his capture was never attempted.

Smith was strange in some respects; his peculiar adaptation to surrounding circumstances and perceptive faculties enabled him to pick up a little knowledge of everything, and to show it off much to his own credit—an unaccountable composition of goodness and evil, cleverness and meanness, caution and recklessness! I used to look at him with astonishment and wonder if he was not the devil incog. He and I often sang hymns, and a more sanctimonious, meek, at-peace-with-mankind look could nowhere be found than in his countenance; at other times, he *sacré-ed* in French, *caraho-ed* in Spanish-Mexican, interpolated with *thunder strike you* in Cheyenne, or, at others, he genuinely and emphatically damned in American.

[2] *Caraho*—a Spanish oath.

I had a backgammon board, brought from St. Louis. Smith kept the squaws of the lodge "chunking" up the fire to give light for us; and "deuce ace," "double sixes" were, probably for the first time, heard in a Cheyenne village. We played for hours, interrupted occasionally by a squaw with a robe to trade; and, attending to her wants, we would resume the board. The Indians laughed at us, saying, "Ten-o-wast?"—"What is it"—which we explained to the best of our ability. My books and backgammon board, paper and pencil, were great novelties to the savages, who would attentively examine them, look at me, shake their heads, and, after a sober pause and sometimes with a puzzled expression of features, exclaim, "*Mah-ke-o-nih ma-son-ne,*" "Big Wolf's foolish." So it was! everything beyond their comprehension was *ma-son-ne.*

Smith's voice was capable of some little harmonious modulation, and we used to sing, "The days when we went gipsying," "The mellow horn," "The minstrel's returned from the war," and other antiquated melodies, interspersed with hymns and our own crude airs and compositions, making the lodge resound, to the infinite amusement of the squaws and children, and sometimes calling forth contemptuous "*Ve-heo mah-son-nes*" (White men are fools") from the ridiculously solemn old men. Frequently, when executing a song in our very best manner, the village dogs chimed in with their original and touching music, forcing us to acknowledge ourselves beaten, in fair fight, and to withdraw, leaving them undisputed masters of the field; our only consolation was in the idea that they, being Indian dogs, were incapable of appreciating our efforts.

The Cheyennes have quite a variety of dishes, some hard to stomach—others quite palatable. Among them, a favorite is of wild cherries, gathered in the mountains in

66

the summer and pounded (stone and all) to a jelly, which, when dried, is put away for the winter, when the buffalo marrow is good—the time for a reunion of the small bands, to trade, feast, smoke, and deliberate. These cherries, incorporated by much manipulation at the hands of the not particularly clean matrons with marrow and pounded meat, and patted in balls, form a principal portion of the feasts.

A buffalo skin is quite thick, which, to make pliable, is stretched to its utmost on the ground (the hair side down), as soon as it is brought in from the hunt, by means of wooden pegs. When it dries, the squaws take the adze-shaped instrument, fitted to the angle of an elk's horn, which has before been described, and, with repeated blows, chip off small shavings of the raw hide until it is the requisite thinness. The shavings are carefully preserved, and, when a very nice feast is wished, these "chips" are put in a wooden bowl and boiling water poured over them, which cooks and reduces the whole to a pulpy mass immediately. This dish tastes similar to boiled Irish potatoes—to which, with the addition of cherries, a fancy flavor is added.

The fungus growing on the sides of decaying logs is gathered by the squaws and boiled with meat for several hours; on tasting the poisonous stuff, as I previously supposed it to be, my thoughts instantaneously traveled to Galveston Bay and its fine oysters. It was first rate, but the appetite soon cloys.

A root growing in the bottoms is much eaten, raw or cooked, partaking both of the flavor of the potato and Jerusalem artichoke.

Before most of the lodges are three sticks, about seven feet in length and an inch in diameter, fastened at the top, and the lower ends brought out so that it stands alone. On this is hung the shield, and a small square bag of *par flèche*, containing pipes, with an accompanying pendant roll of stems, carefully wrapped in blue or red cloth and decorated with beads and porcupine quills. This collection is held in great veneration, for the pipe is their only religion. Through its agency they invoke the Great Spirit; through it they render homage to the winds, to the earth, and to the sky.

Everyone has his peculiar notion on this subject; and, in passing the pipe, one must have it presented stem downward, others, the reverse; some with the bowl resting on the ground; and, as this is a matter of great solemnity, their several fancies are respected. Sometimes I required them to hand it to me, when smoking, in imitation of their custom; on this, a faint smile, half-mingled with respect and pity for my folly in tampering with their sacred ceremony, would appear on their faces, and, with a slow negative shake of the head, they would ejaculate, *"I-sto-met mah-son-ne, wah-hein"*—"Pshaw! that's foolish: don't do so."

It seems strange that these people remain the same untutored, blood-thirsty savages as ever; and so untamable are their natures that contact with missionaries and white men make them only the greater demons—to remain here, as wild, almost, as their favorite buffalo, with no settled purpose, for no apparent good, with no cares but those of providing for themselves and families in the savage way—their fine forms, their intelligent (in spite of their mental darkness) countenances, and noble eyes used for no intellectual purpose, or in any way for the advancement of religion or science. And it appears that all Christian efforts, with extremely few exceptions, instead of humanizing and rendering their homes peaceful and themselves industrious, are so much waste of valuable lives and time.

Religion they (the Cheyennes) have none, if, indeed,

we except the respect paid to the pipe; nor do we see any signs or vestiges of spiritual worship; but, one remarkable thing—in offering the pipe, before every fresh filling, to the sky, the earth, and the winds, the motion made in so doing describes the form of a cross; and, in blowing the first four whiffs, the smoke is invariably sent the same four directions. It is, undoubtedly, void of meaning and unintentional in reference to Christian worship, yet it is a superstition, founded on ancient tradition. This tribe once lived near the headwaters of the Mississippi; and, as the early Jesuit missionaries were such energetic zealots in the diffusion of their religious sentiments, probably to make *their* faith more acceptable to the Indians, the Roman Catholic rites were blended with the homage shown to the pipe, which with the custom of offering, in the form of a cross, is still retained by them; but, as every custom is handed down by tradition merely, the true source has been forgotten. My inquiries were unsatisfactorily answered, owing to want of power to express myself fully: had a reason been assigned, no reliance could have been put in it. The inquiring mind is naturally restless to think that no light can be thrown on their origin and early customs, nor the question settled whether they are the descendants of that race or races by whom the immense turmuli and fortifications were erected throughout the continent; or if they are the progeny of the Aztecs and Peruvians, whose advancement in civilization was so astonishing to the Spanish navigators. But the present Indians are totally ignorant of the most common inventions—a woefully degenerate set, in truth, if they are so descended.

CHAPTER V

THE FORT

On the 29th of November, a party of Mexicans came near camp, with their *mulada*,[1] freighted with corn, beans, etc., to trade for meat and robes. To Smith, the messenger was quite polite. "*Señor; si Señor*"—"Sir, yes Sir"—was prefixed or affixed to their answers to our most trivial question. They were too polite. As they knew Smith by reputation, if not by sight, he was offered whatever he wished—"*a suy disposicion*"—"the whole is at your service"—but he took only that for which he paid in trade a good price. I pitied the poor fellows, though they had no cause for fear; and, after a speedy exchange of commodities for meat and robes, their swarthy faces were turned toward *Las Cumbres Españolas*, whose snow crests could dimly be seen struggling through the fleeting clouds afar off to the northwest.

This side (the west) of the river and a hundred miles down from Bent's Fort is considered, by men who have lived in the country for years (the late maps to the contrary), as New Mexican territory. Undoubtedly our camp was in *Nueve Méjico*. Occasionally we saw government trains, on the opposite side of the river, trailing slowly along, but we did not wish to hail them.

We were a long time without bread, but while buffler's

[1] Train of mules.

fat, we cared or thought little of anything more—better living there could not be. The weather was pleasant toward the middle of the day; and, at night, the lodge fire and pipe contributed, by its genial influence, to make us more than contented to sit cross-legged on warm robes, listening to the traders' yarns (there were several now with us).

William Bent, one evening, wished someone to go to the fort. I proposed to oblige him; and, in the morning, saddling Paint, I was off. A stiff wind, fresh from Pike's Peak, caused me to pull up the collar of my blue blanket overcoat and wrap the pliant buffalo robe around my chilled legs. The fort was thirty to forty miles distant; and, when I clutched more firmly my rifle, as it lay between the saddle pommel and my body, I wanted sincerely to turn back. Chagrined and biting my blue lips with vexation at the last night's rash proposition, I urged Paint in a lope.

In going down a declivity, I espied a horseman in advance; so, putting on a fresh water-proof cap, I spurred up unwilling Paint until within five or six yards of the man, who knew not my approach. Seeing, before nearing him, that he was a Mexican, I took the precaution to turn the muzzle of my rifle toward him, so that, in a case of a hostile demonstration on his part, my gun could be fired in the smallest possible time.

"Hello! *señor*," shouted I at the top of my voice, "where are you going?"

"*Valgame Dios!*" exclaimed he, as he quickly turned his head, much startled at the unexpected sound. Perceiving that I was "white," he bowed his uncovered head, with a respectful *"Buenos le dai, Señor"*—"Good day, Sir."

A response, from me, of *"Gracias, muy bueno"*— "Thank you, very well," was the sum total of our intelligible conversation. He then talked and pointed awhile, and away he galloped through the bottom, while I kept the direct course. My heart felt lighter when he left; he glad to get away, I more than happy, though I had apprehensions he would lie in wait with his *compadres*, whom I knew were in the neighborhood; and, as my horse and rifle were of the best, they would likely not have many intervening scruples as to the propriety of sending an arrow through my coat.

The ground was sparsely covered with grass, and the high wind blew the sand and gravel furiously, blinding both Paint and his rider; but we persevered, sideways and backward, for three or more hours—I trying to see the expected Mexicans through the struggle—until overtaking a United States ox train, with which I traveled and stayed all night.

The teams were unyoked, wood gathered, and soon smoke was rising from the different mess fires. The laugh and oath were mingled with the hungry voices of the men —so different from the quiet, dreamy village. The captain gave me a cup of coffee, and bread, and bacon, at his mess —the two last-named articles great rarities of late. I cut cottonwood limbs from a tree and threw them down before Paint, tied up to a wagon wheel, for him to peel for food. I accepted a sleeping place in the captain's wagon.

The first snow clothed the ground with its chilling drapery. When we arose, shivering with cold, we kindled fires and boiled the coffee. Paint had gnawed off the cottonwood bark quite clean. It affords considerable nourishment and is often given to animals in the spring, when the old grass is rotten and the new not yet fit for use, or in deep snows when grass cannot be reached. Too much of it causes the hair to come out, sometimes leaving the animals quite bare, though it renders them "seal fat."

The Fort

Thanking Captain Fowler for his kindness, I soon was facing the same winds as yesterday—my course pointing to Pike's Peak; and in an hour's ride, *Las Cumbres Españolas*. Near the mouth of the Purgatoire, a deer stopped, with his head turned to look at me, until I was within sixty yards; but my horse, disposed to act foolishly, snorted as I raised my rifle, and away the buck bounded out of sight. Paint traveled pretty fast for an hour or so.

The country in the fort vicinity assumed a bleak appearance; the short grass scantily concealed the cold ground, and the white chalk bluffs, the leafless trees, and the chill air made me feel lonely. The fort mud walls were abominably cheerless. Near were some men digging a grave.

My own unenviable thoughts occupied me through the solitary day; and only when Paint was turned in the corral behind the fort to chew dry hay, and myself with numbed fingers gradually thawing in the long, low dining room, drinking hot coffee, eating bread, buffler, and "State doins," and listening to Charlotte, the glib-tongued, sable fort cook, retailing her stock of news and surmises, did I feel entirely free to throw off care. Shortly following, did I sit by the bright wood fire, in the clerk's office, in a *dolce far niente* state, puffing a Mexican shuck cigarillo, wondering when originated the soothing luxury, until the combined effects of dinner, tobacco, and great change from cold to warmth threw me in a doze, from which I was awaked at dusk.

Mr. Holt, the storekeeper, and I, selected the goods and other articles—the object of my mission—in time for supper.

Captain Enos, assistant quartermaster, and his clerk, Dyer, Doctor Hempstead, Mr. Holt, the carpenter, blacksmith, and a few fort and government employees, constituted the quality and quantity of the male inmates. Rosalie, a half-breed French and Indian squaw (the wife of Ed, the carpenter), and Charlotte, the culinary divinity, were, as a Missouri teamster remarked, "the only female women here." They nightly were led to the floor "to trip the light fantastic toe," swung rudely and gently in the mazes of the contra dance—but such a medley of steps is seldom seen out of the mountains—the halting, irregular march of the war dance, the slipping gallopade, the boisterous pitching of the Missouri backwoodsman, and the more nice gyrations of the Frenchman—for all, irrespective of rank, age, and *color*, went pellmell into the excitement, in a manner that would have rendered a leveler of aristocracies and select companies frantic with delight. It was a most complete democratic demonstration. And then the airs assumed by the fair ones—more particularly Charlotte, who took pattern from real life in the "States"; she acted her part to perfection. The grand center of attraction, the belle of the evening, she treated the suitors for the "pleasure of the next set" with becoming ease and suavity of manner. She knew her worth, and managed accordingly; and, when the favored gallant stood by her side waiting for the rudely-scraped tune from a screaking violin, satisfaction, joy, and triumph over his rivals were pictured on his radiant face.

Doctor Hempstead, however, did not join the festive throng; and his well-stocked library afforded recreation and pastime during the dull intervals of the day.

I met McIlvaine, from the capital of my own state, and, with him, many agreeable reminiscences were gone over. He was in charge of a provision train, and I noticed his command were under better discipline than is usual on the prairie with United States employees.

74

The Fort

In the following afternoon, Greenwood, Jean Batiste—
a Canadian—and myself left for the village with a laden
cart of goods. I never had before seen these men, but, as
the heavy, slow-spoken Française remarked—"*Il est tout
le méme chose ici*"—and, together with shooting at whining coyotes, talking, and the reproving "*sacré*" to the stub-
born tandem-cart mules, we fixed ourselves in good time
near to a heap of logs, which an improvident party of teamsters had collected, set on fire, and left to burn.

The animals were well hobbled, for we knew their failing—that of straying afar, in a spirit of restlessness, and
trouble giving. Paint—the old coon—waited impatiently
for the rawhide strap to be securely fastened, and, at the
first forward lunge, he knowingly turned his white eye
at me.

The foibles and virtues of mutual acquaintances in St.
Louis were freely descanted upon, during the discussion of
some cigars, found, unexpectedly, among my "possibles" at
the fort, as we crossed our legs on the ground that night
before the cottonwood logs. Our taciturn *compañero*
looked at the hot coals for hours, without joining in the
"talk"—with not a muscle of his face relaxed from the
same meaningless rigidity into which they had stiffened at
first—it would be hard to tell of what he thought—and, but
for the vacillating puff, puff, from his thick lips and short
pipestem, one would have supposed him asleep. On the
offer of a cigar, he replied, with a feeling stress on the first
word, without turning his head, as he gave a trial puff for
fire—"*Sa-cré! mon pipe est bon, certainment!*"

Early, Jean Batiste was out for the "cavyard," while
Greenwood and I prepared something to eat. Waiting two
hours in dread of the proximity of the horse-loving Caman-

che or straggling Pawnee, we descried the animals with heads to camp and Jean at their heels.

A hobble is a strip of soft buckskin, or thin *par flêche*, twenty or twenty-five inches in length, fastened to the mule's forelegs, so that both forefeet have to be raised at once in walking; the labor attendant on the exertion generally prevents their straying far.

By five o'clock, we were at the lower end of Tharpe's bottom, where was corralling a United States train. Buchanan, who, in the pride of wagonmastership, directed and superintended, invited us to supper, while our animals grazed unsaddled. A pipe and short talk ensued, and we resumed the trace. By ten o'clock, the baying of the village dogs was distinctly heard across the river. After an hour's wandering in the tangled bottom, Vip-po-nah welcomed us.

The village was in an uproar. The "opposition traders" a mile above had conferred a present of liquor on several chiefs, who, in turn, disposed to their friends, and all were making "the night hideous," in honor of the "rosy god"; for they have songs adapted to their orgies, more noisy and fierce than which none exist. No serious injury resulted from the revel. We saw nothing of the devotees except two squaws in the morning, who tumbled, like wounded "bufflers," in our lodge, pitching on Greenwood, Jean, and I, waking us from our recuperating slumbers. They fell weeping, in drunken seriousness, and the next moment, peals of laughter issued from the mouths, whence but an instant before the blubbering accents of grief had proceeded.

"*Sacré garces! tonnere! sa-a-cré garces!*" rattled out Jean, casting them off rudely with his muscular arm.

Greenwood swore and charged about until he was perfectly awake, but the importunate squaws clung to us.

"*Ten-o-wast? O-ne-a-vokst?*" "What do you want? beads or blankets? What is it?" asked I.

"*Wah-hein! ve-heo-kiss pow-wow nashit, ve-heo mahpe*"—"Nothing. Young white man is very good—want whiskey?"

"Oh, get out, you old hags," said Greenwood; "darn a fool squaw, anyhow; this coon hates 'em naterally, when they act so fool like."

We finally succeeded in making them vacate the premises by dint of threats and persuasion, though sleep was chased effectually, for the time, from our eyelids. There are two objects most repugnant to my feelings—a drunken or an angry woman. She seems to descend from the position of a ministering angel down, down below any scale of degradation conceivable, and imprints such a hideous image of contorted passion, which, notwithstanding the subsequent blandishments of grace and smiles, can never be effaced from the memory.

We began to trade briskly in robes—owing to the cold weather, plenty of buffalo, and liquor, which last seemed to open the Indians' hearts—causing us to drop the backgammon board often to serve the precise savages, who would look at and handle a blanket or other commodity an hour before concluding a bargain. We would have to praise, and feel, and talk of the article in question, and seal the trade by passing the long pipe as a balm to their fastidious tastes.

One evening we were in our places—I was lying on a pile of outspread robes, watching the blaze, as it illumined the lodge, which gave the yellow hue of the skins of which it was made a still brighter tinge; and, following with my eye the thin blue smoke, coursing, in fantastic shapes, through the opening at the top of the cone; my thoughts carrying me momentarily everywhere; now home; now enjoying some choice edible, or, seated by a pleasant friend, conversing; in short, my mind, like the harp in "Alexander's Feast," the chords of which, touched by the magic hand of memory or flight of fancy, alternately depressed or elevated me in feeling. Greenwood and Smith, sitting up, held in "durance vile" the ever present pipe. Their unusual laughter attracted my attention, but, not divining the cause, I joined in the conversation. It was now quite late, and feeling hungry, I asked what was on the fire.

"Tarrapins!" promptly replied Smith.

"Terrapins?" echoed I, in surprise, at the name. "Terrapins! how do they cook them?"

"You know them hard-shell land tarrapin?"

"Yes."

"*Well!* the squaws go out to the sand buttes, and bring the critters in, and cook 'em in the shell alive—those stewin' thar ar cleaned first. Howsomever, they're darned good!"

"Yes, hos, an' that's a fact, wagh!" chimed in Greenwood.

I listened, of course, with much interest to their account of the savage dish, and waited, with impatience, for a taste of that, the recital of whose merits sharpened my already keen appetite. When the squaw transferred the contents of the kettle to a wooden bowl and passed it to us, our butcher knives were in immediate requisition. Taking a piece, with hungry avidity, which Smith handed me, without thought as to what part of the terrapin it was, I ate it with much gusto, calling "for more." It was extremely good, and I spoke of the delicacy of the meat, and answered all their questions as to its excellency in the affirmative, even to the extent of a panegyric on the whole turtle species. After fully committing myself, Smith looked at me awhile in silence, the corners of his mouth gradually making preparations for a laugh, and asked:

"Well, hos! how do you like dog meat?" and then such hearty guffaws were never heard. The stupefaction into which I was thrown by the revolting announcement only increased their merriment, which soon was resolved into yells of delight at my discomfiture.

A revulsion of opinion, and dog meat too, ensued, for I could feel the "pup" crawling up my throat; but saying to myself—"that it was good under the name of terrapin," "that a rose under any other name would smell as sweet," and that it would be prejudice to stop, I broke the shackles of deep-rooted antipathy to the canine breed, and, putting a choice morceau on top of that already swallowed, ever after remained a stanch defender and admirer of dog meat. The conversation held with Smith, the second day of our acquaintance, was brought to mind, and I acknowledged that "dog" was next in order to buffalo.

On the 7th of December, I left, with Smith, for the lower Indian village. His squaw, Wo-pe-kon-ne (Jack), an Indian boy of twelve years, and Pierre accompanied us. A single pack mule carried our small stock of goods and provisions. Smith had his band of five horses, and with two discarded lodgepoles, tied one on each side of a mule, and a basket fastened on a short distance behind the animal, he made an Indian dray, in which Jack was put when tired.

Indian squaws carry very young children on their backs, whether riding or walking. With a twist of the arms, like putting on a coat, the squaw places, or rather flings, the child around, and pulls its little arms about her neck; then,

79

stooping forward until her back is horizontal, she drops her hold of the child, who digs his fingers in her neck, or tugs away at the long braids of pendant hair; and, with a peculiar *hunch* or upward motion of the arms—the same a lady makes in putting a shawl on her shoulders when it has fallen off the neck—the robe is drawn over him, the head only visible. It is a comfortable and desirable position— hence the total absence of one-sidedness, *cross eyes*, and many of the "ills that baby flesh is heir to" through neglect or carelessness of nurses.

We crossed "Big Sand Creek," and camped for the night on what would be an island in high water, and made a cheerful fire of driftwood, leaving the animals well hobbled in good grass. The cold air, after coffee and tobacco were duly disposed, sent us to bed early.

Jack took a crying fit while under way. His mother tried to quiet him gently; Smith endured, impatiently, the fuss for a half-hour; but Jack, keeping it up, was taken from his mother, who looked daggers askance at her unfeeling lord, and jammed into the "dray," where he blubbered, unheeded, for two hours.

Toward sundown we looked for the village; and, when in the "Salt Bottom," a number of lodges, far away to the right, was espied, the river intervening, whose edges were so hard frozen that the animals could scarcely be urged in. Experiencing the same trouble on the opposite side, we forced our way between the high weeds and the trees, emerging into open space not ten yards from a lodge. Smith, fearing that we had stumbled on an Arapaho instead of a Cheyenne village, spoke in a low tone—

"Pull the wipingsticks from your guns, we may have to fight!"

"*Sacré*, dis is von very dam bad affaire—mais here is

mon couteau pour les diables," replied Pierre, loosening his knife in its scabbard, and twitching around the belt.

We kept on much elated. The first man who showed himself caused Smith to turn aside his head and whisper, "Coho! the most infernal and mean of the tribe—the leader of the worst band in the mountains."

Notwithstanding the gloomy aspect, we rode up and offered our hands to Coho, and asked for Warratoria—a chief more friendly than otherwise. We "broke" for the largest lodge; and, giving our horses into the hands of Pierre and the squaw, entered that which proved to be Beardy's, a prominent chief, who, though not on cordial terms with the whites, was not so bad as Coho.

Beardy and others smoked with us, and after a present of tobacco, we left, contrary to their request and desire, under the plea of wishing to reach the Cheyenne village that night, still holding ourselves in readiness for a "brush," determined to save at least one scalp apiece before our own "hair" should go. I kept my horse in motion, looking back for charging Arapahoes; and, before I was aware, he plunged in a rush swamp, so deep I was obliged to dismount and wade through water over my knees, while Paint floundered to the other side, severely straining himself.

We met Indians galloping, who, contrary to custom, did not stop to shake hands, which unequivocal symptom of hostility increased the probability of danger; but we were not molested, and we took care to put a long distance between them and us before night.

On dismounting, my feet were too much frozen to walk, but Smith, by shouting to me to make myself useful, restored the circulation.

Just as the fire was kindled, Long Lade, one of the Company's traders, with a wagon and one man, drove up.

His fine face, strongly marked with the characteristic high cheek bones and broad under jaw, proclaimed him to be of a northern tribe. He has been a trader for many years, and like many of the Far Westerns, he is still poor. Now, in his old age, he has nothing on which to depend for a livelihood but his salary. He speaks French well (he is a half-breed Canadian-French and Indian) and American but imperfectly. From the first time I met the old man, the more tender chords of my heart were touched with sympathy and respect for him. He seemed so lonely, fast growing old, with a few gray hairs struggling through the straight, jetty locks—alone and poor. I have often wondered what has befallen him—he was so sad a picture of taciturn solitude.

Early we separated—Long Lade, with two pack mules and Pierre for the upper village—we for the lower—with his wagon and Mexican—which was reached by ten o'clock, where we pulled off our saddles in front of Se-ne-mone's or "Tobacco's" lodge. Our host was afflicted with sore eyes; but we were welcomed to the "back part," in true feeling of hospitality.

CHAPTER VI

THE DANCE

Four inches of snow greeted our sight on awakening. The wind was cold and furious; but, by the next noon, tranquillity and sunlight were restored.

Toward the middle of the day, the village was in a great bustle. Every squaw, child, and man had their faces blackened,[1] which is a manifestation of joy.

Pellmell they went, men, squaws, and dogs, in the icy river. Some hastily jerked off their leggins and held moccasins and dresses high out of the water. Others, too impatient, dashed the stream from beneath their impetuous feet, scarce taking time to draw more closely the always worn robe. Wondering what "caused all this commotion," and looking over the river, whither the yelling, half-frantic savages were so speedily hurrying, we saw a band of Indians advancing toward us. As the foremost braves reined their champing barbs on the river bank, mingled whoops of triumph and delight, and the repeated discharges of fusils, filled the air. In the hands of three were slender willow wands, from the smaller points of which dangled as many scalps—the single tuft of hair on each pronouncing them *Pawnee*. They were raised aloft, amid the unrestrained bursts of joy from the thrice-happy, blood-thirsty throng.

[1] The blackening mixture is made from a species of plumbago, found on the bare points of hills in this region.

83

Children ran to meet their fathers, sisters their brothers, girls their lovers, returned from the scene of victorious strife; decrepit matrons welcomed manly sons; and aged chiefs their boys and braves. It was a scene of affection, and a proud day in the Cheyenne annals of prowess. The small but gallant band were relieved of their shields and lances by tender-hearted squaws, and accompanied to their respective homes, to repose by the lodge fire, consume choice meat, and be the heroes of the family circle.

Se-ne-mone's son was fortunate enough to take a scalp, which was hung above us; the half-blind father, in parental pride, centered his fond gaze on the features of his son, who, in battle hard-won, emblazoned the Se-ne-mone escutcheon with honorable and fresh devices, as in the days of his own prime.

The drum, at night, sent forth its monotony of hollow sound, and our Mexican, Pedro, and I, directed by the booming, entered a lodge, vacated for the purpose, full of young men and squaws following one another in a continuous circle, keeping the left knee stiff and bending the right with a half-forward, half-negative step as if they wanted to go on and could not, accompanying it, every time the right foot was raised, with an energetic, broken song, which, dying away, was again and again sounded— "Hay-a-hay, hay-a-hay," they went—laying the emphasis on the first syllable. A drum, similar to, though larger than, a tamborine, covered with *par flêche*, was beat upon with a stick, producing, with the voices, a sound not altogether disagreeable.

Throughout the entire night and succeeding day, the voices of the singers, and heavy notes of the drum, reached us, and, at night, again the same dull sound lulled me to sleep. At first, Smith, to whom the ceremonies were no new occurrence, muttered, as he turned in his robes, curses at the "infernal noise." Before daylight, our lodge was filled with ceaseless dancers, and the drum and voices, so unpleasing to our wearied ears, were giving us the full benefit of their compass. Smith, whose policy it was not to be offended, bore the infliction as he best could, and I looked on, much amused. The lodge was so full that they stood, without dancing, in a circle round the fire, and, with a swaying motion of the body, kept time to their music.

During the day, the young men, except the dancers, piled up dry logs in a level, open space near, for a grand demonstration. At night, when it was fired, I folded my blanket over my shoulders, *comme les sauvages*, and went out. The faces of many girls were brilliant with vermillion; others were blacked, their robes, leggins, and skin-dresses glittering with beads and porcupine quillwork. Rings and bracelets of shining brass encircled their tapering arms and fingers, and shells dangled from their ears. Indeed, all the finery collectible was piled on in barbarous profusion, though a few, in good taste or through poverty, wore a single band and but few rings; and with jetty hair parted in the middle, from the forehead to the neck, terminating in two handsome braids.

The young men who can afford the expense trade for dollars and silver coin of less denomination—coin as currency is not known among them—which they flatten thin and fasten to a braid of buffalo hair attached to the crown-lock, and which, hanging behind, outside of the robe, adds much to the handsome appearance of the wearer.

The girls, numbering 200, fell into line together, and the men, of whom there were 250, joining, a circle was formed, which "traveled" around with the same shuffling step already described. The drummers and other musicians (twenty or twenty-five of them) marched in a contrary direction, to, and from, and around the fire, inside the large ring; for, at the distance kept by the outsiders, the area was 150 feet in diameter. These Appolonian emulators chanted the great deeds performed by the Cheyenne warriors; as they ended, the dying strain was caught up by the hundreds of the outside circle, who, in fast-swelling loud tones, poured out the burthen of their song. At this juncture, the march was quickened, the scalps of the slain were borne aloft and shaken in wild delight, and shrill war notes, rising above the furious din, accelerated the pulsation and strung high the nerves. Time-worn shields, careering in mad holders' hands, clashed, and keen lances, once reeking in Pawnee blood, clanged. Braves seized one another with an iron grip in the heat of excitement, or chimed more tenderly in the chant, enveloped in the same robe with some gentle maiden, as they approvingly stepped through one of their own original polkas.

Thirty of the chiefs and principal men were ranged by the pile of blazing logs. By their invitation, I sat down near "Old Bark," and smoked death and its concomitant train of evils to those audacious tribes who doubted the courage or supremacy of the brave, the great, and powerful Cheyenne Nation.

The pipe was lavishly decorated with beaver strips, beads, and porcupine; the mixture of tobacco and bark was prepared with unusual care, for this, their grand gala night.

By this time, I had made the acquaintance of many young men and girls, and often I chasséd up to the scalps and joined in the chorus, much to their gratification and amusement, and no less to my own.

Se-ne-mone's daughter, a clever girl of sixteen or seventeen winters, reveled in a flaming red cloth dress. She was quite a favorite of the beaux, and, consequently, her presence was sought for at all the festivities. But, sleepless night, with continual dancing, fatiguing her, she, on one of these evenings, slipped from her friends to bed. Though it was not more than two hours after dark, we were in our places, to all appearance, asleep.

The red dress was hardly composed beneath her warm robe before she heard the other girls, who had just missed her, coming; so up she sprang toward me, and, ere I was aware, she jerked up one side of my blanket, and accommodated her own form to my recumbent position. Then, pulling it over her shoulders, she quietly nestled her head on my arm, as if indisputably entitled to my sole protection. Her right as to the supporting arm must have been that of occupancy—surely not that of pre-emption!

Why did she not crawl to the robe of her mother, or her little sisters lying around, or even that of her brother? It was one of those unaccountable mysteries not "dreampt of" in my "philosophy," but I bore the affliction quite heroically, and tucked the clothing more snugly than before around us. All this was hardly accomplished when in broke the girls, with merry laughs, bounding toward the lately vacated robe. But "Genevra" wasn't there; and they stood puzzled for a moment, with looks of doubt. They then glanced at the different sleepers; I alone was awake, and the firelight showed my watchful countenance. The fugitive held her breath in suspense, and, as the girls came flying over to me—I, meanwhile, invoking all the saints in the calendar to avert the impending disclosure—out burst the little witch with a shrill laugh, discovering herself. They all chimed in, and insisted on my accompanying them to the dance. I refused, under the plea of fatigue. They pulled me to my feet, perforce. I still persisted in excusing myself; but, peering among the larger girls in front, who stood around the bed, the sweet, oval face of *O-ne-o, Se-hak's* daughter, shaded with an anxious cast of solicitude, decided the point at once. *"Ta-bin-ah!"* ("Come on"), said she, beckoning with her head to the drumming outside. What expressive eyes!—liquid and hazel, with a dish of playful humor, mild, beaming, and loving. Who could help being facinated, magnetized, spirited away, but those imperious souls void of true feeling or soured by adversity!—and, as for me, ever susceptible to genuine loveliness, 'twas nothing less than absolute enchantment; so slipping on my moccasins and throwing a blanket around me, I followed her and companions, to charge through and over the jolting steps and uncertain halts of the grand scalp dance.

The Indian beaux are ridiculous personifications of vanity. With small lookingglasses, vermillion-streaked faces, and decorated robes or blankets, they perambulate the village with looks of supreme self-complacency. I often laughed heartily at their unique costumes and self-satisfied looks. One of the dandies painted my face in the most approved Cheyenne style, but the squaws laughed so immoderately at the grotesque contrast of a white skin and red paint, I soon washed it off.

The trader is treated with much respect by the Indians and is considered a chief—a great man. To retain this respect, he acts with as much dignity as the circumstances permit. Caring for none of the trader's assumed reservedness, I danced with the squaws, mixed in the gaieties, and, in every way, improved my time. It was more than probable I never would wish to trade with them; and why deprive myself of amusement? The squaws were astonished to find a white person so careless of dignity, though they liked me the better for it. With emotions of pleasure are recalled the happy hours passed with this nation—the bright faces of the girls—the pleasant, broad, good-humored countenance of the "Smiling Moon" (O-ne-o Missit's daughter), the dancing eye of "Morning Mist" (Vip-po-nah's daughter), and the low chuckle of the young men as they gained a triumph in the favorite game of "guess."

CHAPTER VII

STRANGERS AND DRAWBACKS

A TRAIN of wagons passed on the 14th of December. Going out to it, I saw Buchanan, who was sent, with others, to meet Captain Murphy, United States express, with a load of corn for his mules. They expected to find him about one hundred miles below. Buck was so pleased with my representations of savage attractions he concluded to remain with us.

Our rifles, the backgammon board, and basking on the sunny-sheltered banks amused us for two days. The Indians quite pleased Buck, who walked about, laughing at everything. His inquisitiveness, together with a red flannel shirt, attracted the squaws, who, naturally hilarious, were much diverted.

On the 18th, our eyes were regaled with a new phase in the dances. The squaws and men were dressed in different and more fantastic styles than ever. Some with the horns and skin of a buffalo attached to their own heads—others, with jackets of red and blue cloth, carried swords and lances. The horse, captured in the same fight for which we had been so festive for the preceding week or two, was brought in and led around the ring, amid the noise of drums, waving of scalps, and dissonant yelling.

One great drawback to the pleasures of an Indian village is that the inhabitants are troubled with a persecuting little animal—a roamer through the unbroken forests of hair on children's heads—now ascending the mountain of self-esteem, or reposing in the secluded vales around about combativeness. These creatures (the bugs), here, are white, and nearly the size of wheat grains. They do not confine their penetrating researches to the caput alone, but traverse the immense surface of the whole body. By being in the same lodge with *les sauvages* continually, it was impossible to keep clear of the *insects*. Of course we came in for our share; but Buchanan, who wore a flannel shirt, was doubly visited.

We were sitting, one day, by the fire, with uncombed hair and unwashed faces (in the mood, physical and mental, to feel unpleasant), when Buck, who "suspicioned" not the true cause of his torment, said—

"I feel something biting, and darned bad, too, let's go and examine. I don't know what's the matter!"

"Biting you!" ejaculated Smith, "there's nothing so mity queer in that when you're in the village, and," added he laughingly, "when that shirt and 'forfarraw' of your'n comes off—Wagh!"

The sun shone out warm, and we went to the river and undressed on a clean sand deposit, hid from the view of the village by intervening weeds, uninterrupted, save by an occasional squaw on an errand for water, with her bright brass kettle. Many families, who do not wish to buy a bucket, or who cannot afford it, use a large buffalo intestine, one end of which is tied, filled with water, and hung to a lodgepole, as it cannot stand on its "own bottom." When a drink is wanted, the thirsty one puts his (or her) mouth to the opening at the top, and with hands on either side of the flabby bucket, compresses it, while the water flows into the mouth. But it always looked so dirty I preferred waiting until reaching the river or our own lodge.

When Buck pulled off his flannel, he uttered an exclamation, coupled with an oath; which, to express on paper with the proper force would require more italicization and more exclamation points than could be given. From the collar seams of his shirt to those parallel to the body, the interstices were lined with ovae, the germs of future tormentors, appearing as so many miniature pearls reposing in the rich setting of red flannel. My clothing was alike infested. As we passed the sentence of death, "Sampson and his jawbone" were brought to mind; but, according to my facetious *compañero*, the aforesaid "jawbone" was totally eclipsed by his thumbnails. What he said on this occasion need not be written. A swim in the icy element ensued, and dressing, we felt much better than before.

It would be superfluous in me to dilate on the changes effected in the way of empires, republics, arts, sciences, and religion during the past eighteen hundred and forty-six years. All know these historical facts; and, as John Smith and myself are but heroes in our own small way, and as historians are so obtuse to a sense of justice as to omit mentioning the hardy souls—the forerunners of civilization—who waste dear life among the savages, teaching them the *pure* English language (to say nothing of the robes we had to take from them), I shall have to be, to rescue our names from the depths of oblivion, narrator for both, to apprise all of our occupation and whereabouts on New Year's Day.

While we, in this village, had neither mince pies, cakes, or any of the good things consumed on like occasions, neither did we hear guns, shooting-crackers, or cannon, or see shops gaily decorated; yet we had good buffalo meat and aromatic coffee (without sugar or bread), which I enjoyed far more than anyone could a most tempting "State" dinner. For music, the village maidens chanted war songs—the harmonious strains of which fell on the ear far more pleasingly to me than Russell's best.

The village, in accordance with an almost invariable custom of the Indians, who undoubtedly have an eye for picturesque, rural beauty, was in a secluded, narrow bottom, overrun with long tangled and matted grass, quite close to the river, and sheltered by the hill in the background, dotted here and there with large cottonwoods, whose outspread limbs, gigantic and gnarled, impressed a sensation of protection. A range—a snow-covered miniature Sierra Nevada—rising above a still lower range of coarse grass-covered hills, combined with the silver sheet of water, way beyond, gleaming through the trees and the lodges, formed a camp at once remarkable for romantic loveliness and its excellent shelter for man and beast.

Buck joined the return party, which he had so unceremoniously left, to stay with us. He was a jovial, open-hearted fellow, and had such an insinuating manner we feared not that the quartermaster would discharge him, or make deduction of pay for dereliction of duty.[1]

Se-ne-mone's squaw gave a dog feast one day. As the Indians are great epicures, the modus operandi of preparation may not be uninteresting to our more civilized gourmands, whose tables are bare of a viand, which, undoubtedly, ranks pre-eminent in the list of delicacies and luxuries.

First, a pup of four months' sojourn in this world of

[1] In this we quite mistook the quartermaster's character; for, in the following spring, on arriving at Fort Leavenworth, Buchanan found all his absences, etc., summed up, and deduction from his pay made in consequence. In the impulse of the moment, he made them a present of the *whole* of his dues, and, in a few hours, left in charge of a lot of mules for the army in the south of Mexico.

sorrow, so fat he could scarcely waddle, was caught by the affectionate squaw and turned, and felt, and pinched, to see whether it would do. Then its neck was invested with one end of a buckskin strap, and the other tied short up to the projecting coupling pole of our wagon, while the poor victim to savage appetite, dangling between earth and sky, ki-ed until his little canine spirit departed for the elysium where neither squaws molest nor dog meat is eaten, to the very apparent satisfaction of the laughing women, and delighted children, and the no small annoyance of many large dogs, among whom was the disconsolate mother of the unfortunate. She sent forth, with head and neck elongated, most piteous bewailings, until receiving a kick from one of the amazons, which sent her off limping, filling the air with discordant yells, fully as painful to us as was the kick to the recipient of the squaw's marked attentions. She sat on her haunches, at a little distance from us, now and then raising her paw—not to brush away the falling tear, but to rub her nose, on which had fallen the cruel blow.

After hanging half an hour, the pup was taken down and laid on the fire. What! thought I, they are not so heathenish as to offer sacrifices? He was kept on the blaze, with constant turning, until the hair was well singed off, and then cleaned, beheaded, and divided into all imaginable shapes and sizes, and cooked in water for six hours. It was then fished out, and a portion set before us—a slimy, glutinous mass, uninviting to the eye, but, nevertheless, most delicate and sweet. Smith laid by one of the hind legs until the next morning; the marbled thin streaks of lean and fat were most tempting. It reminded me of cold roast pig—a faint simile, probably derogatory to the fair fame of "dog," and for which degenerate, civilized comparison, I humbly crave the pardon of Se-ne-mone's spouse and her worthy curs.

Civilized and semi-barbarous nations are represented by flags, on which are their distinctive stars, stripes, or colors. The different Indian tribes have no such distinctions but in articles of dress or marks of the body—using no flag except the white, indicative of peace—a sign, as it would seem, understood by intuition to all the world.

The signification[2] of this tribe, in their own language, is, "cut arm," from the fact that, at a certain period of their lives, the men make three transverse cuts on the upper side of the arm (or that not next to the body) generally equi-distant from the elbow joint and the socket, which leaves three scars, by their uniformity not a little perplexing on first sight. With this "mark," they connect grand flourishes, solemn looks, and much invoking of the unseen Spirit, through the medium of the pipe.

The Arapahoes (an adjoining tribe, with whom the Cheyennes intermarry) have three equi-distant punctures on the breast.

The mode of keeping the hair is another characteristic. The Camanche, Cheyenne, Arapaho, and Utah[3] tribes wear their hair in long, unconfined locks, cutting it off in front close above the eyebrows, so as not to obstruct the vision. The Osage, Pawnee, and Kansas shave the *os frontis* (and, as Buck remarked, the *os backis*), leaving only a topknot at the crown, which is so taut and greasy that it stands erect and trembling with every motion of the body.

The peculiar form of the moccasin, especially in the

---

[2] The term *Cheyenne* is a French derivation, I suppose, from the feminine—*chienne*—of dog.

[3] I speak in this paragraph of Indians I have seen—not from hearsay.

absence of the wearer, is the most certain and usual way of determining the tribe in which it is made.

The Cheyenne, Arapaho, and Camanche, similar in dress and manner, and at peace with each other, use cow-skin[4] moccasins, the inside edge straight, and the extreme point so turned in as to give the wearer the appearance of being what is termed "pigeon-toed," as they really are in a slight degree. The outside edge is brought around in a continuous curve, until it meets the straight edge at the large toe. They are pleasant, though a white man's foot will not fit snugly, unless it turns in more than usual.

The Pawnee moccasin is the same as if one would place his foot in the center of a piece of buckskin and make all the edges meet on top of the foot, in front of the ankle. The hinder part is brought up on the leg and laced to its place by strings. This is the best and easiest shoe, for it fits in every part. Some Mexican-Indian (Pimo) moccasins, that I have worn, are long-toed, with a sole of *par flêche*[5] lapping over on top of the foot, as protection while tramping the cactus-grown plains.

One morning, before sunrise, while soundly sleeping near the fire, Smith's squaw shook me by the shoulder, saying, "V*e-heo kiss, ve-heo kiss! hua, hua 'sst ve-heo mok-ta-bo*": "Young Whiteman, young Whiteman! get up! there's a *black* white man at the door."

I rose to see a genuine specimen of the thick-lipped Negro. The squaw was at a loss for words to call him properly; certainly it was not intended as a compliment to us, to call him a "black white man."

At first I could understand nothing the Negro said, so mixed were his words with Indian terms; but, inviting him

[4] The cowskin is the same as the robe, divested of hair.
[5] All the Prairie Indians use *par flêche*.

in, and paying attention, I learned that he was a slave to a Cherokee Ross, and that he accompanied a surveying party (from his description of the instruments), and were charged upon by a Camanche force, who, killing the most of his party, took him prisoner to their village. Here he stayed for many months, until his captors, having confidence in him, made him a brave. They went to Chihuahua,[6] where, in several battles, they captured hundreds of mules and many prisoners, among them some women, who were taken as the wives of chiefs. For his own prowess, he was given a squaw. But he longed for other lands and watched for every opportunity to escape; but none offered until, in a fatal conflict with the Mexicans, his party were routed. He saved himself from the triumphant lances by plunging into a stream, where he remained for two days, his persecutors on the watch. He showed me a lance wound in his wrist and an arrow mark through his arm. When the Mexicans were gone, he quietly slipped out, and groping around, found a bow and arrows. He took a course, knowing not whither it led; and, after nearly three months constant walking, subsisting on wild rosebuds and whatever could be picked up, he made his way in sight of our village. Lying around for a day, until satisfied that we were not Camanches, he appeared the morning I first saw him. The straightforwardness and simplicity of his story dispelled all doubts as to its veracity.

I traded Paint to an Indian for a mule—the poor grass and my hard riding being too severe. His new owner ran him for buffalo two successive days in the snow, which covered the ground from twenty-five to twenty-eight inches in depth, and not coming up to the game the last day (no

[6] From the direction the Negro gave, and the country described, the color, etc., of the inhabitants, they must have gone to Chihuahua.

wonder! for the horse was turned out after the first hunt, heated, tired, and hungry, to find his food in the snow, so deep that only the tops of weeds were visible), he brought him back to me. I made a "virtue of necessity" and returned the Indian his mule, taking possession again of poor, old, broken-down Pinto. Had I refused to reswap, he would probably have stolen the mule from me at night and retained my horse, too; and, being at the tender mercy of the whole tribe (as there were but two of us and a Mexican), I could not retaliate. What would have been worse, the unfair horse trader might have taken my scalp for presuming to dictate to him, a loyal, pure-blooded Cheyenne. I smothered my feelings of resentment, though my wishes were "pistols for two—coffee for one."

Snow was deep; "fat cow" a luxury not to be thought of; horses too poor to "run" meat; and a scant supply of "poor bull" was all the provision with which to satisfy hunger. In this emergency, the inroads upon the dog population were most alarming and destructive.

On the 6th of January, two Indians arrived from the upper village with instructions for us to join William Bent, with our goods, etc., without delay. A storm arising gave a chilling prospect, and added to the already accumulated snowdrifts.

On the 7th, I traded Paint to Smith by giving thirty dollars in addition. Smith, having several animals, could afford to keep the horse until he fattened, but I needed one for present service. My new exchange was a raw-boned, impetuous piece of mule flesh—her temper, eye, and sharp feet as full of the spirit with which Old Nick is supposed to be possessed as could well be.

We heard from O-cum-who-wurst's village, at the "Buttes" a day's ride hence, that a Pawnee war party had succeeded in running off forty of their best animals. The close proximity of the "horse stealers" caused some trepidation in our village, and even we felt like caching.

CHAPTER VIII

THE SNOW TRAMP

O N THE 8th, we packed our robes and possibles,[1] and, by eleven o'clock, the wagon, with its two yoke of half-famished oxen attached, ready for a start, was on the top of the hill. The sun shone clear, reflecting, in the intense cold, from the encrusted snow points millions of miniature diamonds. We parted cheerfully with our kind-hearted Indian host, Se-ne-mone; and I did not omit to take the hand of his daughter, "red-dress," to tell her "good-bye." At the same instant, the recollections of the gay dances around scalps in her company, with other graceful Houris, enveloped in the same blanket, and our commingled "hay-he-a-hay" (scalp chorus) rising above the other voices, sent a momentary pang vibrating through me. I half wanted to stay. The poor, shivering Indians, standing in the deep snow, saw us off.

The surface of the country, on this (the south) side of the river, was greatly broken. Large sandhills sloped to the river's very edge: others, with a strip of land intervening, were frequent; the loose, slippy nature of which made the footing uncertain, the travel laborious. The poor oxen, toiling through snow up to the briskets, were to be pitied. The Bent's Fort trail was on the opposite side.

We went on for some hours; now on the steep side of

[1] Personal property.

a glazed sand butte, now on top, with the freezing wind shooting pains through our heads; now again stretching across a low bottom, at a tediously slow rate. On the exclamation by the blue-lipped squaw, of *"Po-ome! na-wa'sst,"* we looked the direction she pointed, to perceive an Indian urging his animal through the snow with all speed.

"Ten-o-wast?" ("What is it?") asked Smith, making "sign" as the savage drew rein alongside, most opportunely for his panting animal.

The amount of the conversation was that he had a "big heart" for Pinto; he loved him very much, and, in a few moments, his saddle was changed to Pinto, and shaking hands with us, he urged him back toward the village, while we kept our way.

We talked of the battle of New Orleans (this was the anniversary)—of the bravery evinced—the probability of another war; but plowing through the snow and the tingling cold were no aids to prolonged dissertations on the merits and demerits of Jackson and his army. A little more severe weather would have dismounted us.

With all our steady travel, we made no more than five or six miles, and encamped, as the sun was waning beyond the snowbanks ahead, sheltered in the rear by a sparse growth of stunted willows.

We felt with our feet, on the river's edge, for pieces of wood, and, with numbed fingers, knocked the snow from them. These, with the aid of a few handfuls of dead willow twigs, served as fuel. Watering the animals through a hole in the ice-bound river, they were hobbled in a hollow, and left exposed to the "storm's pitiless peltings," to eke a scanty meal from the weeds and stray blades of grass laid bare by the frame-pervading blasts. We cut brush, and clearing a small space of the snow, laid our robes and blankets on the boughs, and, sitting with crossed legs, stared at the flickering blaze rising through the still and piercing air, our pipes charged with fragrant "honeydew" or "single twist"; the holders every moment blowing out blue clouds of smoke, calculated at most any other time to sicken, but now not a bit too strong. By turning our eyes to the darkness, we could see the dusky forms of our congregated *caballada*, with backs bowed and tails to the blast, too cold to paw for grass, now snorting as a hungry wolf crossed the wind, or feebly answering an inquiring whinney from a timid mule, scared at its own tramping in the dry, frosty snow.

It is strange how self-satisfied one is, when safely in camp. There we, almost at an unapproachable distance from anywhere, amid snowstorms, with scarce a hearty meal, in a barren country, and too freezing cold to hunt, sat on our soft robes, acknowledging the grateful warmth of the coals (shuddering, perhaps, as a cold puff of wind, coursing on the crusted snow, struck our backs and caused us to pull the blankets more closely to our necks)—chatting as unconcernedly as if surrounded by luxuries, such as large fires and plenty to eat. It is by some experience in a prairie voyageur's life that I can say, never was I more contented, silently happy than when, with snow wreaths drifted interminably for miles and miles around, with a choice companion or two, cosily seated by a small comfortable fire, with plenty of tobacco and a modicum of meat to sustain life, I have listened to the baying of wolves and have imagined the Hamadryads' tuneful sighs mingling with the crackling of the frosted tree branches, while the mournful cadences of the wind, sweeping up the vale with wild fury, would burst over our heads with shrieks of crazy delight—now dying away in harmonious deflections, anon increasing in vigor, yet never ending.

And, on composing oneself to sleep, with what care does he place his feet, well-covered by thick moccasins, to the broadest blaze! Then, sitting on his robe, he tucks it around his legs and body, high as the waist, and falls back with his face from rude Boreas, retaining his soft wool hat to serve as a breakwind to his head, resting on the saddle for pillow. There he is, warm, comfortable, and selfish— nothing short of Indians or fire on the dear robe would stir him an inch. Then, in the morning, how hard he is to rouse. His cold blue nose, exposed to the weather, is sensitive enough in its gradations from warm to cold to serve as thermometer—"b'low zero, wagh! too cold," and he draws within himself, shuddering at the bare idea of facing the breeze. "Darn breakfast, when a feller's fixed; I wouldn't git up for the fattest meat as runs on the peraira; t'ain't often this buffler *is* comfortable, an' when he is, he knows it," and off he drops in dreamland,

> *Chasing the stag*
> *From crag to crag,*

indicating, by convulsive twitchings of the hands or contortions of the face, the contending passions by which he is actuated when in quest of game or "raising" the "hair" of a skulking Pawnee who has been audacious and unfortunate enough to steal his animals.

Our Mexican was up first and kindled a fire. All soon rising, we drove the *caballada* to camp from the leeward of a bank, whither they had retreated, standing with low, drooping heads, and indicating, by a glance at their hollow flanks, the scanty meal they had eaten; choosing rather to starve than push away with aching noses or paw with balled feet the cold snow from the withered herbage of this region, at no time remarkable in excellency.

The morning was bitter, bitter cold. The exhaled breath rapidly condensed; which, with the blowing of the animals as they were forced over the deep snow, enveloped us in a cloud of vapor. We strung out, one or the other in front; the Mexican with his ox team following. In the wake was our squaw, astride of a large sorrel horse, muffled in robes. Clinging to her back was the boy, Wo-pe-kon-ne,[2] with his lint white locks, grayish-white eyes, and sallow face visible through an opening—an air hole—in the hairy covering.

About eleven o'clock in the morning, we saw a party of men trailing toward the States. Urging our mules through the snow, nearly breast high, to the river, we were met by one of them, who crossed the ice on foot. He was almost hid in the folds of a robe overcoat, extra moccasins, heavy hat, and his right hand grasped a thick, large-bored rifle. On nearing, he shouted—"How are ye, Smith, old coon. Whar now—are ye makin' tracks to Fort William?"

"Why, Boggs, old hos," rejoined Smith, "what's up? you've got so much 'fofaraw' stuck 'bout you, this child didn't savvy at fust! Which way?"

"Well, old Kurnel Price wanted some one to take the trail fur the States on express; and, as none but mountain men *can* 'come in' now, he gave me six hundred dollars to 'travel' with letters and dispatches. But, I tell 'ee it'll be a chargin' time, fur the snow is bad *some*, now."

"Who's with you; right sort of stuff for this season?"

"Oh! a lot of darned gover'ment men; but as I'm

2 "White Eyes"—Jack.

'bugheway'[3] they do pretty well. Well, I must break—how are ye off for cow meat?"

"H——! cow meat, *this* freezin' time? You've bin down to Santy Fee too long. Why, 'poor bull' is hard to git, boudin out of the question, and 'gras'[4] so scarce we don't think of it. Howsomever, if you want to chaw on lean buffler dried, you can have it 'on the prairie.'[5] *Hombre, Pedro, mira! venica cary por carne, poquita!* [Pedro, look here, want a little meat]," shouted Smith to our Mexican.

"Na-wa! o-ne-a-voke veheo" ("Quick, some meat for the whiteman")—to his squaw.

He took about half—not much to be sure, but seemingly a great deal—and crossed the river, while we started the team, the wagon wheels creaking and singing as they pressed the stalagmitic snow. We were thoroughly benumbed, and rode in a state nearly amounting to torpidity. How I silently wished for the warm and pleasant home left but a few months previous. How we longed for fire—no wood to be had—even coffee would have given comfort. Our pipes were the only solace in this trying time, but one tires of that, or sickens by too frequent use. As far as the eye could reach, on all sides, was a boundless expanse of snow, snow, snow! Above, the dreary, dull-gray winter sky; no sun to cheer us, or to impart warmth. Every step, every motion, every glance bore down instead of relieving us. I shut my eyes, wearied and sick of the white monotonous drapery; which, in my bewildered fancy, seemed to look on unmoved at us stiffening by degrees; and, by mocking, freezing placidity, to check all buoyant hope or retrospect.

[3] Bugheway—bourgeoise—master.
[4] Gras—fat.
[5] "On the prairie"—free gift.

To add to the wretchedness of mind, large, gaunt white wolves, attracted through keen hunger, stealthily followed, or dashed across our way like specters—spirits of the storm wind—and burst, hell-hound like, into prolonged, fearful howls, rousing us from our apathy to cause shudders to pervade our chilled and weakened frames.

Camp at night and its few duties soon were completed, for our provision (if a little dried meat, without bread, coffee, or salt could be called provision) was scanty, requiring no cooking or preparation but thorough mastication.

Sunrise saw us on the tramp. It was so cold, Smith left his gun (a most foolish thing, not to be expected of a mountaineer) in the wagon. Though I hardly had the *sense of feeling,* I retained my rifle in front of the saddle. In the afternoon we were finding a practicable route in the drifts for the team; and, in so doing, strayed several hundred yards ahead, and out of sight of the wagon. Seeing a party approaching, Smith called my attention to it with—

"Look ahead! there's white men."

I gave a shout, at the same moment digging my spurs into the mule's side—"Hooray, we'll have meat and coffee tonight; but look! they wear Mexican hats."

"So they do," replied he, after a scrutiny; "but they won't bother us, they know me too well to cut 'shines'— John Smith's a name not to be grinned at by a darned carahoing 'palou'—Wagh! Indians, 'by beaver!' " hurriedly said he, changing his tone, "keep your eye skinned; I have left my gun in the wagon, and have nothing but a knife."

I put on a fresh cap without changing its position, so as not to excite the attention of the coming party, though one gun was as nothing against thirty Arapahoes. We met them with as little show of trepidation as could be helped, and advancing to the foremost grim savage, offered our hands. The fellow took the proffered advance of amity with coldness, and stopped still. We dared not pass by, and asked him—

"*Ten-o-wast?*" "What is it you wish?"

He looked silently at us, and again we chidingly asked, in the Cheyenne tongue, "*Ten-o-wast?*"

"*Ni-hi-ni, veheo, matsebo, esvone Arapaho,*" answered he. The amount of his answer was, that the "white man was bad, that he ran the buffalo out of the country, and starved the Arapaho."

Smith explained that he had been trading a long time with the Cheyenne, whom he loved, and who was brother to the Arapaho; that he only took what meat he wanted, and, pointing to his squaw, that his wife was a Cheyenne. The Arapahoes must not blame him. It was the white man from the States (government men) with wagons, who scared the buffalo from him and his children. It was always his intention to live and die with the Cheyennes, for he had thrown away his brothers in the States. The Cheyenne lodge was his home—they smoked the same pipe—the broad prairie supported them both.

"The white man has a forked tongue," replied the chief, impatiently, raising his hand to his mouth and sending it in a direct line with two of the fingers open, and stretched far apart, to signify a fork or divergence from a point.

"*I-sto-met, wah-hein*" (P'shaw, no"), said Smith.

"*Ni-hi-ni, ni-hi-ni, Hook-ah-hay*" ("Yes, yes," "Good-bye") and off they rode, trying, yet without much open manifestation, to drive our little band of horses with theirs, but, by a dexterous interposition of Smith, he turned their heads, preventing the quiet trick of our brothers, the Arapahoes.

Smith told me, after they left, that they were just returning from a successful marauding expedition into New Mexico, with several scalps, two prisoners, and thirty or more horses and mules, which they then had with them. Happily was it for us that their vengeance was wreaked on other unfortunates than ourselves. We, however, feared for our swarthy son of Mexico, the ox driver—as he was of the same stripe as those to whom the scalps dangling from the Arapaho lance points originally belonged. We waited, with some doubts as to his safety, until he made his appearance.

The poor wretch! There he came, plying the whip vigorously to his tired yoke. When within hearing distance, we distinguished the fierce spoken words, "Geet up— *caraho! Wo-o ha-ha—los Rapaho.*"

"Did you see the Indians, Pedro?"

"*Si Señor, a-a-h Caraho! los Rapaho; muchos diablos— grandote, muchos, muchos, muchos*"— "D——n the Arapahoes—big devils."

"Did they touch you, the darned niggurs?"

"*Si!*" replied he, in a tone of vexation, "*Si, mucho,* dis a way," jerking himself to and fro by the hair, "dis a way, pull me bout, de dam Rapaho; dey want *carne* [meat], want carabine, dey want mucho; and," added he, ready to burst into tears, "dey want my hair. Me feel for my *cuchillo* [knife], but do one *lancero grandote,* he luk mad—he raise his lance. By by dey mount de *cavallos* [horses], dey go way—"

"Yes!" said Smith, "but, it's too cold here to talk—start up your team, we must be to a good camp before night, for it'll freeze the nose off a feller's face in the morning."

The queerest part of this meeting with the Indians was that after their departure, Smith upbraided me for turning pale and showing fear, while his face was blanched and wore a peculiar rigidity of features and nervous twinkling of the eyelids. The fact is, we were both scared badly.

An hour before the sun set saw us stopping on an island, for the sake of a little dry grass for the animals and the twisted, partly decayed stump of a fallen cottonwood for ourselves—both things quite essential this inclement season.

My mule was an obstinate, foolish animal, and, to keep her from returning to the village, a hobble was necessary every night. The rest of the *caballada* was as usual, snorting and pawing for grass, or wandering around, before mine was let loose; and while I, in the snow, was adjusting the hobble, she was impatiently stamping and frettingly held by the bridle. So soon as I rose to my feet and pulled the headstall from her brow, off she started, with a squeal, the rein still on her neck. To prevent her trampling on the bit, I caught it in my hand and kept up alongside. She rushed in the water, splashing my moccasins and buckskins to the knee; by the time she hauled me in the ripple to her satisfaction and jerked me down several times, my scalp knife was out of its sheath.

To keep my limbs from freezing from the effects of the already congealed water with which my moccasins and pants were saturated, while Smith and Pedro were making a fire, I took a sheet-iron camp kettle—an Indian article of trade—to the river for water, which labor might restore the circulation. Under a bank, several springs kept the water from freezing hard; I broke it with but little difficulty, and, reaching down the bucket to dip and fill it, in I followed. Scrambling out, I hurried to camp with the water in frozen pellets on my clothes and hair.

Smith, standing with back to the fire, shouted as I approached, "Ho, boy! wet? You're more like a ducked beaver 'an anything this hos has seen yet. Cold, eh?"

"*Caraho!*" cried Pedro, looking up from the ground, where he was seated drying his torn moccasins, "*Señor, tu muy freo?*"—"Are you very cold?"

We cleared the snow for several feet around the fire, so as not to melt and make a muddy camp. Spreading down my robe, I wrung and dried my clothes.

For supper each took a little piece of dried buffalo meat and chewed on it until the strength was gone; then, smoking, we went to bed, to dream of the many good things some persons have and know not how to appreciate. Being now not at all fastidious, Pedro and I shared the same robes.

In the morning, seeing that the *caballada* had had but little to eat and the cold being so intense, a day in camp was thought best. A snowstorm, with all its blustering fury, burst upon us during the morning and lasted half the day, driving the rotting-wood smoke in our eyes, so that small comfort was gained by the fire. We would sit in one position until nearly stifled; a change to the opposite side was only for the wind to veer and drive us again away. We had no tent, of course, and the shifting wind monopolized every good position.

What a prospect was in advance! Snow twenty-two to twenty-eight inches deep; our mules starving; the oxen broken down with fatigue; and not more than one day's scanty portion of dried meat, and nothing else; an attempt at hunting almost certain death; and, at least, two days' travel to William Bent's village; although there were but forty miles between the two (one day's trip in pleasant weather; now five for us). Verily, this is the dark side of prairie life!

The Snow Tramp

We ventured to start the following morning, but dared not ride for fear of freezing to the saddles, though tramping in the snow was severely fatiguing.

The few pairs of socks brought with me from the States were long before worn out, and my moccasins coming only to the anklebone left bare part of the foot and leg. The snow soon filled the hollow under the instep, which I, at first, raked out with my forefinger; but, becoming so benumbed, I forgot it, and it congealed, unheeded, in a solid mass.

We kept on foot all that day, without stopping, dragging one weary foot after the other until near night, and encamped on an island with plenty of wood and high grass. Our mules procured their food only by pawing, in which mode they became adepts. With tobacco and a stinted ration of "poor bull," we managed to pass the evening.

We left camp the next sunrise, with keen appetites and nothing to eat, and traveled the entire day without stopping. An hour or two before dark, Smith approached some antelope, leaving his bridle rein in the squaw's hand. The band, afar off, scented us, though they scarcely moved; while we anxiously watched Smith stealthily drawing nigh. Hunger rendered him cautious; and, when within two hundred yards, he fired, bringing down a doe. The others ran across the river, stopping once to gaze back at their fallen companion. I imagined the teardrops glistening in their big dark eyes. Our hearts were now made glad, for we had a prospect of plenty; and, as Fortune never comes single-handed, the snow decreased in depth, enabling us to travel in a fast walk. At camp, we used part of the rather unmasticable and poor goat, which, however, was better than nothing; and, to make up for the deficiency of our larder of the past few days, we lingered by the red coals late.

Did anyone ever hear of the *Gros Ventres* Indians? *Well*, we were the same, so far as the name goes, about the hour for retiring.

The travel improved; snow not more than twelve or fourteen inches in depth. The oxen labored less heavily. Smith's gravity relaxed in a degree; and I, being crammed with goat meat, felt finely.

Near noon the squaw cried out—*"Po-ome, na-wa Cheyennes!"* "Blackfoot [Smith], look ahead, Cheyennes!" pointing to an approaching body of men, women, children, horses, and lodges. It was part of the upper village, on the march.

The first few we merely saluted *en passant*. Then came the "Morning Mist" and her father, Vip-po-nah; and, after them, "Smiling Moon," riding on a lodge dray. Her kind eyes beamed with tempered rays of affection; but Smith marred the pleasurableness of our meeting by informing me that she had, during my absence, married—run off with one of the village exquisites. I was quite unhappy for an hour, rode, in silence, apart from the joking Smith; but, finally, consoled myself with the idea that there was more than one pretty Indian girl left in the world.

We found William Bent in his lodge, with his squaws, children, and goods for trading. A few steps distant was another cone, in which were Fisher and Long Lade, traders, and Pierre, and one other, employees. We abode in the back part. The village was a quarter of a mile off—a desirable distance—for we could trade without the usual bother and throng. No snow, but on the shady declivities, chilled us with the sight; the sun shone joyously; the horses capered on the green sward, and the dull, but comfort-recalling drum notes, in honor of fresh scalps, were heard once more. We reclined that night in the warm lodge, with feet to the fire, new faces to look at, and stomachs filled with "fat cow" and coffee. A casual observer could have seen,

> *By the smoke, which so gracefully curled*

from our pipes, that contentment reigned within.

CHAPTER IX

PROSPECTIVE TROUBLE

T HE CRACK of the ox whip and the "wo ha-a" of the drivers broke the stillness of our quiet retreat. The blow of the ax and the small dwelling for trading goods raised by our puny efforts were but the precursors of a settlement, for already do these Indians talk of tilling the ground.

This particular vicinity is called the "Big Timber"—a strip of woods extending for several miles along the river. As a general thing, there is little or no timber on the Arkansas from the Cimarone crossing to the headwaters, with the exception of this belt, which the Indians consider their future home.

My single pair of pantaloons was completely worn out before I procured others. Being in want of the buckskins, I took my rifle, and, skirting the village, crossed to William Tharpe's trading lodges. In the largest was the owner, reclining on robes and smoking, and judge of my surprise when before me sat a fair-skinned woman and two children. She was the proprietor's Mexican wife.

When Mr. Tharpe was getting the buckskins, I could do no less than stare at his wife and the other appendages of civilization hanging around, in the shape of dresses, etc., but the woman did not compare, in point of symmetry of features, with my faithless "Smiling Moon." With the skins under my arm, I bowed myself out, and "made beaver" for Mr. Bent's lodge, on the way passing through a bottom in hopes of finding deer, several of which were seen disappearing before my gun could be brought to bear on them.

While the pantaloons were being cut out by the enterprising John Smith and sewed by his squaw with awl and sinew, I wore a breechcloth, *à la mode Cheyenne*, manufactured of a leg of my old pants. They were rather the worse for wear than when I sat with them in a daguerreotype room before leaving home, trying to look my sweetest for a fond relative. With breechcloth, blanket, painted face, and moccasins, I made a very respectable looking savage.

O-cum-who-wust, principal chief of the Cheyennes, visited us a few days following our arrival. He was talking with Smith when the kettle boiled over. Instantly, yet deliberately, he laid down the pipe, which he was about to smoke, and, covering his head with the robe, bowed himself to the ground, silently remaining in that position several minutes. On rising, his countenance wore a resigned, though sad, aspect, as one engaged in spiritual devotion.

The notion prevails here that the ashes raised by ebulliting liquid engenders a disease of the eye, and it is with much trepidation they sit until the cloud settles. Often, indeed, their negligent spouses are lodgepoled[1] for such accidents; the fear of punishment keeps them on the alert when anything is cooking. Smith's poor woman had consternation strongly depicted on her face, and he helped her through with looks most grim and menacing.

The Cheyenne marriage ceremony is not a little curious. As in all cases, whether civilized or savage, the matter

[1] Whipped.

is talked of and arranged by the anxious pair long before the friendly or inimical interposition of those deeming themselves the guardians of inexperienced youth. Then follows the formality of asking for the fair one, which, though it may seem mercenary, must not be entirely so considered, as it is the invariable custom.

At night, when all are supposed to be asleep, the lover, selecting his best horse, ties it up to the lodge of his father-in-law to be, where it stays until morning. If it is put with their band, he is accepted; if not, it stays tied, exposed to the jeers of the village boys and the stinging laugh of the girls (who are ever ready to make fun) until night again. Then the jilted youth sneaks up and takes it away, or makes an additional propitiatory offering.

If the father is an inexorable tyrant, the loving couple sometimes take hasty leave for parts unknown.

The queerest oddities with the Cheyennes are gray-haired children. From the age of three up, they can be seen going about, like so many little old men and women. The hair is not white or "tow," but real streaked, black and gray, such as we would see on a man of forty-five. I could neither see nor hear of the cause. The owners of the premature growth had juvenile, healthy faces, as others of their years, though there may be an affection of the roots of the hair. *Possibly*, as there is an edict saying that the iniquities of the fathers upon the children unto the third and fourth generations shall be visited, these innocents have to don the venerable locks before the proper time because their great-great-grandfathers happened to stick their tantalizing lance points the eighth of an inch too far in some poor devil of a Pawnee prisoner. *Qu'en sabe?*

On the morning of the 28th, Smith and I were in the log house, trading *o-ne-a-wokst* (beads) to an old squaw for *o-ne-a-voke* (a piece of meat). While asking for an addition to our already large contribution, she pointed with her mouth to an approaching object, saying, "*Po-ome! num-whit veheo*" ("Blackfoot! look yonder, there's a white man").

Coming close, he hailed us, "How are ye, John?"

"What! Louy, old coon, down hyar? How's times to Fort William!—but let's see, you's the one as run 'meat' for them gover'ment fellers to Bent's ranch—eh?"

"Yes! an' this child was mighty nigh losin' his har, *he* was."

"How?"

"Them darned Spaniards!"

"H——! anybody 'gone under' to Touse?"

"Yes! Guvner Charles."

"Wa-agh! but them palous 'll pay for their scalpin' yet, I'm thinkin'."

We went in the lodge, where the men, after recovering from the surprise of seeing an old *compañero*, were told the sad news of Governor Bent's death, and while Louy was stowing away huge pieces of buffalo, he was interrogated by the anxious traders—

"Louy, tell all 'bout the whole consarn; it's all over now, an' can't be worse. I 'spect the niggurs got my woman too," said Fisher, who was a resident of Taos, the scene of the massacre, "Who else is under, 'sides Charles?"

"*Well*, you see the Purblos [Pueblas de Taos] was mity mad fur the 'Mericans to come in thar diggins an' take everything so easy like; an', as Injun blood *is* bad an' sneakin', they swore to count coups when they could. So when Charles was down to Touse to see his woman, the palous[2] charged afore sunrise. The portal was too strong

[2] *Pelado*—loafer—corrupted into *palou*.

117

fur 'em, an' they broke in with axes, an' a Purblo, cached behint a pile of dobies, shot him with a Nor'west fusee twice, an' skulped him."

"Scalped *him*—scalped Charles?" cried the men, partly swinging to their feet and clutching their knives, "Thar be heap of wolf meat afore long—sartain!"

"Yes! an' they took the trail for Santy Fee; but afore they left, Stephe Lee dropped in *his* tracks too. 'Hell!' says I, the palou as threw that arrer is marked,' an' so he is—Wa-agh!"

"Was Narcisse Beaubien killed, Louy?" asked I.

"Who? that young feller as kem with the wagons, last fall, with St. Vrain?"

"Yes, the same."

"Oh! he's gone beaver 'long with the rest. He was Mexican blood, an' so much the better fur them. They had a big dance when his topknot was off. Well, you see," commencing once more, "a band of the devils got to the Poinel ranch, over Touse Mountain, and back agin with the biggest kind of cavyard. Maybe *coups* wasn't counted that trip. The sojers—a lot of greenhorns and Dutchmen—came to Purgatoire, this side of Raton. Frank De Lisle had the company's wagons, an' the boys thar. We cached along the train fur the Arkansa—*well* we did! Mule meat went a wolfin' that spree—Wagh!"

"Where is Drinker [the Cincinnati editor]? He was at the ranch, I believe."

"Out in the pinyon, that morning, with his big Saint Loui' gun—a Jake Hawkins gun, *she* was, eh? He had bullets an inch long, with a sharp piint—be doggoned ef they wasn't some, eh?—We had to leave him, but I guess he'll come in safe."

"Will they take Santy Fee, think ye, Louy?" inquired Fisher.

"Now that's more than this hos kin tell. He hasn't made 'medicine' yet; but I'm afraid the 'Mericans *will* 'go under.'"

Louy was called from the lodge by William Bent. We pitied William. His murdered brother, being much older than himself and George, was loved and respected as a father.

The news had quite a depressing effect upon us. We were even apprehensive of our own safety in case the Santa Féan forces were overpowered; for it was probable the country, from El Paso to El Valle de Taos, had revolted; and, as Bent's Fort contained much of value and was an important post, a Mexican expedition might well be expected.

When the Indians learned the death of their old friend, W*oh-pi ve-heo*—"the gray-haired white man"—criers were sent out, and the people harangued. After consultation, the chiefs proposed that the young men should march to Taos and scalp every Mexican within reach. But Mr. Bent, thanking them, declined, saying that the soldiers at the fort would go if necessary.

At the following dawn, Mr. Bent and I left for the fort, some forty miles distant, taking no baggage but the robes strapped to the saddles.

The morning was cold and cloudy, in consonance with our moody taciturnity. Keeping the south bank of the river for some miles, we attempted a ford. Our fractious mules gave much trouble, detaining us a vexatious half-hour; we then broke the ice, and dragged and pushed in their unwilling feet by main strength.

While breasting the strong wind, which keeps the trail nicely swept as with a broom, we saw, emerging from a patch of high marsh-grass, skirting a belt of cottonwoods on the river's margin, a Mexican, mounted on a strong, iron-gray horse. He wore, in lieu of a hat, a handkerchief bound over his head, under the edges of which long jetty locks flitted to the breeze. His right hand grasped a short bow and a few arrows. He was passing at a gallop, when Bent, with his cocked rifle, shouted in Spanish to stop. The man stated that he belonged to William Tharpe's company; but the skulk's restless eye and his every motion seemed to indicate more than he told. After a searching cross-examination, Bent told him to "*vamos, prento!*" ("go quick"), or he would send a ball through him, anyhow. I expected to see the Mexican pitch from his horse through the aid of a bullet. Bent turned to follow him, expressing a regret at not having taken a shot.

By sundown we reached the fort, having traveled the entire day without ten minutes' halt, or scarcely a word of conversation. Fifty dirty, uncouth, green-looking Missourians, in command of Captain Jackson, hung about us as we left the saddles.

There was much excitement in regard to the massacre, some expecting a Mexican army to appear on the hill across the river; others, strutting inside the high and secure fort walls, gasconaded and looked fierce enough to stare a mad "buffler" out of countenance, declaring themselves ready to wade up to their necks in Mexican blood. Everyone, however, had cause for fear, as the American force was known to be small and much weakened by being scattered in small herding parties throughout the province. The traders, etc., proposed to push right on to Taos: steal all the animals, "raise" all the attainable Mexican "hair," burn every ranch, and "charge" generally.

A while before dusk, an express from the Arkansas

Pueblo,[3] seventy miles above, arrived with the news that the United States detachment of volunteers stationed there were awaiting orders from Jackson, the superior in command. But the Captain (Jackson) would not act without orders from Colonel Price, at Santa Fé, at that time likely a prisoner. So the idea of aid in that quarter was reluctantly abandoned.

Louy Simonds, on leaving the ranch, cut across the country, by that means preceding the wagons several days. The morning after our arrival, Frank De Lisle's wagons corralled in front of the fort. My old friends, the Canadian teamsters, shook my hand heartily—finer fellows were never soaked by the prairie storms.

About ten o'clock, as I was standing at the far end of the court, a tall man stalked in the gate, looking wildly around. A long-browned rifle rested on his shoulder, with that exquisite *negligé* air—firm yet careless-appearing—his long, black, uncombed hair hung in strings from beneath his greasy wool hat; and a frowning moustache gave a Satanic cast to his features. On his feet were thick moccasins, and to judge from the cut, of his own fashioning. His pantaloons, of gray cassinet, were threadbare and rudely patched with buckskin. Instead of a coat, a blanket was thrown over the shoulder and fastened, at the waist, by a black leather belt, in which was thrust a brass-studded leather sheath, sustaining a "Green River" of no small pretensions as to length; and which, had it the power of speech, might dwell with ecstatic pleasure on the praise of choice morceaus of "fleece" severed by its keen edge—perchance astonish with the recital of the number of "Yutes,"

[3] A settlement of Mountaineers, with their Indian and Mexican wives, and the station of a detachment of the Mormon Battalion.

whose "hump ribs" have been savagely tickled with its searching point. His quick eye, wandering, alighted on me, followed by—

"How are you?"

"Why, Drinker!" exclaimed I, in the utmost surprise, and taking his outstretched hand, "I'm glad to see you— Louy Simonds told us that the Spaniards had taken your 'hair.' "

"Oh p'shaw! not yet, I can assure you."

"Did you travel by yourself all the way?"

"No, not quite. I went out hunting that morning, and became so interested in a beaver dam that it was night before the ranch was reached again. Our men were gone, but I cooked some of the "goat" I had that day killed, and on Louy's old deerskins, lying about camp, I slept until morning. I then followed their trail, on foot, toward the Vermaho. The second day I caught up to a train, but they being too slow, I pushed ahead by myself. I overtook the company's wagons yesterday, and have been alone the rest of the time."

"That's a quick trip for a pedestrian. How long were you in coming? It's about 170 miles."

"Oh! a little over six days. My moccasins nearly gone the way of all flesh"—replied he, looking at his feet.

Mr. Bent determining that something should be done, called his men together; and, stating the facts of the case, ended by saying they could go or stay—as they choosed. Every one offered his services.

CHAPTER X

EL RÍO DE LAS ANIMAS

IT WAS in the afternoon of the next day that the party was started, consisting of twenty-three men. Bransford was in charge of the seventeen employees and the wagon; the other five were free. One was Lucien Maxwell, a hunter to Frémont's expedition in 1842, a resident of the valley of Taos, and a son-in-law to Judge Beaubien (Narcisse's father). Manuel Le Févre—Lajeunesse and Tom—claimed a local habitation in Taos. They, very fortunately for themselves, happened to be on the opposite side of the mountain at the time of the massacre.

We crossed the river into Nueve Méjico at the fort ford, and followed the Santa Fé Trail, which kept the river bank. Five of us were mounted; the rest were to get animals at the Purgatoire, ninety miles distant. The object of the expedition in which we were about to engage was to travel as far as we could toward Taos; kill and scalp every Mexican to be found, and collect all the animals belonging to the Company and the United States.

Where the route diverged from the river at right angles for Santa Fé, we camped. On the west, white chalk cliffs cropped out from the brow of the hills; the soap plant spread its green fan here and there, and dead-seeming sage bushes, harsh and stiff, were dispersed in irregular patches.

No sun appeared; the chilling winds blew fitfully over the bleak plain, indicating an approaching snowstorm.

Most of the Canadians were those with whom I journeyed from the States. As they trudged along, chattering in French, overflowing with boisterous mirth, they thought not of the fatigue of walking. All were equipped with nor'-west fusils; with them, every prominent object in the road was *un sacré Mexican*. When any one of them raised his fusil to fire, all stopped; some leaned forward on tiptoe, others drew back and sighted with one eye, and others again, with half-open mouths, in anxious expectation, would wait until the report of the gun rang out. Then all would start forward at a run to the target. If a good shot, a *sacré bon* of approbation might be heard; if not, they would look carefully around, then examine the bushes twenty and thirty feet from the target, in tones of solicitous irony, condoling and praising the marksman with such exclamations as *"un beau garçon"*; *"votre fusil tres bon, wagh!"* *"One Mexican he go ondare too, parceque you put de ball through son tête."* *"Pauvre Mexican!"*

The wagon contained one barrel of flour for provision, but no meat. Wood was scarce; with chunks from old camps around, we cooked. We sat by the coals, I talking to my Canadian friends of their trip to Santa Fé; they to me of Indians. Our short clay pipes were again and again filled before retiring. Bransford and I slept together. With blankets and robes, in a depression of the ground, to keep off the wind, we made a snug bed.

An hour before daylight I awoke, and raised my head from under the clothes (we always covered them, to keep off the winds) when a mass of snow filled the vacated pillow. Bransford, hearing me moving and talking to myself, told me with a grunt to "be still."

"But the snow is all under my head, and I'm as uncomfortable as possible."

"Ah, boy! you'd better mind what I say; you get to fooling and let the snow in on you, and you'll freeze. Take care, old fellow," and off he dropped asleep.

I interposed my right hand between my head and the snow, until it was benumbed; then my cheek would be pillowed on the snow, until it was quite chilled. Lying on my right side, I dared not turn; my left hand could not be raised, and in that awkward position, Bransford's tantalizing snores constantly recalled me to a sense of my misfortune.

Some little effort was required to throw off the clothing when getting up, by reason of the accumulated snow. A warmer covering could not have been made, as it effectually excluded the chill winds sweeping the hill behind us. The men, with their feet, found the wood and rekindled the fire.

What a sight greeted our eyes on rising! The hills, ourselves, and saddles were covered with the white drapery; bitter cold winds penetrated our clothes, while far off to the northwest, the twin mountains—*Las Cumbres Españolas*—glittered with snow. The mules were starving, for the scanty grass was hidden early in the night with the same frigid envelope which contributed not an atom to our personal comfort; and they stood trembling over their picket pins, pricking their ears at any noise, without moving their heads.

From the impossibility of journeying with any degree of warmth, and the fact of the total absence of wood at the next two camps, and the probability of more snow, it was decided by the leaders that we should stay in camp—choosing the least of two evils. Succeeding an unpleasant day of freezing on one side of our bodies and scorching on the other, with our eyes red, blinking, and weeping, by reason of pungent wood smoke, we rolled in our robes to get warm all over—a desideratum not attainable outside of them. We slept in the open air, the sky our canopy, as usual. Trouble and many inconveniences, both great and small, are invariably attendant on the exposed life we were leading; and though there were too many harsh ejaculations and expressive curses at the "ill luck" for true philosophers, yet, from the frequent occurrence of mishaps, we learned to endure them as pains inevitable.

Here we have nothing but bread and coffee, which, in truth, is less nourishing and acceptable to us than meat alone.

We were again on the road, the mules no better for their stay. The pedestrians, comprising four-fifths of the company, had a laborious time walking through the snow, which, toward the middle of the day, melted, and rendered the ground slippery; but being Canadians was a sufficient guaranty for their acting with the proper spirit. Unpleasant matters will sometimes end; and, following a tedious day's tramp, we made camp on La Río Timpa—a stream three or four feet in width, which, in pools and ripples, coursed along a tributary to the great Mississippi. The Timpa rises in New Mexico and is the beginning of a series of streams whose names are much more euphonious than those in the American territory.

Leaving the wagon on the bank, we descended to the margin of the rivulet, to be free from the wind. The greasewood, so called from the crackling, eager flame in burning, afforded the only fuel, for the creek has ever been sparsely wooded, and General Kearney's division, *en route* to Santa Fé, used the little that was left. The above-mentioned bush here grows to the height of four and five feet, starting from the ground in uniform wiry stems, which, by a quick, bending motion, can be broken. It makes a hot, sparkling, though short-durating fire, and, to judge from the odor exhaled, contains a large proportion of resinous matter. The green bush burns as well as the dry, and is well designed to supply the traveler with fuel. The teamsters and soldiers on the Fort Leavenworth and Santa Fé trail are so improvident that not many years will pass ere the timber now standing will disappear.

Unfortunately for our coffee, the waters of the Timpa were so impregnated with salt as to be scarcely drinkable, though not so brackish now as in dry weather.

The fellows were strung close along with their blankets and robes for sleeping; our mules hobbled, jumped among the grease-bushes on the bluff above for the sparse herbage, and by the expiring embers of the campfire sat Lajeunesse, without hat, which he never wore or possessed, puffing the dear pipe thoughtfully. A queer genius was this same Lajeunesse. For years a voyageur, undergoing between the Platte and Arkansas even more than the usual hardships, he now was settled in the quiet vale of Taos with a wife; but, like his brother Canadians, no better off in property than when a young man, he first came to the Far West.

True to the mountaineer's characteristics, he was kind-hearted; for, of seemingly unsociable dispositions, they are generous, even to a fault. The fewness of their numbers seems to create an interchange of kindly feeling, and the more one learns the nature of the hardy frequenters of the Rocky Mountain hunting grounds and beaver streams, the more will he be pleased. To judge by his frankness and reckless life, his sole aim appears to be freedom of person and speech in its fullest import. Considering his neighbor's "possibles" "on the prairie" with him—his own at their entire disposal; and, though coffee, sugar, tobacco, and other luxuries are high-priced and often purchased with a whole *season's* trapping, the "black water" is offered with genuine free-heartedness, and the last plug of tobacco subjected to the rapacious knife of the guest as though it were plenty as the rocks around.

In consonance with the Divine provision, the mountaineer deems it not good that he should be alone, and a visit to the Mexican settlements, or a trading tour to the Indian lodges, often results in his returning a quiet, contented Benedict, with, perhaps, the village belle to grace his solitary campfire, to mend his moccasins, or to spread the warm robes in the least smoky spot—the lonely pair as devoted in their love and as tranquil in their affection, in the midst of blood-thirsty enemies, howling wolves, and chilling snows, as in the saloons of a metropolis.

The easy manners of the harum-scarum, reckless trappers in rendezvous and the simple, unsuspecting hearts of these mountain nymphs cause him to be ever jealous of the attentions bestowed on his wife; and often serious difficulties arise, in the course of which she receives a severe drubbing with the knot end of a lariat, or no very light lodge-poling, at the hands of her imperious sovereign. Sometimes, the affair ends in a more tragical way than a mere beating; not infrequently, the gay gallant pays the penalty of interference with his life.

One instance, partaking of the spirit of chivalry, was related to me by a witness. It was about two years before my visit that, at the *Pueblo* (the mountaineer settlement), a man suspected his squaw of cherishing greater affection for a handsome young fellow than for himself, and jealousy once fairly possessing him, no difficulty was found in sending a challenge. It was accepted; and, on the succeeding morning, the two mounted their horses, rifles in hand, and faced each other on the plain, two hundred yards apart. During the momentary pause before the signal to advance was given, the younger one (and the transgressor) watched, with unmoved features, the bright sun looming up through the prairie to the east, then directed his eyes to the cold, gray spur of the Wet Mountain above. He gave one thought to his friends, a calm smile to his antagonist, gathered the bridle rein more tightly, and moved forward at an easy gallop, sitting as lightly as though he was out for a buffalo hunt. The simultaneous discharges rang out in the clear morning air; the wronged man turned in his saddle to behold a riderless steed clattering wildly over the dry plain, and, a puff of wind uplifting the smoke, discovered, outstretched, the form of his opposer.

We were off again on our way. The small hills were thick set with a heavy growth of "greasewood" and sage, whose leafless, dead-appearing stems, protruding through the snow, gave a desolate, barren cast to the scenery. On our left were high bluffs, their tops crowned with stunted pine and cedar. The black-tailed deer, said to browse there, incited me to a trial for "meat"; and, after much toiling, up and down indentations and around chasms, the summit was reached. Reining in the mule, with forefeet on the highest rock, I looked around.

Far off to the northeast was the well-known Pike's Peak, connected toward the south by a low range to the Wet Mountain, so famed for the game within its very shadow; and, still further to the south, the White Mountain, out-topping all; and yet below it, the twin *Wah-to-yah,* one beyond the other, rising until the furthest floated as clouds, their white crests apparently touching the sky—

the whole view including a stretch of 150 miles. From my position to the nearest was 90 miles or more; yet, such was the extreme purity of the atmosphere, any one peak seemed attainable by a few hours' ride. How simple, how imposingly great are these distant works of Nature!

As the men (shortly after) pointed out the different spurs, they expatiated more particularly on the Wet Mountain, with its lovely savannas, its cool springs and murmuring rills, its shady bowers of fragrant cedar and sheltered spots of grass, its rocky retreats and tumbling brooks, its grizzly bear and mountain sheep, its silky beaver and black-tailed deer with wide-spreading antlers, its monster elk and fleet-footed antelope, its lucious plums and refreshing grapes, its juicy cherries, delightful currants, and other attractions, making it the hunter's paradise. Warming in their descriptions, Bransford and I, enamored with the joys of a hunter's life, made our plans for the coming summer.

We obtained a view of the effulgent snow-piled Raton, at whose base our road runs. At noon, in came the hunters with two antelopes, scaring, as they descended the precipitous hills back of camp, a band of "black-tail," who, clattering adown, with graceful motions sped across the hunters' saddles, gave avidity to our decidedly carnivorous appetites, as we had been two days without meat. The repast finished and washed down with strong coffee, the officiating butcher knives were wiped across our buckskins, with that deliberate languid air which plainly proclaimed *j'am satis*.

Tom wanted some bullets—in lieu of a ladle he cut a shallow place in a stick of wood—a hunter's expedient—where, laying in the lead and piling on coals, it soon melted.

Bransford's dog, whose fierce growls this night made

me long recollect him, was of the Mexican-shepherd breed, somewhat larger than the Newfoundland, with white, coarse, and long hair. This dog had often been seen around Bent's Fort in company with wolves, on the watch for offal and other refuse. The men, wishing his skin, shot at him many times without effect. One morning early, the fort gates were opened, and the dog, cautiously passing the first portal,[1] entered the yard, and pulled at the bait of meat, starting with it for the prairie, but not before the gate was secured. The infuriated dog, far more strong and savage than the largest wolf, turned on his assailants, who safely stood on the roof (which shelved toward the courtyard on all sides), with lassos to noose him as he ran from one side to the other. He gnawed and bit several *riatas* in two; but, at last entangling him, he was fastened with a heavy iron chain and secured in a bastion for two days; he continually making desperate, though ineffectual, efforts to break loose, which severe straining drove the blood to his not yet clear eyes. He resisted all attempts at friendship with growls of decided anger, until the third morning when Bransford, walking up without show of fear, patted him on the head. He followed him every step, but allowed no one else to make friendly advances. Bransford and I occupied the same bedding; and, if I wanted to sleep first, he had to accompany me until safe between the blankets, for the faithful guardian always asserted his right to coil himself on Bransford's property and growl at those who approached. His warm body was quite an acquisition to the comfort of our feet.

The wind rose at dark, driving the most of us down by the water's edge; where, sheltered by the high banks, we

[1] Portal: in the mountains, the accent is on the last syllable, por*tal*.

talked and smoked. The Canadians were above us, chattering in their usual glib style, when a sound like distant thunder filled the air. Down they rushed, all talking at once. We knew that it could not be thunder at this time of year, and the conclusion at which we soon arrived was that a battle was taking place in Taos.[2] Although it is a long distance there by the road and a lofty mountain intervenes, it is not more than thirty-five or forty miles in a direct line. It was a hazardous trip for us to venture so far in the Mexican territory, with no knowledge of affairs at Santa Fé and elsewhere except those of an alarming nature; and we knew too well the carelessness and paucity of the American soldiery. We felt the Mexicans to be an injured people, possessed of vindictive tempers, who would, with a prospect of success and under the guidance of brave leaders, revolt and fight well.

We were apprehensive that a Mexican force had overpowered the Americans at the Purgatoire (a day's ride in advance), and was on its way to Bent's Fort. Our position was anything but enviable. Maxwell, Le Févre, Lajeunesse, and Tom were cast down with thought of their families, who might, at that moment, be subject to the lawlessness of the infuriated populace. It was a gloomy night to those who, in anxious wakefulness, passed the long, dark hours till morning.

On awaking, our spirits revived with the appearance of the happy sun; and, being thawed enough to raise a laugh and smoke a pipe good-humoredly, we hitched up and rolled over the prairie in earnest haste.

Now, although at night all the extra clothing was required as protection from the piercing winds, yet, toward

[2] That evening Colonel Price commenced the attack on the Pueblo de Taos.

noon, the heat was quite uncomfortable, and we encamped after a long and warm drive through a barren waste, save for an occasion stalk of cactus and scattering plants of the *pamilla*, from under whose sickly-green leaves loped, awkwardly, large gray hares. We stayed in camp, without water, for the oxen to rest; and, while waiting with thirsty impatience in the shade of the wagon, we saw advancing from the direction of the Raton an object, which was immediately pronounced a grizzly bear. At the starting announcement, every man arose quickly to his feet, gun in hand, to encounter the unwelcome visitor. But the bear proved to be a worn-down ox with "U.S." stamped in seared letters on the left foreshoulder. The beast, though not grizzly by nature, was grizzly with age and hard work, his sharp bones nearly protruding through the lifeless-looking skin. He was, no doubt, journeying the prairie trail, on home intent, to the land of fodder and tall grass—the Platte purchase in Missouri; and how the poor thing came this far without being hamstrung by rapacious wolves is a wonder. We, with self-interest at heart, detained the homesick youth, and that afternoon drove him, with many a harsh *"sacré,"* and "wo ha-a," along the same road he had just languidly traversed; this time, with his head bowed in submission to the galling yoke of servitude, no more to see his land of promise but in dreams, while chewing the cud of hunger and disappointment.

Toward evening, we came to a *cañon*,[3] or enclosed creek, with bluffs forty, fifty, and even eighty or more feet in height. A diminutive streamlet trickled along the uneven bottom, in places disappearing, to reappear after a dark passage under the flat stones, and to find its way, with

[3] Pronounced "Kanyon"—a Mexican word, signifying a tube, or hollow, ravine, etc.

numerous tiny accessions, to the brackish Timpa, thereby constituting the headwaters of that insignificant stream.

A camp, known as the "Hole in the Rock"—so called from the pools of water in the dry channel—was our resting place for the night; the huge. detached masses lying around, the thick groves of cedar, and the shelving ground formed a good stopping place, but in our present state of insecurity somewhat undesirable. We fixed ourselves according to fancy, built cheerful fires, drank plenty of the mean water, ate considerable of the slim stock of poor provision, and smoked frequently, conjuring up, in the wreaths of strong smoke as they ascended, shapes both blessed and *au contraire*.

The fires grew low; all were in bed but poor Maxwell and Lajeunesse, both too uneasy to sleep for thought of their homes, when we were startled by the bark of dogs and the almost simultaneous rush of Bransford's hound from my feet. What a thrill dashed through me! The men sprang to their feet, and ran from the fire in every direction, and I, following suit, cached myself behind a large stone, with ready rifle. Everyone was in the bushes, ready for the attack, in a moment from the time the dog barked, though not a shout of warning was heard from any of us. We reconnoitered, now with faces flat to the ground, to listen for footsteps, now dashing through the bushes. After a quarter of an hour, we ventured to return. Guards were set and continued through the night. What a train of new thought does an affair like this bring! The anxious state of suspense, the strain of the eyes in the endeavor to penetrate the Cimmerian darkness, the dodging behind rocks and trees, and the stealthy crawl of the older Indian fighters combined to work up to a greater tensity our already high-strung feelings.

El Río de las Animas

The following morn, ere the mists were fairly dispersed, we were again in our hard saddles, trotting down the little hills and walking up the elevations, in the same old way. A new variety of cactus appeared; round stems covered with innumerable sharp spines being the peculiarity. When dead, the spines can be broken and the main stem used barely to boil a cup of coffee or cook a piece of antelope meat, for the heat is but of short duration. The *pamilla* here dots the plain, its bayonet-like leaves diverging from the center as rays; and looming up in the ever-distant and receding mirage, in increased proportions, was often supposed to be a deer, or horse, until a change of position dispelled the idea. We came in sight of the groves of dead cottonwoods on the Purgatoire by noon, and, diverging to the right of the trail, took a short cut for the camp of United States teamsters, whom we expected to find in a bend of the stream. The animals sank up to the fetlocks in the loamy bottom soil, and stumbled more than once in the numerous gopher burrows, or shied around the prairie-dog hillocks, and continually pricked their ears at the lively chirpings of the well-fed inhabitants.

Las Cumbres Españolas were now to our right, but a few short hours' ride distant; to our left was the long descried Raton Peak, which, though smaller from its proximity, seemed more towering than its superior on the opposite side of the valley—the Spanish Peaks. We traced with the eye the sinuosities of the Purgatoire, by the cottonwoods on the margins, with abrupt cliffs and alternate prairie, far up to the mountain gap, whence it emerged. Manuel Le Févre pointed to us the route which he, with a party of *ciboleros*—buffalo hunters—years ago came from El Valle de Taos on the search for buffalo. He spoke of the deep snows in which they ran the noble animal with lance and bow, and of going up in the neighborhood of the "Peaks," where they found great numbers, killing enough in two days, to load their large train of pack mules. In one race, he lanced three, and two of the *ciboleros*, five apiece.

The fine hunting grounds and the pleasures of the chase he dwelt upon with commendable fervor. *"Mais sacré,"* said he complainingly, with a suppressed heave of the breast, "les American, dey go to de Missouri frontier, de buffalo he ron to de montaigne; de trappare wid his dam fusil, he follow to de Bayou Salade, he ron again. *Dans les Montaignes Espagnol*, bang, bang! *toute la journee! toute la journee!* go *de sacré voleurs*. De bison he leave, parceque des fusils scare im vara moche—ici, la, all de sem —*sacré!"*—and while telling it, he worked himself in a great heat, as if the prairie and mountain peaks were made exclusively for Frenchmen and *ciboleros*, through which to chase buffalo in yelling barbarity forever.

We found the United States teamsters encamped on an elevation above the creek, strongly fortified with wagons placed in the form of a hollow square, and a ditch and breastwork dug on the inside, behind which to fight. A few volunteer soldiers, who fled from the ranch at the same time Bent's employees left, were here encamped; they and the teamsters faring well on government rations, of which there were fifty or more wagonloads, and doing nothing but herding their oxen, in momentary expectation of a Mexican army to come sweeping down the mountain, and, amid the blasts of trumpets and the roar of *escopets*, take them unwilling prisoners to the mountains beyond *El Río Grande del Norte*.

We made camp in a small grove of dead cottonwoods, sheltered in the rear by a gentle hill and surrounded by long bottom grass. We were as far from the teamsters as safety dictated, for the never satisfied inquisitiveness of the government men was unbearable. Some soldiers of Captain Fischer's artillery company were here. They, too, left the ranch, driving with them large droves of horses and cattle belonging to the United States and Bent, St. Vrain & Co. When we claimed the Company's (B. & St. V's) animals, they murmured and disputed much, in which the teamsters sided with them. They endeavored to secrete the most valuable in a distant valley, but, through our vigilance, they were found and brought back to camp. Hard words were uttered, and anger engendered on both sides. Not a few of our men were "for open war." Numerous were the curses showered on the "Neds"[4] by the mountain men of our party; and, still more frequent, the *"sacrés," "cochons," "enfants des garces,"* etc., hissed between the voluble lips of the Canadians, for their hatred was of the deepest dye toward these unfortunate wights, so far from the "land o' corndodgers"—Missouri.

On the 11th, a fall of snow covered the ground a few inches in depth. Toward night our party was increased by the arrival of Sublette, an old *compañero*, accompanied by Bill Garmon and Fred Smith, both clever fellows. They had ventured from the States with the United States express this inclement season of the year, bringing with them the news that General Wool had been ordered to join General Taylor, and that forty thousand men were enrolled for Mexico.

We now felt badly indeed—Doniphan's regiment was in Chihuahua, with no force to support it, and its certain defeat would give the Santa Féans additional courage. A

[4] Among many farmers, pork is familiarly called "Ned," and as pork forms a principal portion of the government rations, the United States employees were so termed by the mountain men, in derision.

month had passed since Governor Bent was murdered, several expresses had been sent from this side into New Mexico, but none had returned. Our position, more than a hundred miles in the Mexican territory, was unsafe.

CHAPTER XI

EL RÍO VERMÉJO

Aᴌᴌ were busied through the day in catching mules from the *caballada* for a start toward the Valley of Taos, though the snow on the mountain above was forbidding. On the 13th of February, the younger portion of our company, mounted on mules, with a few pack animals, left La Barge and two more in camp with the wagon, to follow on the receipt of orders from Bransford. We bade a gay farewell to the Purgatoire encampment, and, leaping the narrow stream and spurring the rejuvenated mules, gained the old trail, when, after a series of hill and dale, we turned to the left and commenced the ascent of the Raton Pass!

The route was up a steep valley, enclosed on either side by abrupt hills covered with pine and masses of gray rock, our course now along the points of hills, now in the rough, stony bed of the creek itself. The sparkling, flitting waters, leaping and foaming against the mules' feet, now gliding under large flat stones, and now reappearing, bounding impetuously down the uneven flinty bed, mingled itself with the pure stream La Purgatoire, hundreds of feet below. As we ascended, the scenery partook of a bolder, rougher cast. Sudden turns in the intricate windings gave views of the great valley below.

Toward four o'clock we, fatigued with the incessant

climbing, spurring, and walking, came to a valley gently sloping to the summit of the pass on the west and rising on the east immediately by a continued succession of acclivities and terraces to the bare cliff, which, overlooking the country for leagues around, is known and designated as the Raton Peak—a familiar landmark to the trappers and traders.

The packs were deposited on the ground, and the mules, with trailing lariats, quietly continued, single file, further up the nook; where, gradually diverging on the wayside to crop a stray bunch of grass, they busied themselves in feeding.

Dry sticks were gathered, water was brought, and so far on the "community system," with provision and work in common, we progressed to our utmost satisfaction. A lookout was placed a hundred feet above to notice the approach of friend or foe.

After eating, Bransford, Maxwell, and I took our guns to relieve the guard. The side of the mountain from which we kept watch declined toward the western horizon; as we lazily laid on the crispy, brown grass, sheltered from the cold winds, the waning sun shed its warm rays upon us and pervaded the air with a subdued mellow luster. White fleecy clouds, tinged with rosy hues, flew across the view, and between the etherial mottling was seen the placid blue.

Below, beyond the low range of mountain, was the valley—*Río de las Animas* or River of Souls—and to the further extremity of the great depression uprose the peerless snow-wreathed twin peaks *Las Cumbres Españolas*, the first of the Sierra Blanca, guardian-spirit-like, keeping constant vigils over the western plains; watchers of the fierce Indian skirmishes 'neath their shades; quiet lookers-on of the army which a short time before passed this point; and, by mere force of simple grandeur, inspiring a sentiment of friendship and protection in the breast of the lonely trapper, who, in momentary danger of losing his scalp, builds his little fire, cooks his meat, and smokes his pleasant tobacco, not without first offering to the towering crests the mouth of his pipe and the freely given homage of the first and most honorable whiff.

This is the acme of life. With fat, sleek mules, plenty[1] of provision and tobacco, the undisturbed possession of our scalps in doubt, we traveled and camped, always on the alert and ready for any emergency, caring little for foe, nor keeping guard; for a mountain man is supposed to always have his ear open to impending danger. In the present case, however, we had a guard, for the purpose of intercepting the express from Santa Fé, which we might reasonably expect.

After coffee, the mules received their packs, the riding animals ready saddled, stood while the owners, with lariat ends in their hands and the rifle held between the legs, raked out coals from the smoldering fire to light a pipe preparatory to starting.

The summit of the ridge was reached after an hour's toil; and, stopping a moment for the fatigued animals to blow, we rapidly descended. The immense precipices of bare rock and earth, the confusion in which nature seemed involved, caused all to remark the forbidding aspect on the *Canadiano* side of the summit. At some steep hills, near the pass terminus, we picked our way over a road, which, in verity might be termed rough. Pine trees interfered with the free use of the whip; large rocks obtruded their rude fronts in the tortuous road; one "wo ha-a" too many or a

[1] How full of import is the word "plenty"!

"gee" too few here endangers the safety of the unwieldy teams and burdens. The debris of wagons, such as fellies, loose tire, and tongues snapped short off shewed unmistakable signs of mismanagement, and told plainly that "government" was a loser in the Raton Pass.

Once more on the plain, rapid travel gave place to the late tiresome mule wriggling; and, at noon, the saddles were pulled off the warm and thirsty animals under a cottonwood, on the banks of *El Río Canadiano*, at this point a glassy, snow-fed streamlet, fifteen feet in width.

On crossing the stream, Maxwell, who had heretofore stayed with the crowd, kept some distance in advance, as scout. We were strung carelessly along, when he, jerking his mule around quickly, spurred her in a gallop and diverged from the route, at the same time motioning to us to ride *à la Camanche*—with our bodies so that nothing is seen on the opposite side, but part of the leg with which, and the heel of the same, we held on to the saddle cantle. There was no hill, but the gradual rise of the ground served to conceal any object approaching from the other side. We were quite excited, thundering along at full speed, able to sweep the ground with the free hand, our rifles ready to jerk up to the face, not knowing whether the run was from Mexicans or a band of Utahs or Apaches, or whether we were trying to surprise a party ourselves. But, too well versed were we in Indian warfare, through practice or hearsay, to question at such a time or to utter any noise, except, indeed, a Canadian's impatient *"sacré diable"* to his shying mule, or a smothered curse from a less conscientious American.

On making the rise, we espied a man unconscious of our proximity, going at half-speed on one horse and leading another; but so soon as he caught a glimpse of the foremost hat, away he lashed his animals in a full run. With wild yells, we straightened in the saddles, and, with the report of two or three fusils, in the hands of as many half-frantic Frenchmen, we charged after him, endeavoring to escape; but seeing that it would be of no use, he fired his gun in air, in token of submission, and rode slowly toward us. It was *Haw-he,* an Indian belonging to George Bent, now on his way to the fort with the joyful news that Colonel Price had marched into Taos at the head of 250 men, and, in battle, had killed 200 Mexicans and Indians, and had bombarded and knocked down the Indian walled town of the Pueblos de Taos. On mentioning that Mr. St. Vrain commanded a company which did considerable service, cheers of exultation burst from us again and again. The *Moro,* another town, was razed to the ground, and several thousand dollars' worth of grain burnt. The Mexicans fled to the mountains, but being pursued, several prisoners were taken.

As Haw-he spoke American in broken sentences only, our information was gained through the services of our Taos companions.

Said he, "I see you come on de cavallos, and de mules poco tempo[2]—me tink you los 'Utes,' *caraho!*—me hair gone—me rubbed out,[3] but *quien sabe el cavallo colorado esta bueno,*[4] me be off prento; *you* fire de carabine, den I fire—me no want nada." Maxwell knew from experience that no prairie traverser will permit a body of men to approach him for fear of undergoing the painful scalping operation. By surprising this man, we would be sure of

[2] "Cavallos poco tempo"—horses and mules coming fast.

[3] "Rubbed out"—killed; "rubbed out" of existence.

[4] "Quien sabe el cavallo colorado esta bueno"—"who knows but that my red horse is good and fast."

him. Bransford hastily writing a few words to our men at the Purgatoire to come on, sent Haw-he on his way.

The animals were watered at dark, and, pushing on, we stopped at a hill, amid groves of *piñon*. In honor of the late victories, we made a blazing pine fire, which cast a strong light for miles around. Heretofore, we had been careful, having but small fires, sufficient only for cooking, though now there was as much danger as ever from the marauding bands of Mexicans and Pueblos in the mountains near. The most gratifying result of the intelligence was the satisfaction to our Taos friends to learn the safety of their families.

Without breakfast or other solace, we saddled our mules for the Vermaho (Verméjo) ranch, one of Bent, St. Vrain & Co.'s herding establishments. In an hour's ride, a hill, rocky and sterile save a few stunted pines, presented itself, which overlooked a valley a mile in width, devoid of trees or bushes, and carpeted with brown "bunch" or "grama" grass. On either side of the dale rose mountains precipitous and rugged, presenting a wilderness of verdure; to the north, a high-defined point, clad and shaded by the everlasting pine, stood in softened relief; the narrow nooks on either side were dark and cool with the somber shades of the forest above and around, and toward the further extremities of which herds of sleek, fat, bright-spotted cattle ran bellowing on our near approach.

In a recess of the mountain, completely sheltered from the chill winds and at a sufficient elevation to command a view of the animated plain below, was the site of the *rancho*. As few persons, probably, out of Mexico, understand but vaguely its definition, a description will be essayed. First, an eligible site for wood, water, shelter from the winds, and a full view of the herds is chosen; then the adjacent aspen or pinyon[5] groves furnish two forked poles, which are generally driven upright into the ground, as far apart as occasion requires, with four feet or about, visible. A pole is then laid from one fork to the other, and other small ones, seven or eight feet in length, laid, the smaller ends on the cross pole, the butts resting on the ground. On top of these are spread raw hides of beef and the skins of game, and under the frame the soft ends of the pinyon and cedar branches are spread to the depth of a foot or more. On top of that, deerskins are laid, and then the bedding surmounts that, which, altogether, makes a springy mattress, equal to the best "hair" or "moss." In front is the blazing pine fire, and at one side a small stick driven in the ground, an inch or two of the branches remaining, on which the tin cups are hung when not in use. A short distance beyond is a pen of logs and brush, in which the *caballada* is driven when an animal is wanted.

This constitutes a New Mexican *rancho*, where the herdsmen of the poorer class stay, far remote from their homes, living for months on *atole* (thin mush of unbolted flour) or, perchance, a deer or antelope which they have been fortunate enough to kill, and performing severe and dangerous duty: exposed to the rains, the winds, the sleets, and snows; liable at all times, whether in the gray of morning or the shades of evening, the bright glare of noonday or the dark hours of the howling night-tempest, to the incursions of the numerous fierce, savage tribes, whose visits from the Mexican mountain glens are the immediate precursors of bloodshed and death. These perils do they endure, always in thought and too often in deed, for a small compensation, ranging from four to eight dollars per

[5] "Pinyon." I have preferred writing these words as they are pronounced.

month, frequently payable in dry goods and other imported articles, at exhorbitant prices.

The *rancheros* generally have no firearms; but, in lieu, a bow and quiver of arrows. With saddle, lasso, *hojas,* and *ponche*—shucks and tobacco—they seem content to lead this desultory life. They are always in the saddle, and a *ranchero* has the rare faculty of making the unhappy quadruped he bestrides, if there is the least life in it, answer his purpose by means of murderous spurs, the rowels of some of which measures five inches in diameter.

Manuel Le Févre, Maxwell, and Tom left for Taos. The rest made camp by the ashes of the old ranch fire; and, shortly after, the band of cattle which had been driven up, startled with the report of one of our rifles, ran to the mountain again, leaving one of their number stretched on the ground. With the aid of a half a dozen scalp knives, its skin was stretched on a pole frame, the meat hung on a pinyon tree near, and ere the warmth of vitality had passed away, sundry pieces of tenderloin and fat links of *boudin,* hastily browned by the quick pine blaze, had glided down the "grease-hungry" throats of the independent party at the Vermaho ranch.

The following morning, Bransford started, with two men, for the Poinel ranch (also one of Bent, St. Vrain & Co.'s), three or four hours' ride distant. I accompanied them. Each one tied a piece of beef to the saddle strings for our only provision. Our course lay along the foot of the mountain; every step, in crossing from one point to another, disclosed quiet, lovely vales, on whose grassy undulations reclined herds of clean, well-fed cattle and droves of dusky-colored, gamboling deer and antelope; who, on our approach, started forward and with graceful bounds re-

treated into the fastnesses of the almost impassable bar-
riers of rock in the background.

A large bird, soaring from its eirie in the crag far above,
denoted the name of the great depression—the *Eagle Park.*
The low, level prairie, with its salt marshes and solitary
stalking game, stretched far away to the southeast, its
monotony somewhat relieved by the mirage into which it
merged. In the direction we were traveling, the Senegee
Mountain rose before us, snow-clad and overshadowed
with a drapery of mist; and, from its side, a long line of
smoke, from a signal fire, trailed upward, reminding us of
the Apache—no reliable friend to the American. Turning
in our saddles, we beheld the Raton Peak, and many minor
ones to the southward, heaped with gathering snow.

We crossed the Cimarone, a rushing, limpid stream,
issuing from the yawning mountain gorge, foaming and
tumbling over the rocky channel and imparting additional
cheerfulness to our already lively spirits, for the Indian boy
(Haw-he) had told us much to quiet our fears. Another
half hour brought us to the Poinel Creek, where we found
a *caballada* of mules and horses, bearing the brand of B.,
St. V. & Co. and that of "U. S." A mounted *ranchero,* on
guard, at first afraid, but finding who we were, directed us
down the creek a half mile, to a party of five more, all sent
from Taos by "Señor San Bran" (St. Vrain) to herd the
flocks, etc. The majordomo[6] was an intelligent-looking
Mexican, in a blue roundabout, leather pantaloons, and
peaked oilcloth hat. Between the thumb and forefinger of
his right hand was held the universal accompaniment of
this olive-complected race—the shuck cigarillo. All were
extremely polite through habit and through fear, as Col-

[6] *Majordomo,* pronounced "Myordomo."

onel Price had given them quite a fright. To our inquiries, their answers were invariably ended with *"señor, si señor"* —"sir, yes sir."

With a portion of their unbolted flour for *atole* and our beef, we made an excellent dinner. After a shuck and some horridly pronounced Spanish with the *rancheros*, we remounted for a grand cattle hunt. By night the small drove was augmented to hundreds.

Shortly following the sunrise next morning, we, with many a "heh-hep-ya" urged the scattered drove in a walk down the Poinel, where it debouched into the Cimarone. A band of deer, roused from their lair in the long grass at the junction, gave opportunity for a flying, though unsuccessful, shot. A mile below the mouth, we camped in a sandy, weed-grown bottom, near the wagons, which had been left in the flight by Frank De Lisle. They were much injured by the rapacious guerillas in obtaining the iron rods.

"Friendly relations" and a perfect understanding having been established between the *Rancher-hosses* (as one of the men facetiously called them) and us, Bransford sent our two men back to the Vermaho for the main party and all the cattle; he and I stayed with the Mexicans, to pass the three most miserable days yet recorded. Our meat gave out during the first twenty-four hours, leaving us dependent on *atole* for sustenance. The camp was in a sandy spot; fitful gusts of wind spent their petty fury against our shrinking bodies, filling our eyes, noses, and hair with the gritty particles, and a light fall of snow made the ground and air uncomfortable and chill.

My worthy fellow sufferer had a wiry, whitish-red beard. As we sat by the few sticks, once on fire, but now smoking and blown out by the strong wind, hungry and disgusted with the flour mush, eyes red and weeping with the smoke and sand, he would despondingly raise his rueful face from his knees, on which it rested twice as long as usual. Once, after a protracted, dreary silence, he lifted his drooping head, tantalized by the elements, and, in a tone of vexation, exclaimed—

"Oh, *darn* the country anyhow! *Don't* you wish you were in the Planters' House?" and then we talked of the table, the pleasant streets, and the ladies; on contrasting those momentary hallucinations with our wretched condition, we were indeed unhappy.

One of the Mexicans—a dreamy-looking fellow of twenty-two or three years of age—sang in a low, dulcet tone, in his own harmonious, flexible language, melodies of a plaintive, yet pleasing character, indicating by the expression of his countenance the sentiment of the song. Sitting by the dim blaze of our campfire, enveloped in the *sarape*, and uttering the strange words, his costume and complexion, together with our situation in the wild mountain, impressed me with a vagrant fancy that he was a Spanish exile, bewailing the decay of his country's glory and his own bereavement of friends and home.

Sometimes, when the weather was mild and the trees and grass enlivened by joyous sunlight, we could see up in the mountains snowstorms raging furiously; and often, while the snow was beating mercilessly on our unprotected selves, the bright sun gilded the snow-clad peaks, as if in mockery of we poor mortals on the Cimarone.

CHAPTER XII

EL RANCHO

T HE MEN from the Vermaho joined us on the fourth day, and Louy Simonds, the indefatigable, to our supreme delight supplied us with antelope meat. The baggage party arrived from the Purgatoire (the 9th), and all changed their habiliments for something cleaner, with the exception of myself and two others, who left Bent's Fort with no clothing but that on us—not even a spare shirt. Though my garments were, in all likelihood, soiled after such a length of time, *il est tout le même chose* here. In this country of hardships, dress is of small importance; and although the mind is not concentrated on the lore of the past and present generations, it is not the less employed; as the voyageur has to know locations, ascertain, by almost imperceptible "signs," the presence of friend and foe, exercise skill in approaching game, and, when so unfortunate as to lose his animals, to resort to some expedient suitable to his emergency. Here, where the mind is stretched to its utmost tension by reason of the continually impending dangers of starvation, thirst, or the wary Camanche, Arapaho, Digger, or Apache, his perceptive faculties are quickened, his judgment brought into constant use, and his courage daily tested.

On the 4th of March, all were busied in making a large corral in which to drive the stock, so as to count and send a report to Colonel Price, commanding the army at Santa Fé. Before the insurrection, one thousand head of beeves for the government forces, several hundred yoke of oxen, and four hundred and more horses and mules, bearing the United States brand, which, with a considerable number of each kind belonging to Bent, St. Vrain & Co., were here herded by their employees, with the aid of a few soldiers. When the Mexicans rose in arms and killed the Governor, a party of guerrillas was sent to this ranch, over the mountain from the valley of Taos, the greater portion of the animals driven away, and the remaining scattered in all directions. The wagons were abandoned; the soldiers and employees fled toward the Arkansas, and everything within the influence was involved in seemingly inextricable confusion. The Mexicans, however, were defeated; our hardy little spy party reached the Poinel and Cimarone, charged among the hills and valleys for cattle and horses, and soon order reigned on the east side of the Taos Mountain.

We drove the congregated herds in the corral, and Bransford and myself, on blank pages of my journal book and with bullets hammered out and sharpened for pencils (for I had lost the pencil procured at the fort), noted the different brands, and the number, as the cattle were permitted slowly to walk out. We now stopped our depredations on Uncle Sam's flocks, with the prospect of lean deer and antelope, which meats, though palatable with the usual accompaniments of a well-conducted *cuisine*, were not so good when cooked by an open fire in a sandy country, with nothing but its own scanty gravy and no salt.

We had true March weather: spitting, fuming, flirting, blowing, snowing, raining continually. We were so encompassed by mountains that the wind came from no particular quarter any length of time. Several of the energetic made a half-face tent of a wagon sheet. To protect us from the wind, we shifted it three times during the day—no small affair—and, after dark, changed again. On arranging our robes comfortably within, a snowstorm in ungovernable rage burst directly in the mouth. This was too much for the men to bear patiently, and, with curses ranging from the lowest to the highest in the scale of force and acrimony, with the commingled, never ending, ever present "*sacré*," we hung blankets in front, which, in some measure, warded the unwelcome tempest from our beds. It was really amusing to listen to the Frenchmen swearing in their vernacular. For a while, *diables, virgins, sacrés*, etc., would roll out with the facility of voluble tongues, until, becoming quite excited, the more expressive and inelegant American oath would follow with all imaginable vehemence and accompanying gesticulation.

A short distance from us was the shanty of the Canadians (for ours could not contain the whole party), pitched rightly, and its inmates snugly ensconced within, some reclining, a few cross-legged with the pipe, others singing and talking away, full of life, merriment, and fat beef! What happy temperaments these fellows possess— rather too volatile and easily depressed, but like confined watch-springs, they regain the former elasticity of spirits with the least freedom. My friend, Petout (the one who procured the water for me the thirsty night, on the route out), was here among the rest, as kind and polite as ever, which, I trust, was, in some measure, reciprocated.

From Pablo, one of the Mexicans, whom we retained (the others were sent home), I purchased *por un rial*—for twelve and a half cents—the skin of a wildcat, which he, the day before, saw an eagle pounce upon. By dint of running and shouts, he made him drop it.

In an excursion one day for ducks on the Cimarone, a few miles below camp, while lying in expectation for a flock to come floating with the current, my attention was drawn to the musical sound of gently falling water, which proved to be the stream running over a beaver dam. After a shot at the handsomely plumaged mallards, I examined this specimen of animal ingenuity and skill, which extended from one bank to the other. The sticks composing it, from one to two inches in diameter, were laid parallel to the stream, and the interstices filled with mud and leaves. With teeth for saw and ax, and tails for hod and trowel, these enterprising creatures accomplish much for their own safety and convenience.

We were one evening lounging in camp when an eagle, soaring with graceful gyratory motions, which "grew small by degrees and beautifully less," settled with a proud flap of his wings on the topmost branch of a dead cottonwood, and in self-conscious majesty viewed the setting sun, whose rays clad the trees and hills around with golden hues. *Ad interim*, I was cautiously approaching under cover of large trees and bushes, and when ready, with steady aim, I pulled trigger. "What a vandal am I," rose in my mind, as the report rang out sharply; but the ball, speeding its aerial flight without harm, the magnificent "baldhead" unfolded his wings slowly, as if to retire, at least, with dignity, darted upward, and with a wild scream disappeared.

Charles McCarty and brother, "Ike," Santa Fé traders, arrived in advance of their main train, with an assorted load of commodities, such as alcohol, tobacco, etc., in hopes of "striking" advantageous trades with our comfort-bereft party; and, a few mornings following, camp was enlivened by the sight of Hatcher's comical phiz. He had been absent during the winter with George Bent and com-

pany in the interior of Mexico, on a mule-trading expedition with the Utah and Pomo tribes, who levy heavy con-
tributions on the Mexican *caballadas*. These trade to the
whites. Hatcher had an inexhaustible fund of anecdote
and humor, which kept his camp circle in a continual roar,
and which rendered him always a valuable acquisition to
any party. He was about the cleverest fellow I met; always
cheerful, ready to hunt and do his duty; a good temper,
with an occasional dash of impatience, quickly relieved,
however, by a well-delivered, hearty, though harsh exclamation, and an unerring shot. With a short "dudeen"
in his mouth, he would sit cross-legged by the warm coals,
scintillations of wit flowing from his lips, his mirth-provok-
ing countenance contorted in mockery of the poor butt of
his jests, his keen, gray eye half-closed with inward enjoyment. He was the beau ideal of a Rocky Mountain man.

The company's mules were not in good flesh; so I lent
Hatcher mine to make the trip to Bent's Fort, 180 miles
distant. I commissioned him to get me three shirts, for my
single one had been on my back nearly long enough. I have
read that the Turkish ladies never apply water to their
faces, for it tarnishes, in their estimation, the brilliancy of
the complexion: somehow, it so happened that myself and
several others had not washed our faces, combed our
Medusa-looking hair, or changed hickory shirts since leaving Bent's Fort—forty-one or two days. Whether *our* complexions were improved or not by the banishment of water
is not to be said; the beef grease and sand certainly excluded the browning effects of the wind. We concluded
to take "von grand swim" in the creek; the beneficial effect
of the hydropathic treatment was quite visible. Pulling off
our shirts and dipping them in the running stream, the
objections were, in some degree, removed; with a double

154

twist, they were wrung, and hung on bushes to dry, while we poor *sans culottes* kept in the warm sun.

Louy Simonds returned after an absence of several days with the choice parts of a wild Mexican steer. It is the opinion of those who have eaten beef fattened on the bunch (festuca) and grama grasses that the meat is nearly as good as buffalo. In my own experience, both surpass the beef of the States; yet between the two (mountain beef and buffalo), the latter has the preference.

Our camp became old and dirty, and we moved further up the stream; where, in a grove of blighted cottonwoods, we once more settled down. McCarty's camp was a few steps distant. Greenwood, who has been mentioned before, stayed with him.

Two days after the removal, the *caballada* was driven up, six mules roped, and the same number of men mounted on them, went to the "Springs," a few miles distant, to tend a large drove of cattle. Herding is not arduous duty; the keepers merely have to ride two or three times a day to collect the stragglers; except that in storms, which are of frequent occurrence, there is much trouble and vexation of spirit. Nevertheless, one is naturally impressed with a feeling of loneliness, greatly increased by the knowledge of the proximity of marauding bands of refugee Mexicans.

The Canadians reported several cows, with their calves, among the beeves. The thoughts of "milk" roused our drowsy camp to alacrity, and after considerable spirited chasing on the part of our Mexican, Pablo, seven calves were lassoed. We hastily constructed a pen to hold them, and the dams then gave little trouble. All the pans, kettles, and tin cups were put in requisition. The cows were milked from behind, instead of at the side, with heads drawn up to a wagon wheel; with hindlegs tied and fearfully rolling eyes, they looked quite differently from the patient, chewing "Suke" of the American farmer.

How we feasted! A pot of rich milk was put on the fire, and when it boiled, the ground coffee was poured in, staying for a moment on top, to contrast the more strongly with the foamy fluid, until it sank; while we stood around, watching with eager eyes the grains as they were thrown to the surface by the ebullition. It was splendid!

Grizzly bear are plenty in this vicinity. Two years before this time, Hatcher and Boggs built cabins near this, with the intention of farming. To protect their corn from these bold depredators, they erected scaffolds in the fields, from which secure position they could fight off the marauders from the crops. A combination of unfavorable circumstances induced them to abandon their agricultural project, and the bears now roam unmolested through the deserted ranch.

One day a party of horsemen were seen coming toward camp at full speed, who, on a near approach, were found to be a band of thirty well-formed, good-looking Utahs. General Kearney effected a treaty with the nation; but they are, in common with all savage tribes within my knowledge, friends when weakest, enemies when strongest. Such is their frequent intercourse with the New Mexicans, they being at war with them, that many of the Utahs speak the Spanish-Mexican language.

McCarty's wagon still remained with us; and as the men's drafts on Bent, St. Vrain & Co. were good, cards and liquor passed freely; which latter is alcohol, but, mixed with water, constituted a passable beverage, its principal use being, in mountain parlance, to "make drunk come."

Fitzgerald and Bill Gramon came from Taos with a report of the excitement occasioned by the numerous arrests. Fitz was a private of Captain Burgwin's company of dragoons at the battle of Pueblo de Taos. When the breach was made in the church, whither the enemy had retreated as a last resort, the dragoons attacked with bombs, holding the shells in their hands until the fuses were nearly burned, and then tossing them in to do their work of devastation. The first two Americans who entered the breach fell dead, the third was unhurt, the fourth killed, and Fitz was the fifth. He was a man of good feeling, but his brother having been murdered by Salazar while a prisoner in the Texan expedition against Santa Fé, he swore vengeance, and entered the service with the hope of accomplishing it. In the fight at the Pueblo, three Mexicans fell by his hand; and, the day following, he walked up to the *alcalde* and deliberately shot him down. For this cold-blooded act, he was confined to await a trial for murder.

One raw night, complaining of cold to his guard, wood was brought, which he piled up in the middle of the room. Then breaking through the roof, he noiselessly crept to the eaves. Below, a sentinel, wrapped in a heavy cloak, paced to and fro to prevent his escape; but, when the guard's back was turned, he swung himself from the wall, and, with as much ease as possible, walked to a mess fire, where his friends in waiting supplied him with a pistol and clothing. When day broke, the town of Fernández lay far beneath him in the valley, and two days after, he was safe in our ranch.

Our "hos guard" came hastily into camp one morning, saying that thirty of the *cavyard* were stolen. Mounting the few mules grazing around, we started in hot pursuit; but the trail led up a steep part of the mountain, rendering an attempt at rescue both unsafe and uncertain, so giving the Apaches or Mexicans the credit of a successful *coup* hunt and binding on our hearts the proverb of "prudence the better part of valor," we returned.

As the spring advanced, the sun's rays grew more genial, and green grass peeped from under the heavy tussocks of the past year's vegetation. The air, bracing and fresh, was tempered by the increasing warmth; no dew fell to dampen or make disagreeable the walking; and, in the heat of the day, we, perfectly inactive, laid about camp fanned by the gentle zephyrs.

Hatcher, with Captain Jackson, Company D, Price's regiment, his first lieutenant, and one private, arrived from Bent's Fort on the 2d of April. On the 3d they, with the addition of Louy Simonds and myself, jogged along at a quiet mule pace for the pass, *en route* to Taos. Two hours' ride brought us to the foot of the mountain, where, dismounting to rest, we permitted the mules to wander and nip the dried yellow blades of grass in the many crevices of the rock. The country adjacent was exceedingly rough and forbidding. Isolated buttes and abrupt cliffs caused us often to turn aside; the ground was thickly strewed with fragments of coarse sandstone, and huge masses of scoriaceous rock, thrown up as by internal convulsion, reared their flinty fronts. So remote is this region, and so incapable of production is the soil but in the narrow valleys, that many years must elapse ere it can become attractive to the farmer.

The path up which we rode wound around rocks and under the shadows of beetling cliffs, now facing and now with backs to the sun, its tortuous sinuosities and uneven steep surface causing the sure-footed mules to pant and frequently rest. At one side, stuck in the heavy stones, were several rude wooden crosses planted by the Mexicans during the descent on the ranch. When fear overcame their audacity, a prayer *en passant* was offered to the Virgin

Mary, which commendable act of piety finished, they proceeded, much relieved, on their way, leaving the honored emblem of Christianity for some other consistent worshiper.

In the States, the smooth bark and slender branches of the aspen, with its glossy leaves, looked beautiful; but here the scene was one of barrenness, and the white-leaved aspen, springing from the ground bereft of verdure, and the cold gray rocks, with the mournful pine interlaced, induced other and sadder sensations. I even wondered how so spectral a foliage could ever have been admired.

At the side of the trail, at intervals of fifty and a hundred yards, were piles of stone, which, from their uniformity, excited our attention. Hatcher told us, that years since, the Camanches, at that time warring with the Pueblos de Taos, sent a party over this mountain on a foray. To enable them to find their way back in case the snow should cover the trail, these piles were made. Admirable forethought! But their tawney hides not being arrow-proof, the scalps of the greater portion were swung aloft in the furious dance, to the booming sound of the Pueblo drum.

We rode over snowbanks five feet in depth—occasionally breaking through. The air grew chilly as the sun declined; our exertions in walking up the steeps warmed us but little. On the summit, a level, bare spot and a brackish body of water—El Laguna—presented itself—its margin grown with slime-covered sedge. Riding to the edge of a precipice, we saw the valley we that morning left. Thousands of feet below, tall pines appeared mere bushes, and the Río Rayada, a silver thread. Pursued with the eye, it was lost among the numerous hills, whence, after many windings, it coursed over the plain, a considerable stream, the channel marked out by trees on either bank.

Sheltered by an elevation of ground and a pine thicket in the rear, we encamped by a snowbank, from which was scooped the water for our coffee. The horses had been, before sunset, watered, while the melted snow ran in the path; they were left for the night in a sheltered grassy spot, to luxuriate on festuca.

On leaving the *rancho*, Hatcher, Louy, and myself tied beef to the saddle strings; the captain and companions had their rations. The blending of their salt with our fresh meat was agreeable to both. From some pines, we clipped, with knives, the soft ends of the boughs, and before the fire, in a depression of the ground, spread them down with blankets and robes on top, making a couch, whose ease repaid our trouble.

An old Mexican trudged up to camp after dark, who, when we hailed him to know his business so far from any place, replied that he was going to Señor San Bran's *rancho*. He ate some proffered meat and coffee, and, after rolling up and smoking a shuck cigarillo, coiled himself before the fire in his one blanket, to sleep. A common person would have frozen with so slim an amount of covering, but *Valgáme Dios!* these *rancheros* can undergo that which would kill a dozen respectable white men.

CHAPTER XIII

EL VALLE DE TAOS

Though the wind was piercingly cold, Hatcher was up early, making a fire, "for," said he, "this hos is no b'ar to stick his nose under cover all the robe season,[1] an' lay round camp, like a darned Ned; but," he added in an undertone, as he looked to see if the government men were awake, "thar's two or three in this crowd—wagh!—howsomever, the *green is* 'rubbed out' a little. This child hates an American what hasn't seen Injuns skulped, or doesn't know a Yute from a Khian mok'sin. Sometimes he thinks of makin' tracks for white settlement, but when he gits to Bent's big lodge, on the Arkansa, and sees the bugheways, an' the fellers from the States, how they roll thar eyes at an Injun yell, worse nor if a village of Camanches was on 'em, an' pick up a beaver trap, to ask what it is—just shows whar the niggurs had thar brungin' up—this child says—'a little bacca, if its a plew[2] a plug, an' Dupont an' G'lena,[3] a Green River[4] or so,' and he leaves for the Bayou Salade. Darn the white diggins, while thar's buffler in the mountains. Whoopee!" shouted he to us, "are you for Touse?

---

[1] *Robe season* means cold weather—winter—as the robes are fit for dressing only at that time.

[2] *Plew*—a pelt, a beaver skin—a plug is one pound of tobacco.

[3] DuPont powder and Galena lead.

[4] Green River knife—the name of the manufactory.

This hos is thar in one sun, wagh! Louy, the cavyard's out picking grass—half froze to travel."

We dispatched a cup of coffee, and, driving our shivering mules to camp, saddled and packed them—the Captain and companions fixing their American saddles with a frail buckle and girth; while Hatcher and Louy first laid on their mules the half of a robe, and on that a bare Mexican tree, without pad, cover, or other appendage, save a few long buckskin thongs tied to the back part of the cantle, and a pair of huge wooden stirrups dangling directly *under*—not forward—the seat. With an *adios* to the Mexican, who, returning the salute, started for the *rancho*, we mounted.

The transition from the valley was sudden for us, in substantiation of which fact our blue limbs gave irrefutable testimony. Gaining the summit of the hill, at whose base we had been sheltered from the fiercer blasts during the night, the animals would scarcely be persuaded, through severe digs of long-rowelled spurs, to face the wind. Words intended for each other were borne unheard along the breeze, which rushed down our throats, nearly stifling us. To walk was impossible. To ride was exceedingly unpleasant, but we were forced to retain the saddles.

While riding up a narrow path, toward the warmer part of the day, a small, reddish-gray squirrel, jumping nimbly from limb to limb in the bright sun it had left its winter quarters to enjoy, attracted our attention.

"Thar's a gone beaver," shouted Louy, as he discharged his rifle, though without effect, at the diminutive animal disappearing among the swaying pine branches, "it's many a time this paw's hild a forked stick, with an old nor'-west fusil—one of dads, that's 'under'—when his arm wasn't no bigger an' a beaver tail, to shoot at sich varmin as them [the squirrel]. An' when the old shootin' iron 'ud flash in the pan, I'ud say—Doggone the old thing; you ain't wuth a cuss (I was afraid to swear then), but then, I would git as chargin' *fâché* nor an old buffler an' out 'ud rip dam! Then this old hos would feel kinder like a sick beaver in a trap, or a 'cow' with a G'lena pill in her lights—the dark wasn't the place for me then, I tellee; but this coon has 'raised har' so often sence, he keers fur nothing now. Mind the time we 'took' Pawnee 'topknots' away to the Platte, Hatch?"

"Wagh! ef we didn't," chimed in the interrogated, "an' give an owgh-owgh, longside of thar darned screechin', I'm a niggur. This child doesn't let an Injun count a 'coup'[5] on his cavyard always. They come mighty nigh 'rubbing' me 'out', 'tother side of Spanish Peaks—woke up in the mornin' jist afore day, the devils yellin' like mad. I grabs my knife, 'keels' one, an' made for timber, with four of thar cussed arrows in my 'meatbag.' The Paches [Apaches] took my beaver—five pack of the prettiest in the mountain —an' two mules, but my traps was hid in the creek. Sez I, hyar's a gone coon ef they keep my gun, so I follers thar trail, an' at night, crawls into camp, an' socks my big knife up to the Green River,[6] first dig. I takes t'other Injun by the har, an' 'makes meat' of him *too. Maybe* thar wasn't coups counted, an' a big dance on hand, ef I was alone. I got old bullthrower, made 'medicine' over him, an' no darned niggur kin draw bead with him since."

Crossing a valley a mile in width, with a stream calmly meandering through, we commenced the final ascent, here more steep and rugged than hitherto. Stopping at the summit for the animals to regain breath, a rapid descent for some miles lay before us. A spot of grass presented itself by

[5] Make a successful stroke.
[6] Factory name, near the hilt.

a clump of willows, and on Hatcher's exclamation of, "Hyar's for camp," we turned our mules to wet their mouths in the cool running water, and, with long, trailing lariats, wander in quest of grass. With a few dead willow twigs, fire was kindled, and while the coffee boiled, we reclined on outspread saddle blankets in the warm sun, thoughtfully puffing "Old Virginia" from time-worn clay pipes. Partaking of the nectar-like Java—every drop worth its weight in "beaver"—we smoked, until Louy Simonds proposed that "if we wanted to dance with the Mexican *squaws* that night, we'd better be making 'tracks' fur thar lodges."

"Wagh!" responded Hatcher, looking up from the wreaths of smoke he had been watching curling and melting around his lips, "this hos has been making medicine— good medicine—an' he's fur Touse tonight—'*comme la va, señorita!*'" added he, in a gentle tone, rising to his feet, and bowing to an imaginary Mexican lady—"'*Comme la va, no cary por fandango*'"—"How do you do, Miss—Wish to dance?" and, with a genuine war cry, he started for his mule.

With comparatively easy travel and a more genial atmosphere, we were again journeying down the Cañon de Taos; which, like the route passed over, has never been traversed by wagons—a mere mule path—difficult and dangerous. We saw where Colonel Price had entered the further end of the pass on the march to fight the insurgents —the marks of the cannon and baggage wheels were still visible.

My sentiments were akin to the romantic that afternoon, with my merry friends, who, with quick rifles, fired at trees for targets, or caused their voices to reverberate from the high walls of rock.

El Valle de Taos

The sighing of the wind—zephyr-like, bland, and re-freshing—mournful yet pleasing—the pine-clad hills above, around, and below—the mystery in which the customs of the present and the past inhabitants of this region have been kept through paucity of knowledge or descriptive powers of visitors—the thoughts engendered by the perusal of Prescott's *Conquest*, and Stephens's Central American researches, and the fact of traversing the same road along which the munitions of grim-visaged war were, but a few days before, transported, rendered strange my fancy, and gave my wandering imagination many a theme for instant, yet lengthy, discussion.

Ere long, the sun's rays were excluded by reason of our continual descent; turning a sharp corner of the tortuous path, we surprised two goatherds tending a large flock of the sure-footed creatures, browsing among the gray lichen-covered rocks or perched on the crests of detached fragments, gently giving utterance to the peculiar bleat, as, with heads thrust forward, they snuffed our approach. With a passing *"Buenas le dai"*—"Good day"—to the flock keepers, who, abashed and timorous, quietly and reluc-tantly returned the salute from under the shade of their weighty, broad-brimmed, leather *sombréros*, we kept on, oft riding in the pebbly bed of the rivulet, which by con-stant accessions grew to a noisy brook. The mules, though not thirsty, stopped often to dip their noses in the laughing stream, as if to say—"*We* know good water."

Some hundreds of feet above, in the niche of a cliff, Hatcher pointed out the site of a large reservoir; we were too much wearied to attempt a closer inspection. The pre-vailing impression is that it was built by a people contem-porary with the Aztecs.

The mountain at the pass termination was quite bared

of trees by the Mexicans; who, with axes and patient, diminutive *burros*—jackasses—clamber the steeps for fagots of the dry, resinous pine. A train of these animals, loaded, look like walking brush heaps, so completely is the burro hid by the bulky wood from view.

On emerging from the canyon, the view expanded to a valley nearly circular to the casual glance, hemmed in by a snowy range, while *El Río Grande del Norte*, a few miles distant, rolled between sand banks to the southwest. The level plain below wore a cultivated, civilized aspect. Reposing quietly at our very feet was the hamlet, *El Ranch*, to the west the village *Ranchita*, and toward the northwest, *San Fernández de Taos*, its walls, as well as those of the minor towns, mica lime-washed to a dazzling whiteness. To the northeast, at the base of a contiguous mountain, was the dismal *Pueblo de Taos*, but a few weeks since the scene of fiercest strife.

The brook down whose channel we had kept the preceding few hours was, at its egress, directed into a large *acequia*, or ditch, and from that, in numberless smaller ones, through the valley, to serve in lieu of the grateful showers in which the American farmer puts so much dependence.

The first house we passed was a distillery, where the "mountain dew" of New Mexico—*aguardiente de Taos*—is made; and such is the demand, it is imbibed before attaining a very drinkable age, by both foreigners and residents, with great avidity.

A fiercely moustached native, with broad-brimmed, glazed *sombréro* and gay-colored *sarape* disposed in graceful folds on his lithe figure, and a woman in gray *reboza* enveloping her head and shoulders, leaving unhid and peering through, her piercing black eyes, replied gayly to

one *"buenas le dai, Señorita"*—"good day, Miss"—Hatcher
and she entered upon a colloquy, while the tired mules
trailed slowly on, with drooping heads and vacillating ears,
seemingly too weighty for the thin necks to which they
were attached.

The sun fast sank behind the western peaks, and groups
of swarthy-skinned laborers lined the road on their way
home, greeting us respectfully as we passed, with the accustomed salutation. To the left, a number of men, with implements of labor, were still at work on an *acequia*, under
the supervision of the *alcalde*. Reaching the suburbs of
Fernández, I recognized a *ranchero*, driving before him a
mule laden with shucks.

He exclaimed, as he doffed his hat—*"Comme la va
Señors, esta buen—ah, Bonita!"* "How are you, Sirs—ah,
Bonita"—(to my mule). *"Señora una fandango grandote,
esta noche,"* his eye brightening as he spoke, *"muy Señoritas bonita."* "There's a big *fandango* tonight; a great
many pretty ladies there, too—wish to go?"

"Certainly we do," replied Louy, " 'specially if thar's
liquor on hand."

Passing some low, flat-roofed mud structures, several
American soldiers on guard near, we met at every step
gracefully moving women and *sarape*-enveloped men, the
shuck cigarillo between the lips of many; and turning to
one side of the plaza, drew rein in front of a house, where
were numbers of Americans talking and smoking. Fisher
came forward, with his hand outstretched before reaching
us, with a hearty, "How are ye? I swar' you look tired; come
in and take a 'horn'—a little of the *arwerdenty*—come—
good for your stomach!"

Mr. St. Vrain, at this juncture, approaching, took me
kindly by the hand, coupled with an invitation to his own

house. Leading my mule by the bridle, we crossed the south side of the plaza and entered a courtyard enclosed by high walls. A Mexican took Bonita, and, pulling off the saddle, led him to a pile of shucks and corn.

I was ushered into an oblong, handsomely furnished room, with a fireplace in one corner and the walls hung with portraits of holy characters, crosses, etc., showing the prevailing religion; and to furnish additional evidence, a *padre* (priest) was taking his *congé* as we opened the door. An introduction to Señora St. Vrain—a dark-eyed, languidly handsome woman—followed my appearance. The Mexican mode of salutation is to meet, and one arm of the gentleman or lady is thrown around the other's shoulder; then stepping back one pace, they shake hands, accompanied with the usual "*Comme la va.*" But I did not understand this most cordial mode of greeting, and when the Señora sidled alongside, in expectation of the usual embrace, I thought how strangely she acted, and only extended my hand, saying in American, "How do you do?" Most assuredly, such a fashion with our ladies would meet with enthusiastic followers.

At supper, I sat at table and ate potatoes for the first time in several months. A *fandango*[7] was to be held that night, but declining an invitation to attend, a mattress was unrolled from the wall, where, in daytime, it served as a seat, and I turned in between sheets. Yes! sheets! For months I had enveloped myself with blankets in the open air, pulling off no clothing but the blue blanket topcoat, which, with my saddle, served as pillow—but now a change came over the spirit of my dream. A house, table, vegetables, and sheets—to say nothing of the charming smiles of woman and the Taos *aguardiente*.

[7] *Fandango*—dance, fight—any occupation giving excitement.

Shortly after lying down, the room filled with gay ladies, revelling in the excess of paint and flaunting dress, and partaking of the favorite *aguardiente* by way of support against the fatigues of the *fandango*. I looked at them through my partially closed eyes, to notice more closely without an imputation of rudely staring. The musical tone of their voices, uttering their sweet language, fell gently on my ear, and, as perception gradually failed, amid a delicious reverie, I sank to sleep.

CHAPTER XIV

EL CONSÉJO

At a late hour for a mountain man I dressed by a blazing fire, although Señora St. Vrain and sister—a handsome brunette of some sixteen years—were in the room; they probably being accustomed by the "free and easy" manners of the valley to this liberty, which they themselves took an hour before. After breakfast, the ladies rolled up several shuck cigarillos, which they presented with smiles and a persuasive "*Señor?*" I did not refuse.

The shuck is scraped to free it from roughness and cut in slips, one and a half inches broad by three in length; then moistened, to prevent splitting, by putting it in the mouth and drawing out with compressed lips. The tobacco of the country—bland and fragrant—is sprinkled on one edge and, with a slight-o'-hand motion of the fingers, rolled up. The ends are pinched to retain the contents. In the pocket is carried a roll of raw cotton the size of a common goose-quill, bound with calico, which, with the flint and steel in everyone's possession, is produced, and, with a dexterous blow, fire imparted, from which the cigarillo is lit. A tin tube, three inches long, is fitted to the cotton, and when the shuck lights, the burning roll is drawn in the tube; and, by placing a finger on the end to preclude the air, the fire is extinguished, leaving a cinder to which the steel spark imparts its fire. Some use a silver or even a gold tube, while the poor *pelados* have to content themselves with a tin one, or nothing.

Though smoking is repugnant to many ladies, it certainly does enhance the charms of the Mexican *señoritas*, who, with neatly rolled-up shucks between coral lips, perpetrate winning smiles, their magically brilliant eyes the meanwhile searching one's very soul. How dulcet-toned are their voices, which, siren-like, irresistibly draw the willing victim within the giddy vortex of dissipation! And these cigarillos they present with such a grace, and so expressive an eye, so musical a tongue, and so handsome a face, that it was impossible to refuse. To use a Scotch phrase, "It's na sae bad."

I must say that there is much romance to a superficial observer in having a Mexican wife; but, were we to come down to sober reality, the affair would show forth in a different light. From the depraved moral education of the New Mexicans, there can be no intellectual enjoyment. The only attractions are of the baser sort. From youth accustomed to a life of servitude and vitiated habits, we look in vain for true woman's attraction—modesty—that attribute which encircles as a halo the intelligent, virtuous, and educated woman. Surely 'twas pardonable pride in me to notice, by contrast, the superiority of those of my own country.

Court assembled at nine o'clock. On entering the room, Judges Beaubien and Houghton were occupying their official stations. After many dry preliminaries, six prisoners were brought in—ill-favored, half-scared, sullen fellows; and the jury of Mexicans and Americans—Chadwick, foreman—being empaneled, the trial commenced: F. P. Blair, Jr., prosecuting attorney, assisted by —— Wharton, a great blowhard. The counsel for the defense, whose name I have forgotten, was, as well as Wharton, a volunteer private, on furlough for the occasion. They had, no doubt, joined the ranks in hopes of political preferment on their return home, and the forests of Missouri may yet re-echo with Wharton's stentorian voice, proclaiming to his hero-worshiping constituents how he "fought, bled, and *died*" for his country's liberties—a recapitulation of all the bravado with which many of the military leaders of the discreditable Mexican war have been gulling the "sovereign people" since their return from their easily-won fields of glory.

Mr. St. Vrain was interpreter. When the witnesses (Mexican) touched their lips to the Bible, on taking the oath, it was with such a combination of reverential awe for the Book and fear of *los Americanos* that I could not repress a smile. The poor things were as much frightened as the prisoners at the bar.

It certainly did appear to be a great assumption on the part of the Americans to conquer a country and then arraign the revolting inhabitants for treason. American judges sat on the bench, New Mexicans and Americans filled the jury box, and an American soldiery guarded the halls. Verily, a strange mixture of violence and justice—a strange middle ground between the martial and common law.

After an absence of a few minutes, the jury returned with a verdict of "guilty in the first degree"—five for murder, one for treason. Treason, indeed! What did the poor devil know about his new allegiance? But so it was; and, as the jail was overstocked with others awaiting trial, it was deemed expedient to hasten the execution, and the culprits were sentenced to be hung on the following Friday—hangman's day. When the concluding words "*muerto,*

muerto, muerto"—"dead, dead, dead"—were pronounced by Judge Beaubien in his solemn and impressive manner, the painful stillness that reigned in the courtroom and the subdued grief manifested by a few bystanders were noticed not without an inward sympathy. The poor wretches sat with immovable features; but I fancied that under the assumed looks of apathetic indifference could be read the deepest anguish. When remanded to jail till the day of execution, they drew their *sarapes* more closely around them and accompanied the armed guard. I left the room, sick at heart. Justice! Out upon the word, when its distorted meaning is the warrant for murdering those who defend to the last their country and their homes.

CHAPTER XV

SAN FERNÁNDEZ

Every nation has some peculiarity of dress; and, although the New Mexicans and the States people are geographically so near each other, the marked difference in dress renders a notice of it but proper.

The women (giving them the preference) do not wear bonnets, using instead the *reboza* or mantilla—a scarf of cotton and silk, five to six feet in length, by two or more in width—which serves as covering for the head and body. So dexterous are they in its management that in cooking or walking it is retained, forming a graceful and pleasing contrast to the bonneted and hooded civilized lady. A skirt is worn a trifle shorter than the present States fashion, so that it can hardly be called a dress; the figure, above the waist, is invested with a chemise, with short arms; but, so sparing were they of material, or so bound to follow unrelenting fashion, or through a desire to show their fair shoulders, etc., the chemises were too low-necked. The Cheyenne maidens, on the contrary, wore their buckskin sacques fitting closely around the throat; but the graceful *señoritas de Taos* were pleased to make a more prodigal display, which, to my unaccustomed eyes and taste, was uncomely, and, in fact, satiating.

The men, generally speaking, wear pantaloons open on

the outside seam of the leg and lined with buttons, to fasten at pleasure; while underneath, a pair of white drawers is disclosed to view—a fancy colored shirt and vest, and an oblong blanket (of Mexican or Navajo Indian manufacture, the wool of which being hard-twisted turns the rain effectually), with a hole in the center for the head. A tall, peaked, oilcloth-covered hat of straw or brown wool and yellow *zapotes*—shoes—complete the costume. In one vest pocket are carried shucks, cut to the requisite length; in the other is ready crumbled *ponche*—tobacco. The flint and steel have their place in the pantaloons pocket.

In front of many dwellings is a mud oven, in shape like a cupping glass, in which is baked the whitest bread it has ever been my fortune to taste. No bolting cloths are here used; and those wanting white bread sift for themselves. The hard bread, *biscoche*, is light, porous, and sweet—a perfect luxury with a cup of coffee by a mountain-pine fire. Probably long-continued abstinence from all kinds of farinaceous food influenced my judgment—but, without doubt, it would meet with favor at the Planter's House. On Mr. St. Vrain's table was the national dish—*chile colorado* —a compound of red-pepper pods and other spicy ingredients; a hot mess at first; but, with the aid of *tortillas* (a thin, soft cake of flour and water, baked on a griddle), of which we consumed a great number—a new taste was soon acquired.

Many houses have windows or mere holes in the wall; and, in lieu of glass, large plates of mica are used, which serve the purpose well. The court in front of each house brings everything within a small compass, besides excluding thieves, except in case of a regularly burglarious attempt. From the outside nothing but bare, high walls are visible, thus allowing no scope for architectural display and giving an antiquated, foreign air to the town in the eyes of all from the States.

It was amusing to see the diminutive, long-eared *burros* —jackasses—slowly drawing themselves—one tired foot after the other—up and down the streets, munching bones and other refuse of the kitchen. With noses trailing the ground, long lob ears falling back and forth with every motion of the animal, as if without life, rough, gray hair, and misshapen legs, they formed a most ludicrous picture. What is done with them in summer, where, as here, there are no fences, I did not ascertain; perhaps *los burros* are endowed with sagacity enough, coupled with the fear of the cudgel, to refrain from touching the forbidden grain.

With Hatcher, I visited the house in which Governor Bent was murdered, who, with the district attorney, J. W. Liel, came from Santa Fé to issue a proclamation. While here in Fernández with his family, he was, one morning early, roused from sleep by the populace; who, with the aid of the Pueblos de Taos, were collected in front of his dwelling, striving to gain admittance. While they were effecting an entrance, he, with an ax, cut through an adobe wall into another house. The wife of the occupant, a clever though thriftless Canadian, heard him; and, with all her strength, rendered him assistance, though she was a Mexican. He retreated to a room, but seeing no way of escaping from the infuriated assailants, who fired upon him through a window, he spoke to his weeping wife and trembling children, clinging to him with all the tenacity of love and despair; and taking paper from his pocket, endeavored to write, but fast losing strength, he commended them to God and his brothers, and fell pierced by a Pueblo's ball. Rushing in and tearing off the gray-haired scalp, the Indians bore it away in triumph.

The district attorney, Liel, was scalped alive and dragged through the streets, his relentless persecutors pricking him with lances. After hours of acute suffering, he was thrown to one side in the inclement weather. He entreated, implored them earnestly to kill him—to end his misery. A compassionate Mexican at last closed the tragic scene by shooting him. Stephen Lee, brother to the General, was killed on his own housetop.

Narcisse Beaubien, son of the presiding judge of this district—the same young man in our company last fall—with his Indian slave, hid in an outhouse at the commencement of the massacre, under a straw-covered trough. The insurgents, on the search, thinking they had escaped, were leaving, but a woman—servant to the family—going to the housetop, called them, with the words—"Kill the young ones, and they will never be men to trouble us." They swarmed back and cruelly putting to death and scalping him and his slave, thus added two more to the unfortunate victims of unbounded passion and long-cherished revenge.

Narcisse had been to Cape Girardeau college, below St. Louis, for five years; and, when he left, was a proficient in the French, Spanish, and English languages, as well as versed in the usual college studies. During the route he often dwelt, with delight, on his return home, and of the different duties and pleasures to be performed and enjoyed. When we parted at Bent's Fort—he for the Valley of Taos, I for the village—his last words were warm and pressing invitations to pay him a lengthy visit; but two short months had scarcely passed ere he was numbered among the slain. His being a native—his mother a Mexican—and the advantages he possessed over his fellow citizens by a liberal education would have given scope for his undoubted talents, to be exerted in his own land and for its material benefit.

The church in this place (Fernández) was an adobe structure, with towers and bells, and not attractive in architecture or ornament. The valley, in every direction, was cultivated, and in the total absence of fences, presented the unusual sight of one large field stretching away for miles, intersected by numberless ditches, similar to the Louisiana plantations; only that, in the latter state, the ditches are to drain, here to water, the land.

The melting snow from the mountain flows to the valley, where it is turned into large *acequias*; from these into branches, and again through each man's possession. When a plat needs watering, the ditch below it is stopped with a few shovels full of earth, water suffered to flow in, and, there being no egress, it inundates the plat, thereby giving the vegetation a more effectual and well-timed flooding than the uncertain showers. This means a preferable mode; for the ditch once dug, with an occasional cleaning, serves forever. When it does need scraping out, the *alcalde*, or mayor, issues an order, and the work is done by the people conjointly, so the labor is but slight to any one man.

The New Mexican plows, for the most part, are of the primitive kind—the same as those used by the Egyptians thousands of years ago—being but the fork of a small tree, with only one handle. The point entering the ground is sometimes shod with iron. Last fall, Bent, St. Vrain & Co. brought out several American plows. It is to be hoped the *natives* will learn something from these models.

The soil, by long-continued cultivation and absence of stumps, trees, and other impediments to easy culture, is highly arable; consequently, there is no great need of better implements of tillage. The return for the grain sown is good. Wheat and corn form the principal products. The former is used extensively in the manufacture of "Taos whiskey," with which everyone becomes well acquainted, more particularly if he forms one of a mountaineer party. Were we to drink the wheat liquor as an American distillation, it would be called poor stuff; as Mexican *agua ardiente*, it was excellent.

I understood that Le Févre had a saddle for sale; and one day, entering his courtyard, I perceived him at the further end, assisted by a nearly-grown son, making one of the old-fashioned plows. He invited me to the house, where we were welcomed by his daughter into a nicely furnished, comfortable room.

Señorita Le Févre was one of those beauties, fair to gaze upon—impressive in her simple, quiet manner of conducting herself. Though we could not converse, eloquence was in her silence, persuasion in her eye. A look at her frank, intelligent countenance made me wish for her a better home and more refined company than that of San Fernández. Her mother is a Mexican woman, of matronly, pleasing proportions; her father a Canadian Frenchman, clever enough.

The saddle came from Chihuahua originally—high cantle and pommel, with ponderous, fancifully-carved, wooden stirrups. It suited me well, and I paid a high price for it, though I thought it cheap. It was certainly worth nine dollars, and the sight of Le Févre's daughter made me consider the remaining nine as nothing. The stirrups of wood have the preference over those of iron here, in cold weather, beside presenting a broader surface to the moccasined foot.

At the house of George Bent (brother to the late governor, and partner of the firm of Bent, St. Vrain & Co.), I met Judge Houghton (of the Santa Fé district, and associate of Judge Beaubien), F. P. Blair, Jr., and Mr. Bent himself, who is married to a New Mexican lady. Mr. Blair was slight-formed, young, and agreeable in his manners, and, to judge from his labors in the courtroom, possessed of some legal talent and adroitness. His age was not much, if any, past twenty-two.

At the foot of a slope were several springs, and toward sunset I used to walk out that way, and, seated on a bank or adobe ruin, watch the women procuring water. Their peculiar style of dress displays the form to advantage; and with well-filled, antique-fashioned earthen jars—manufactured by Indians inhabiting the country between this and California—poised on the head, with arms folded, the *reboza* in graceful plaits on the shoulders, and erect, dignified carriage, they, indeed, formed a picturesque and pleasing sight. My thoughts were directed to the Bible descriptions of drawers of water, and of the fair daughters of Jerusalem coming to the wells—how they lingered about the fountain to exchange salutations.

Court was in daily session; five more Indians and four Mexicans were sentenced to be hung on the 30th April; but, exciting as were the court proceedings, very few of us spent much time in the room; we wanted to be moving about.

A remarkable circumstance was that whenever Chadwick was on the jury as foreman, the prisoners were returned "guilty in the first degree."

One little Frenchman, Baptiste —— by name, with not two ideas above eating and drinking, was duly empaneled as a juror, to try the first six subsequently sentenced.

On going into the consulting room, Baptiste went to Chad and asked—"Monsieur Chad*wick!* vot sall I say?" "Keep still man, until we talk awhile to the rest about it," rejoined Chad, "don't be in such a hurry."

"*Oui! oui! eh bien! c'est bon; tres bien! mais Monsieur,* vot sall ve do *avec sacré prisonniers—sacré enfants—*"

"Baptiste! man, keep still; why, hang them, of course; what did you come in here for?" angrily replied he, much annoyed, "Wait till I am done with these Mexicans [part of the jury], and I will tell you what you must do."

The last cases—the nine just mentioned—Chadwick and Baptiste were again in their relative positions. As soon as the jury-room door was closed, he sung out—"Hang 'em, hang 'em, *sacré enfans des garces,* dey dam grand rascale," now getting excited and pacing the room, "*parceque* dey kill Monsieur Charles [Governor Bent], dey take *son* top-knot, vot you call im—skulp; *dis enfant,* he go ondare too, *mais,* he make beevare—run, you Merican say—*pour le montaigne—*wagh! A-ah! *oui,* Monsieur Chadwick, you no tink so!—hang 'em, hang 'em—*sa-a-cré-é!*"

In the courtroom, on the occasion of the trial of the above nine prisoners, were Señora Bent, the late governor's wife, and Señora Boggs, giving in their evidence in regard to the massacre, of which they were eyewitnesses. Señora Bent was quite handsome; a few years since, she must have been a beautiful woman—good figure for her age; luxuriant raven hair, unexceptionable teeth, and brilliant, dark eyes, the effect of which was heightened by a clear, brunette complexion. The other lady, though not so agreeable in appearance, was much younger. The wife of the renowned mountaineer Kit Carson also was in attendance. Her style of beauty was of the haughty, heart-breaking kind—such as would lead a man with the glance of the eye, to risk his life for one smile. I could not but desire her acquaintance. The dress and manners of the three ladies bespoke a greater degree of refinement than usual.

The courtroom was a small, oblong apartment, dimly

lighted by two narrow windows; a thin railing kept the by-standers from contact with the functionaries. The prisoners faced the judges, and the three witnesses (Señoras Bent, Boggs, and Carson) were close to them on a bench by the wall. When Mrs. Bent gave in her testimony, the eyes of the culprits were fixed sternly upon her; on pointing out the Indian who killed the Governor, not a muscle of the chief's face twitched or betrayed agitation, though he was aware her evidence unmistakably sealed his death warrant—he sat with lips gently closed, eyes earnestly centered on her, without a show of malice or hatred—an almost sublime spectacle of Indian fortitude and of the severe mastery to which the emotions can be subjected. Truly, it was a noble example of Indian stoicism.

CHAPTER XVI

LOS PUEBLOS

Hatcher, Louy Simonds, and myself walked up to the Pueblo, by way of variety, as court was dull; and though without guns, we retained our scalp knives, more through force of habit than necessity. After a walk over the fields and crossing *acequias* fringed with bushes and sparkling with cool water, we came in sight. Two irregular, immense piles of adobes—towers and loopholes everywhere visible—and a broken, blackened ruin composed the celebrated Pueblo de Taos—the stronghold of bravery and the terror of the vale of Taos. A clear stream of water flowed between the two structures, over a green, white and gray pebbly bottom. Crossing on large flat stepping-stones, at irregular intervals, the crystal fluid breaking and foaming, murmuring softly over—here a cascade—there an eddy—in which the foam-bubbles glided round and round, we passed by a Pueblo woman washing, her kettles hanging over some pine sticks, the vaport blue smoke from which waved upward in the bright sun. Around were the accumulated ashes of years, embedded and hardened by frequent rains and constant tramping. The palisade, composed, in part, of wooden puncheons, and part thick adobes, formerly connecting the two great houses and the church (making a large enclosure), was broken down in many places by the Americans in battle and by neglect; the puncheons, stick-

183

ing up at every angle, gave an old, tumble-down aspect to the whole.

The church was the most important, as well as first, feature in the town, from the fact of its having been the principal scene of action in the fierce and sanguinary conflict between *El Norte Americanos* on the one side and the combined forces of the Pueblo Indians and Mexicans on the other.

It (the church) was an adobe building, parallelogram-shaped; high, thick walls, with no openings on the outer one or those facing the yard, save embrasures and loopholes, rudely cut for the occasion—the late battle. The front entrance faced the south; the west and north sides (as I have mentioned, devoid of windows), the open fields toward the Río Grande, the town of San Fernández and the Ranchita.

As this was the culminating point of all the differences between the Americans and the New Mexicans, an account may be essential to a portion of the readers of this narrative, of the origin, progress, and termination of the then pending difficulties; and, while seated on a broken baggage wagon, to the south, and in full view of the town, looking and musing on the devastating effects of war, the requisite information will be succinctly given. —

General Kearney, in command of the "Army of the West," marched to the capital of this province (Santa Fé) and quietly took possession, claiming it as United States territory. By him, the oath of allegiance was administered to many of the inhabitants in *propria persona*; in many cases, the *alcaldes* or mayors of the small towns received it for themselves and people. In this way the province was Americanized; a governor and a complement of judges, attorneys, sheriffs, and other appurtenances and impertinences of even-handed justice appointed; and, as the people appeared to be well contented, it was thought a bloodless conquest had been made, reflecting credit, alike, on the character of the provincials and the Army of the West! Leaving Colonel Price in command of the military force and Governor Bent as the civil head of the territory, Kearney left New Mexico for California, to add fresh laurels to his wreath of victory, taking with him a small armed force. Of the results of this latter expedition all are cognizant.

In New Mexico everything was in a peaceful, prosperous condition, to all outward show; the people traded freely; small foraging and herding parties of American soldiery were everywhere scattered, placing confidence in the inhabitants. It was afterward seen that designing men —artful and learned natives—were busily, insidiously sowing the seeds of discontent among the more ignorant class of the community, more especially the Pueblo Indians. The result was, they soon considered themselves outraged —their lives at stake—their possessions in danger. With inflamed passions, perverted minds, the brutal attack upon Governor Bent was commenced; and, with cries of extermination, they advanced on Santa Fé, receiving constant accessions in their triumphant march. Meanwhile, in other towns massacres were frequent; and the perpetrators of these, joining the main body of insurgents, met Colonel Price in the cañon El Embuda, where they were defeated with a small loss. They rallied in a few miles, and again they were forced to retreat. Colonel Price, marching with his cannon and baggage train over a new-cut road, through deep snows, followed them to the Pueblo de Taos, the place best calculated, in all the valley, for an obstinate resistance. Here the enemy, barricading themselves in the houses, bid defiance to their pursuers; who, coming on them late in the evening, commenced a bombardment with twelve-pound mountain howitzers. But night forced them to withdraw to San Fernández, two miles distant, amid the cries and jeers of the securely posted foe. In the morning, Price, with his command, moved forward in fine order over the intervening plain, first sending Captain St. Vrain, with whom the reader has become fully acquainted, and his troop of volunteers for the occasion, of mountaineers, traders, etc., skilled in Indian warfare, to the fields between the pueblo and the mountain, a half-mile distant, to intercept the retreat. A fire was opened by the howitzers at four hundred yards, and, after some skirmishing by the infantry and Burgwin's command of dragoons, the enemy retreated to the church, from the numerous loopholes of which they poured out a galling fire. The battery was now ordered up within a hundred yards, which had some effect; but the balls striking the tough mud walls did not always penetrate. Burgwin's dismounted men then stormed the front door of the church. After a spirited attack of several minutes, they were repulsed with the loss of their brave leader. The command devolving on Lieutenant McIlvaine, they were ordered to the west side; where, with axes, a breach was cut, through which they entered, several losing their lives. The cannon were run up to the breach—the bursting of the bombs in the small space, in which so many were crowded, caused great destruction of life. "The mingled noise of bursting shells, firearms, the yells of the Americans, and the shrieks of the wounded," says my narrator, an eyewitness, "was most appalling."

A Delaware Indian, "Big Nigger" by name, a keen shot, was the most desperate of the enemy. When the roof was fired and the Americans poured in, he was pursued to the room behind the altar, where he fell, riddled by thirty balls. Many of the foe fled toward the mountain. Captain St. Vrain, with his company, gave many their final quietus. The American loss was seven killed—that of the enemy 150, with a number of prisoners, among them the leader, Montojo, hung the next day by drumhead court martial in the plaza of San Fernández. Others were committed to jail to await a trial by civil law. Colonel Price returned to Santa Fé, leaving a strong force to support the civil authorities in pursuance of their respective duties. To resume the thread of our narrative—

We stood on the spot where fell the gallant Burgwin, the first captain of the First Dragoons, and then passed to the west side, entering the church at the stormers' breach, through which the missiles of death were hurled. We silently paused in the center of the house of Pueblo worship. Above, between the charred and blackened rafters which leaned from their places as if ready to fall on us, could be seen the spotless blue sky of this pure clime—on either side, the lofty walls, perforated by cannon ball and loophole, let in the long lines of uncertain gray light; and strewed and piled about the floor, as on the day of battle, were broken, burnt beams and heaps of adobes. Climbing and jumping over them, we made our way to the altar, now a broken platform, with scarce a sign or vestige of its former use; and in the room behind, we saw where "Big Nigger" and others, after a determined struggle, bravely met their certain fate. Hatcher was acquainted with the Delawares in former years. On emerging into the enclosure, we looked around.

A few half-scared Pueblos walked listlessly about, vacantly staring in a state of dejected gloomy abstraction. And they might well be so. Their *alcalde* dead, their grain and cattle gone, their church in ruins, the flower of the nation slain or under sentence of death, and the rest—with the exception of those in prison—refugees, starving in the mountains. It was truly a scene of desolation. In the strong hope of victory they made no provision for defeat; in the superstitious belief of the protection afforded by the holy Church, they were astounded beyond measure that, in the hour of need, they should be forsaken by their tutelar saint —that *los diablos Americanos* should, within the limits of consecrated ground, trample triumphant, was too much to bear; and, pitiable objects, they fled as if *diablos* from *los regiones infiernos* were after them, in sooth.

The two *casas grande*, or large houses, in which the Pueblos live are worthy of examination, being constructed of adobes—the universal building material—seven stories in height, each story somewhat smaller than the one below it, sloping gently inward—but not terrace-shaped. The mode of egress is at the topmost story. Ladders are used on the outside, from which they descend to the rooms inside. So subject are the Pueblos to attacks from hostile neighbors that they have, from time to time, thus strengthened their habitations; and as the ladders are pulled to the roof in case of danger, they are safe from their enemies' lances and scalp knives; for should an attempt be made at scaling, they would be exposed to the fire of the besieged from loopholes. An engineer might suggest the plan of undermining the soft building; the Indian besiegers, devoid of invention, have yet to try the plan.

As a mode of defense from their common enemy, the Indian, it certainly is admirable; but what fort or foe can withstand the assaults of the energetic Anglo-Saxon, aided by consummate skill and the most destructive engines of war?

Los Pueblos

The adobe, or sun-dried brick, is, I think, even better than burnt brick, or stone, to resist a bombardment; as the ball either passes through, making but a small hole, or the force is spent against the wall, without shattering the building. In several places where the cannon ball had penetrated three, four, or five inches, it rolled out again without cracking or shattering the wall in the least. Being tenacious and yielding, the mud brick serves as a good bulwark, not capable of being fired, and, in this dry climate, resists the trials of time and rain exceedingly well. Much credit is due the Pueblos de Taos for their determined and manly resistance to what they considered tyranny and for the capital manner in which their fortifications were planned; but, as a matter of course, they were defeated by the Americans. Who could, for a moment, expect anything else?

For years the Pueblo, by reason of fierceness of disposition, has held the balance of power in this district. It was the Pueblo who first revolted, and committed the late outrages—the Pueblo who, several years since, rose in arms, to put every American to death—the Pueblo who has kept this district in a continual ferment; but, at last! at last, he has met his conqueror.

They approach nearer to civilization than any of the nomadic tribes of the west—profess the Roman Catholic religion; which, by reason of ignorance, is mixed with a large share of superstition; submit to civil law under the guidance of an *alcalde*, of *sangre regular*; cultivate the ground; and, in many points, assimilate to the manners and customs of civilized man.

CHAPTER XVII

EL MUERTE

On Friday, the ninth, the sky was unspotted, save by hastily-fleeting clouds; and, as the rising sun loomed over the Taos Mountain, the bright rays, shining on the yellow and white mud houses, reflected cheerful hues, while the shades of the toppling peaks receding from the plain beneath drew within themselves. The humble valley wore an air of calm repose. The plaza was deserted; woe-begone donkeys drawled forth sacreligious brays as the warm sunbeams roused them from hard, grassless ground to scent among straw or bones their breakfast: a *señora* in her nightdress and disheveled hair—which, at the *fandango*, was the admiration of the moustached *señors* and half-wild *voluntarios*—could here and there be seen at this early hour, opening her house, previous to the preparation of the fiery *chile colorado*.

As onward sped the day, so did the crowd of morning drinkers at Estis's tavern renew their libations to Bacchus. Poor Mexicans hurried to and fro, casting suspicious glances around; *los Yankees* at *El casa Americano* drank their juleps and puffed their cigarillos in silence.

The sheriff (Metcalfe, formerly a mountaineer, son-in-law to Estis) was in want of the wherewith to hang the criminals, so he borrowed our rawhide lariats and two or three hempen picket cords of a teamster. In a room adjoining the bar, we put the hangman's noose on one end, tugging away quite heartily.

A while after we had been talking of the propriety, etc., of taking the Mexicans' lives, said Hatcher—"This hos has feelin's hyar," slapping his breast, "for poor human natur in most any fix, but for these palous [*pelados*] he doesn't care a cuss."

"Yes," replied I, "they scalped Liel alive, and butchered innocent persons."

"This coon," remarked Hatcher, "has made Injuns 'go under,' some—wagh!—but he's never skulped 'em alive; this child's no niggur, an' he says its onhuman—agin natur —an' they ought to choke. Hello, Met, these riatas mity stiff—won't fit; eh, old feller?"

"I've got something to *make* 'em fit—good 'intment— don't ermit very sweet parfume; but good 'nough for greasers; freeze into it, boys," said Metcalfe, producing a rial's worth of Mexican soft soap, "this'll make 'em slip easy—a long ways too easy for them, I 'spect."

We rubbed in the " 'intment" until the nooses could have been "warranted" to serve the intended purpose without hitching; on the teamster's hard ropes, we used an unusual quantity. One item in Met's bill of expenses, was:

"To soft soap for greasing nooses, ... 12½."

Our fee for loan of lariats consisted in the proffered *aguardiente* produced after washing our hands—not of the pleasant transaction of tying hangman's nooses—but of the soap sticking to our fingers.

With newly-lighted cigarillos between our teeth, we walked with the sheriff to the jail, taking along the halters —the significant loops, conspicuous, drawing the attention of both soldier and native, eliciting from the former familiar exclamations, such as—"Go it, my boys," "them's the *doky*ments"—"sarve 'em up brown"—from the latter wondering looks.

Entering a portal with a nod to the sentinel on duty, we found ourselves in a court. In a room fronting this was a ragged, ill-looking *pelado*, conversing with a miserably-dressed old woman—his mother—and discussing greenish-blue *tortillas* and *chile colorado*, under the espionage of a slouchingly-attired, long-haired, dirty, and awkward volunteer, who, to judge by his outward show, was no credit to his corps or silver-gild eagle buttons. He leaned in a most unsoldier-like position against the door frame; and, on our near approach, drew his feet somewhat closer to perpendicular, accosting us with—"Well, strangers! how are ye?"

"Quite well, thank you," replied one of us.

"Them's great briches of yourn," broke in he abruptly, after eyeing my fringed buckskins for some moments, "whar d' they riginate—Santy Fee? Beats linsey-woolsey all holler, down to Callaway County."

"Santa Fé!" replied Hatcher, disgusted with the fellow's simplicity, "why hos, them's Californy!"

"Cal-y-for-ny! my oh! let's look at them, stranger. Calyforny! way over yonder!" halfway soliloquising and staring at me doubtingly, with a side twist to his head and a knowing squint from his porcine eye, "Now, you don't mean to say you was *in* them briches when they was in Calyforny?"

"Him?" interrupted Hatcher, wishing to astonish the man, "that boy's been everywhar. He's stole more mule flesh from the Spaniards[1] an' 'raised' more Injun har than you could tuck in your belt in a week!"

"How raise Injine hair? Like we raise corn and hemp to Callaway County, ur jest like raising hogs and y'oxens?"

[1] Common term for Mexicans—as they speak the Spanish language.

"Oh! you darned fool," retorted Louy Simonds, "a long ways the greenest Ned, we see yet. No!" rejoined he imperatively, "when an Injun's a 'gone beaver,' we take a knife like this," pulling out his long scalp blade, which motion caused the man to open his eyes, "an' ketch hold of the topknot, an' rip skin an all rite off, quicker an' a goat could jump!"

"What's a 'gone beaver,' stranger?" again spoke up our verdant querist.

"Why, whar *was* you brung up, not to know the meanin' of sich terms—we'ud show you round fur a curiosity up in the mountains—let's go, fellers."

We started to another part of the jail, but were stopped by a final question from our brave volunteer to Hatcher— "Stranger! what mout your name be, ef I mout be so free-like?"

"Well, hos!" returned the questioned, "my name *mout* be Bill Williams, or it mout be Rube Herring, or it mout be John Smith, or it *mout* be Jim Beckwith [Beckwourth],[2] but this buffler's called John L. Hatcher, to rendevoo— Wagh!"

We strolled to the room in which were the condemned and other prisoners, to the number of eighty and more. A brass howitzer, the muzzle within four feet of the door, stood always ready to quell a tumult.

It (the prison apartment) was a long, chilly room, badly ventilated by one small window and the open door, through which the sun lit up the earth floor, and through which the poor *pelados* wistfully gazed. Two muscular Mexicans basked in its genial warmth, a tattered and dirty *sarape* interposed between them and the ground. The ends, once fringed, but now nearly clear of pristine orna-

[2] Well-known Rocky Mountain characters.

ment, were partly drawn over their breasts, disclosing in
the openings of their fancifully-colored shirts—now glazed
with filth and faded with perspiration—the bare skin covered with a wilderness of straight black hair. With hands
under their heads, in the mass of stringy locks rusty-brown
with neglect, and their attenuated smutty fingers coming
through, revealing uncut nails, filled with dirt, they returned our looks with an unmeaning stare, and unheeding-
ly received our salutation of—"*Comme la va!*"

These men were the condemned. In two short hours,
they hung lifeless on the gallows.

Along the sides of the room, leaning against the walls,
were crowded the poor wretches, miserable in dress, miserable in features, miserable feelings—a more disgusting
collection of ragged, lousy, greasy, unwashed *pelados* were,
probably, never before congregated within so small a space
as the jail of Taos.

About nine o'clock, active preparations were made for
the execution, and the soldiery mustered. Reverend *padres*,
on the solemn mission of administering the "blessed sacra-
ment" and spiritual consolation, in long, black gowns and
meek countenances, passed the sentinels.

Lieutenant Colonel Willock, commanding the military, ordered every American under arms. In accordance
with the requisition and with a desire to participate in the
fight, should there be any (at least not to be helpless), I
went for my gun, which had been delivered to one of the
household for safekeeping.

Seeing Señora St. Vrain, in my best Spanish, I said to
her—

"*Señora! onde esta riflero? cary mucho.*"—"Madam,
where is my rifle? I want it very much."

"*Ah! quien sabe señor?*—"Who knows, sir? Care you a

great deal for it?" with a smile and shrug of the shoulders, "Esta"—"here"—said she, handing it to me; "*Vamos— prento, por el rancheros*"—"Go quick for the *rancheros*."

"*Si, gracias Señora—adios*"—"Yes, Madame, thanks,— farewell," replied I, touching my battered wool hat.

"*Adios, Señor Americano*"—"Farewell, Sir American," returned she, tenderly.

On the houses, as I walked to the jail, were women trying to catch a glimpse of the prisoners and soldiers. As I passed by an *azotea*, on which were two acquaintances, one cried out—"*Señor!*"

"Quien?"—"What is it?"

"*Eh Señor! los rancheros muy diablos, muy tiefas, caraho!*"—"The *rancheros* are very great thieves—great devils!"

"Yes, ladies"; and I passed on with a low bow in acknowledgment of their salutation.

The prison was at the edge of town; no houses intervened between it and the fields to the north. One hundred and fifty yards distant a scaffold of two upright posts and a crossbeam was erected.

At the portal were several *compañeros*, discussing, in a very light way, the "fun," as they termed it, on hand—they almost wishing a rescue would be attempted so as to gratify their propensity for excitement.

The word was passed, at last, that the criminals were coming. Eighteen soldiers received them at the gate, with their muskets at port arms—the six abreast, with the sheriff on the right—nine soldiers on each side. Hatcher, Louy Simonds, Chadwick, myself, and others, eight in all, formed in line a pace behind, as the rear guard, with our trusty mountain rifles at rest in the bended elbow of the left arm, the right hand resting on the stock, to be drawn up to the face, and all ready to fight on our own responsibility at the least intimation of danger.

The poor *pelados* marched slowly, with down-cast eyes, arms tied behind, and bare heads, with the exception of white cotton caps stuck on the back part, to be pulled over the face as the last ceremony.

The *azoteas*—roofs—in our vicinity, were covered with women and children, to witness the first execution by hanging in the valley of Taos, save that of Montojo, the insurgent leader. No men were near; a few, afar off, stood moodily looking on.

On the flat jail roof was placed a mountain howitzer (the same piece had done the "state some service" at the battle of the pueblo), loaded and ranging the gallows. Near was the complement of men to serve it, one holding in his hand a lighted match.

The two hundred and thirty soldiers (deducting the eighteen forming the guard) were paraded in front of the jail and in sight of the gibbet, so as to secure the prisoners awaiting trial. Lieutenant Colonel Willock, on a handsome charger, from his position commanded a view of the whole.

When within fifteen paces of the gallows, the side guard, filing off to the right and left, formed, at regular distances from each other, three sides of a hollow square; the mountaineers and myself composed the fourth and front side, in full view of the trembling prisoners, who marched up to the tree, under which was a government wagon with two mules attached. The driver and sheriff assisted them in, ranging them on a board, placed across the hinder end, which maintained its balance, as they were six—an even number—two on each extremity and two in the middle. The gallows was so narrow they touched. The ropes, by reason of size and stiffness despite the soaping given them, were adjusted with difficulty; but, through the indefatigable efforts of the sheriff and the lieutenant (who accompanied us from the ranch), all preliminaries were arranged. The former, officiating as deputy sheriff for the occasion, seemed to enjoy the position—but the blue uniform looked sadly out of place on a hangman.

With rifles grounded, we awaited the consummation of the fearful tragedy. No crowd was around to disturb; a death-like stillness reigned. The spectators on the *azoteas* seemed scarcely to move—their eyes directed to the painful sight of the doomed wretches, with harsh halters now circling their necks.

The sheriff and assistant sat down; and, succeeding a few moments of intense expectation, the heart-wrung victims said a few words to their people.

But one said that they had committed murder and deserved death. In their brief, but earnest appeals, which I could but imperfectly comprehend, the words *"mi padre, mi madre"*—"my father, my mother"—could be distinguished. The one sentenced for *treason* showed a spirit of martyrdom worthy of the cause for which he died—the liberty of his country; and, instead of the cringing, contemptible recantation of the others, his speech was firm asseverations of his own innocence, the unjustness of his trial, and the arbitrary conduct of his murderers. With a scowl, as the cap was pulled over his face, the last words he uttered between his gritting teeth were, *"Caraho, los Americanos!"* The atrocity of the act of hanging that man for treason is most damnable; with the execution of those for murder no fault should be found.

Bidding each other *"adios,"* with a hope of meeting in Heaven, at word from the sheriff the mules were started, and the wagon drawn from under the tree. No fall was given, and their feet remained on the board till the ropes drew taut. The bodies swayed back and forth, and, coming in contact with each other, convulsive shudders shook their frames; the muscles, contracting, would relax, and again contract, and the bodies writhed most horribly.

While thus swinging, the hands of two came together, which they held with a firm grasp till the muscles loosened in death.

After forty minutes suspension, Colonel Willock ordered his command to quarters, and the howitzer was taken from its place on the prison roof. The soldiers were called off; the women, children, and population in general collected around us—the rear guard—whom the sheriff detained for protection while delivering the dead bodies to the weeping relatives.

We made a collection among ourselves of five dollars and dispatched a messenger to *el casa Americano* to prepare for us, when relieved from duty, an eggnog in honor of the occasion, for the Mexican has long been the dislike of the mountaineer, for overbearing conduct. Now that they have, for once, triumphed, a merrymaking must be given. We helped the sheriff to take down the bodies and untie the ropes—a most unpleasant business, too, for the cold, clammy skins and dead weight were revolting to the touch.

We were cutting a rope from one man's neck—it was in such a hard knot—when the owner (a government teamster), standing by waiting, shouted angrily, at the same time starting forward—

"Hello there! Don't cut that rope; I wont have any thing to tie my mules with."

"Oh! you darned fool," interposed a mountaineer, "the

palous' ghosts'll be after you, if you use them 'riatas—
wagh! They'll make meat of you, sartain."

"Well, I don't care if they do. I'm in government service; an' if them picket halters was gone, slap down would
go a dollar apiece. Money's scarce in these diggins, an' I'm
gwine to save all I kin, to take home to the old 'oman and
the boys."

In accordance with the fellow's earnest request, we
spared the ropes, on which was soap enough for a dozen
good washings, which he much needed.

Shouldering our rifles, we walked to the tavern—discussing the length of time a man will live after he is swung
off—where the fellows, washing, *primed* with the "raw"
(real American brandy, from Estis's personal store, less
adulterated than that at the bar), and, seating themselves
in the family room, near the handsome *señors*, were regaled
with the best eggnog it is possible to manufacture from the
materials. Who *would* blame a man for making a temporary sacrifice of himself to Bacchus, on such an occasion
and in the presence of such dark-eyed beauties? We had,
besides, brandy *à discrétion*.

"*Sa-cré!*" ejaculated a Canadian, after imbibing a glass
of the foamy beverage, with a strained, half-grunt of approbation, "*Tonnére de Dieu! ce liqueur est tres bon—ah, oui!
trop bon*," added he, in a higher key of delight.

"Wagh!" chimed in a hardy, self-pleased mountain
man, "this knocks the hind sights off of Touse [Taos
whiskey]. I'se drunk," continued he, in a musing tone of
voice, "a heap liquor in *my* chargin' lifetime. Thar's alky-
hol as makes drunk come mity quick; but 't ain't good—
burns up the innards; an' a feller feels like a gut-shot
coyote. Then thar's Touse arwardenty; it's d——d poor
stuff—kin taste the corn in it—makes me think I'm a hos,

a feedin' away fur plowin' time; an' I allers squeals, an' raises my hind foot to kick, when any *palou* comes about my heels. Then thar's—thar's [his strong potations of the "raw" affecting him] State brandy; that's good, too—kin drink on it all night; but this coon wants to dance Injun when he hides that in his meatbag." Rising to his feet, and commencing an Indian dance: "Here's luck, boys! sho-oop! ow-ow-gh! hay a hay—hay-he-ah-hay—ow-ow-gh-he-a, whoop! I'm drunk, boys—*muy borachio* [very drunk]—as the darned Spaniards say." Here he fell on the floor and went to sleep. The rest looked on in drunken merriment.

It is the opinion of eyewitnesses that the chivalric, noble, and patriotic "rear guard" knows little or nothing of the transactions of that eventful day subsequent to one o'clock, or the time of entering Estis's private room.

A nervous, fidgety Canadian—living, I believe, in Taos —came to us, shortly after the bodies were taken away for burial, declaring that "von prisonnier to de Ranchita vas come to de life encore."

We replied, not if there was any virtue in seventy minutes' suspension with rawhide riatas.

To the Ranchita is something less than a mile. The little fellow kept himself in a fume for two hours, running back and forth to see whether "de prisonnier" had yet opened his eyes.

CHAPTER XVIII

ADIOS!

H<small>ATCHER</small>, concluding that we had better return to the ranch, proposed to do so, and one afternoon we left, first loading our packmule at George Bent's with a bulky bag of *biscoche*—hard bread. While they tarried behind to exchange farewells with their *señoritas* and take a parting drink, I drove on the pack mule, so as to gain time. He was an ungainly, vicious animal; and, on a severe application of my gunstock to his dusty hide, he laid flat his ears to his neck, raised his hind legs, and with a petulant squeal shot them out, rattling against my hard saddletree, barely missing my body; and, before I could turn out of reach, the heel battery was again brought to bear, this time taking effect on my right leg. I felt like chewing up all the donkey flesh in Taos.

My friends soon caught up. Keeping our pack mule in front and riding abreast on the level road, we jogged along finely, half-screaming, half-scolding whenever the mule attempted to dodge oneside. Sometime he would stop stock still in the full career of a fast trot; we would shoot by, and then would ensue a race, sundry curses, and much belaboring with gun rods.

We saw, to our surprise, at the large distillery near the mouth of the cañon, Sadler, an old acquaintance, with as big a heart as any man in the mountains, attired in a cos-

201

tume claiming originality with the Indians, Mexicans, and *himself!* He welcomed us—

"Walk in, boys, hyar's old Touse—not so old, but good —and I'm distiller."

Within, the interesting process of whiskey making was in progress. Sadler drew a quart cup of the new liquor and handed it to us, which we merely tasted; had we partaken every time the free-hearted fellow passed the cup, the valley of Taos might have been our resting place for one more night. The beer, manufactured from wheat, was tolerably good.

Bidding Sadler "good-bye," we made our way up the pass. Attaining to some elevation, I turned in my saddle to take a last view of the beautiful valley, where were passed a few days so replete with interest and diversified with scenes tragic, comic, and domestic.

Nature had done much to render acceptable the country—

> *'Tis only man that's vile.*

The New Mexicans, when weakest, are the most contemptibly servile objects to be seen; and with their whining voices, shrugs of the shoulder, and dastardly expression of their villainous countenances, they commend themselves unreservedly to one's contempt. But, when *they* have the mastery, the worst qualities of a craven's character are displayed in revenge, hatred, and unbridled rage. Depraved in morals, they stop at nothing to accomplish their purpose. The extreme degradation into which they are fallen seems a fearful retribution upon the destroyers of Aztec Empire.

Woman *is* woman the world over, no matter where she

is found. Though we were strangers and enemies, the Mexican women stood ready to greet us with a smile; and food, lodging, and the fragrant cigarillo were ever at our disposal. Take the valley and its people all in all, there was much to admire and more to condemn—my mule's head, however, was turned to the mountain with some reluctance.

The sun and water cheered us, and we felt pleasure in the anticipated prospect of sleeping in the open air—a perfect luxury after having been "cabined, cribbed, and confined" in a tight adobe Mexican *casa.*

The green cedar and pine, the mellow light of the sun gleaming through the branches, and the twittering of dusky-colored birds induced a dreamy state; for long intervals naught but the pattering of our mules' feet or the quick, metallic clink of the flint and steel of Louy lighting a pipe broke the silence. We were under the influence of the harmony of nature, tobacco, and Taos whiskey.

Our course was in deep defiles, where moss covered the rocks dank and green and the spreading pine overlapped its twining boughs; now winding along the tortuous pathway, around huge rocks and stunted, bushy trees, or up steeps, compelling us to cling to the manes of our animals for support.

As the shade of the mountain to the west crept over us, we came to the place where, on our journey in, we last drank coffee. Near the willow bushes we pulled the saddles from our jaded mules, placing them on the brown sward; and, watering and hobbling the animals in a sheltered spot, sat down to the beef and *biscoche* soaked in aromatic Java from the time-honored little tin kettle. We were all gratified with the idea of being "free" once more, and so few of us made camp desirable. That night, I with a bunch of cigarillos from a Castilian-descended *señorita,* and they with pipes sat by the blaze in a decidedly musing mood. In my dreams, *rebozas,* black eyes, and shuck cigars were mixed in admirable confusion.

CHAPTER XIX

WAH-TO-YAH

No mules to be seen in the morning; Louy had been out an hour for them; so, partaking of a cup of coffee, Hatcher and I started in search.

"Them Purblos have *câched* our cavyard, I 'spect; howsomever, mules *is* mules, an' they *will* stray about—'specially when tired. You know the pass was rough yesterday, an' we'd better look good—many's the time my animals have strayed in the timber, and me a lookin' for 'em, a cussin' for darned niggurs, all the Injuns atween the Heely [Gila] an' Bayou Salade."

By this time we were at a point of the mountain on either side of which diverged a valley of gradual slope, bare of rocks and cedar and carpeted with russet-brown grass, with small thickets of the smooth-barked aspen studding the easy declinations—presenting an inviting walk in comparison to the rugged, scoria-strewn mountainside up which we had just been laboring. On Hatcher's saying—"You take that pass, an' I'll take this [he started up the left one from our position], the cavyard's maybe gone up one or t'other—guess you'll find the trail of a rope, or some kind of 'sign.' If you do, shoot your rifle—this child's heerd it so often crack 'gainst buffler—an' Camanches, too, wagh! —he knows the sound, an' he'll come an' help you."

A fatiguing walk of half an hour brought me to greater aspen groves and almost impenetrable cedar thickets. My close scrutiny for "sign" was, at length, rewarded, while examining a leaf deposit. The foot of a mule, lately sunk in the soft ground and a tiny print, not far distant, convinced me of being on the right trail.

In front, an isolated peak towered two hundred feet above, affording a good view of the contiguous small valleys; a tiresome clamber over stones and encounters with the bristling cactus brought me to the apex, where I fell carelessly down with momentary exhaustion of strength.

I espied the stray *caballada* below, in a sheltered oasis, quietly cropping the sweet grass—a grateful change from the scanty portion of corn at Taos; for it was scarce, and worth nine dollars the fanega. Untying the hobbles, I drove them in a trot down to camp, with shouts, first discharging my rifle for Hatcher. Saddling up, we soon were wending our way.

As we left Taos, Bill Garmon went in. He was to stay one night and overtake us, so we expected him all day to clatter at full speed down the mountain behind us. At sundown, crossing a wide valley, we camped amid huge, detached rocks, in a bower of pine branches made by some vagrant *ranchero*.

The spiral smoke, turning gray in the twilight, rose from the brush fire through Louy's exertions; the *caballada*, in single file, slowly returned from water, followed by Hatcher, with gun on shoulder, whistling abstractedly, and through habit, searching the hills and the plain with his eye for game or foe; and I, by the fire, undid the leathern bag of *biscoche*, filled the little kettle from a bubbling rill, and, with butcher knife in hand, cut thin slices of beef along (not across) the grain, in most approved style, and laid them on a wisp of grass; for we had no plates or other superfluous kitchen furniture—the only articles requisite to a mountaineer's *cuisine* being a long knife and tin cup.

During the convenient disposition of the meat and coffee, Louy detected a horseman approaching at a lope, from the direction of Taos.

"Wagh! Bill Garmon!" ejaculated he.

"How are ye?" shouted Bill at the top of his voice, as far as he could be heard, at the same moment waving his old white-wool hat—"How are ye old fellers? lookee hyar," he spoke in a less audible tone, as he threw his leg off the saddle, and held up a black flask of *aguardiente*, "Hi, hi-i, hi, he-he, he-he-a, hay a hay [rung out a Bacchanal song]. Who-oopee! horray for Taos an' arwerdenty, eh, old hos," said he to Hatcher.

"*Well* now, you is *some*, I swan. Do'ee hyar, this beaver went down to Taos without bringin' a pint of 'bald-face,' as is only in his meatbag [patting his stomach]; howsomever, you have more'n enough for all; besides it's bad idee to bring *much* of the cussed stuff whar a feller *has* to keep his eye skinned an' his ears picked for the Rapahoes, an' other Injun varmint; but, as you *have* it, old hos, this child doesn't refuse, 'specially from a *companyero!*"

"Now, hobble your cavyard," said Louy, relaxing in a smile at the liquor and at calling Garmon's one mule a whole cavyard, "an' drink coffee with us—*you* is true grit, an' them's the sort as kin have everything 'on the prairie' as belongs to me."

"Yes!" pulling off the saddle and depositing it beside ours, in its proper place for the night, to serve as pillow and protection for his head—"Yes! I know that, without you telling it to me, Louy; you've been in the mountains too long, old feller, to have the meanness in you yet; it's 'rubbed out' beaver season outen mind"—time whereof the memory runneth not to the contrary.

Notwithstanding Cassio's eloquent soliloquy on "putting that in a man's mouth which stealeth away his brains," the *aguardiente* gurgled out, amid the stifled grunts occasioned by throwing the head too far back when the bottle was applied to the mouths of the jovial, yet quiet, group of mountaineers. Perchance a sweetened dram was wanted, and the pattering of the liquor on the bottom of the tin cup could be heard—a sharp click for the first few drops and in filling more confused and indistinct. With brown sugar fished from the open bag and stirred in with the broad butcher knife, it was tossed off with the hunter's toast of, "Luck, boys!" There was not enough to leave unpleasant effects. It put Hatcher in a story-telling and the rest of the group in a good-natured listening humor.

Hatcher was always full of stories of an amusing, serious, and often of a marvellous cast; and we easily persuaded him to recount a few scenes in his wayward, ever changing life. Though he frequently indulged in rough slang, he did not partake of the Western's unsubdued nature altogether. I have chosen to select the more strange parts of his conversations as being the more strikingly illustrative of mountain character. He, at times, for his own, as well as our, amusement, would yarn in the most approved voyageur's style, or tell the hardest story of sights in his range; in short, Hatcher was *au fait* in everything appertaining to the Far West; whether mimicking a Canadian Frenchman, cowing down a score of Mexicans in *fandango* row, "lifting" the "hair" of a Pawnee, playing poker for beaver at rendezvous, or trading a robe, or sitting, with grave face, in Indian council, to smoke the long pipe and discuss with the aborigines the many grievances to which they consider themselves subject by the innovations of the whites, or the rapaciousness and cruelties of their enemies of their own copper complexion.

"Hatch, old hos! hyar's the coon as would like to hear of the time you seed the old gentleman. You's the one as savvys[1] all 'bout them diggin's."

"Well, Louy, sence you ask it, and as Garmon's *aguardiente is* good, I don't care ef I *do* tell that yarn; but it's mity long."

"What one is that?" asked Garmon.

"Why, the old beaver says as how he was in hell once —eh, Hatch?"

"Sartain! this old hos wasn't anywhar else—wagh!" replied Hatcher to Louy's doubting remark; "an' I tellee, it's me *kin* tell the yarn."

He kept the pipe in his mouth, the stem hard held between the teeth, using his hands and knife to cut from a solid plug of "Missouri manufactured" a fresh pipe of strong tobacco. His eyes were fast fixed on an imaginary object in the yellow-pine blaze, and his face indicated a concentration of thought to call back important items for the forthcoming incongruous story, attractive by reason of its improbability—interesting the manner of delivery.

"*Well!*" taking a puff at his pipe to keep in fire, "it's me as had been to Fort William [Bent's Fort] to get powder, Galena, an' a few contraptions, one beginning of robe season. I stuck around, waitin' for my possibles, which Holt was fixin' for me. Only a small train was from the States, an' goods were high—two plews[2] a plug for bacca, three fur powder, an' so on. Jim Finch, as went under on the 'Divide,' told me thar was lots of beaver on the Purga-

---

[1] *Savvy*—Fr. *savoir*—Sp. *sabe*—"to know."
[2] A *plew* is one beaver skin.

toire. Nobody knowed it; they think the creek's cleared. At the kanyon, three suns from the fort, I sot my traps. I was by myself; fur you know beaver's not to be trapped by two—they're shy as a coyote as runs round camp to gnaw a rope, or steal an apishamore. I'll be darned if ten Injuns didn't come screechin' rite onter me. I cached—I *did*—an' the niggurs made for the prairie with my animals. I tellee, this hos was *fawché* [mad], but he kept dark fur an hour. I heerd a trampin' in the bushes, an' in breaks my little gray mule. Thinks I, them Rapahoes ain't smart; so I ties her to grass. But the Injuns had skeered the beaver, an' I stays in camp, eatin' *par flêche* and lariat. Now I 'gan to feel wolf-ish an' squeamish, an' somethin' was pullin' an' gnawin' at my innards, like a wolf in a trap. Jest then an idee struck me, that I'd been hyar afore, tradin' liquor to the Yutes.

"I looked round fur sign, and hurraw fur the mountains, if I didn't find the cache. An' now, if this hos hasn't kissed the rock as was pecked with his butcher knife to mark the place, he's ongrateful. Maybe the gravel wasn't scratched up from that cache *some!* an' *me*, as would have given my traps fur '*old bull*,' rolled in the awardenty—wagh!

"I was weaker an' a goat in the spring; but when the Touse was opened, I fell back, an' let it run in. In four swaller' 'cluded to pull up stakes fur the headwaters of Purgatoire for meat. I roped old Blue, tied on my traps, an' left.

"It used to be the best place in the mountains fur meat —me an' Bill Williams *has* made it *come*—but nothin' was in sight. Things looked mity strange, an' I wanted to make back track; 'but,' sez I, 'hyar I ar, an' doesn't turn, surely.'

"The bushes was scorched an' curled, an' the cedar was like fire had been put to it. The big brown rocks was covered with black smoke, an' the little drink in the bottom of the kanyon was dried up. We was now most under the old twin peaks of Wah-to-yah; the cold snow on top looked mity cool an' refreshin'.

"Somethin' was wrong; I must be shovin' backards, an' that afore long, or I'll go under; an' I jerked the rein, but I'll be doggone—an' it's true as there's meat a runnin'— Blue kept goin' forrad. I laid back, an' cussed an' kicked till I *saw blood*, sartain; an' I put out my hand fur my knife to kill the beast, but the Green River wouldn't come. I tellee some onvisible sperit had a paw thar, an' it's me as says it—bad 'medicine' it was that trappin' time.

"Loosin' my pistol—the one traded at 'Big Horn,' from Suckeree Tomblow, time I lost my Yute squaw—an' primin' my rifle, I swore to keep rite on; fur, after stayin' ten year that's past in these mountains, to be fooled this way wasn't the game fur me, no how.

"Well, we—I say 'we,' fur Blue *was* some—good as a man any day; I could talk to her, an' she'd turn her head as ef she onderstood me. Mules *are* knowin' critters—next thing to human. At a sharp corner, Blue snorted, an' turned her head, but couldn't go back. Thar, in front, was a level kanyon, with walls of black an' brown an' gray stone, an' stumps of burnt pinyon hung down ready to fall onter us; an', as we passed, the rocks and trees shook an' grated an' creaked. All at oncet Blue tucked tail, backed her ears, bowed her neck, an' hinnied rite out, a raring onto her hind legs, a pawin' an' snickerin'. This hos doesn't see the cute of them notions; he's fur examinin', so I goes to jump off, to lam the fool; but I was stuck tight as ef tar was to the saddle. I took my gun—that ar iron [pointing to his rifle, leaning against a tree], an' pops Blue over the head, but she squealed an' dodged, all the time pawin'; but 'twasn't no use, an' I says, 'You didn't cost moren two blankets when you was traded from the Yutes, an' two blankets ain't worth moren six plews at Fort William, which comes to *dos pesos*[3] a pair, you consarned ugly picter —darn you, anyhow!' Jest then I heerd a laffin'. I looks up, an' two black critters—they wasn't human, sure, fur they had tails an' red coats (Injun cloth, like that traded to the Navyhoes), edged with shiny white stuff, an' brass buttons.

"They kem forrad an' made two low bows. I felt fur my scalp knive (fur I thought they was 'proachin' to take me), but I couldn't use it—they were so *darned* polite.

"One of the devils said, with a grin an' bow, 'Good mornin', Mr. Hatcher?'

" 'H——!' sez I, 'How do you know me? I swar *this* hos never saw you afore.'

" 'Oh! we've expected you a long time,' said the other, 'and we are quite happy to see you—we've known you ever since your arrival in the mountains.'

"I was gittin' sorter scared. I wanted a drop of arwerdenty mity bad, but the bottle was gone, an' I looked at them in astonishment, an' said—'the devil!'

" 'Hush!' screamed one, 'you must not say that here— keep still, you will see him presently.'

"I felt streaked, an' cold sweat broke out all over me. I tried to say my prayers, as I used to at home when they made me turn in at night—

> *Now I lay me down to sleep—*
> *Lan'lord fill the flowin' bowl.*

"P'shaw! I'm off agin, I can't say it; but if this child *could* have got off his animal, he'd tuk 'har' and gone the trail fur Purgatoire.

[3] *Dos pesos*—"two dollars"—Spanish term.

"All this time the long-tailed devils was leadin' my animal (an' me on top of her, the biggest fool dug out) up the same kanyon. The rocks on the sides was pecked as smooth as a beaver plew rubbed with the grain, an' the ground was covered with bits of cedar, like a cavyard of mules had been nippin' an' scatterin' 'em about. Overhead it was roofed; leastwise it was dark in thar, an' only a little light come through holes in the rock. I thought I knew whar we was, an' eeched awfully to talk, but I sot still an' didn't ax questions

"Presently we were stopped by a dead wall—no opening anywhar. When the devils turned from me, I jerked my head around quick, but thar was no place to get out—the wall had growed up ahind us too. I was mad, an' I wasn't mad nuther; fur I expected the time had come fur this child to go under. So I let my head fall onter my breast, an' I pulled the old wool hat over my eyes, an' thought for the last of the beaver I had trapped, an' the buffler as had took my G'lena pills in thar livers, an' the 'poker' an' 'euker' I'd played to rendevoo an' Fort William. I felt cumfortable as eatin' 'fat cow' to think I hadn't cheated anyone.

"All at once the kanyon got bright as day. I looked up, an' thar was a room with lights, an' people talkin' an laffin', an' fiddles a screechin'. Dad an' the preacher to Wapakonnetta told me the fiddle was the Devil's invention; I believe it now.

"The little feller as had hold of my animal squeaked out—'Get off your mule, Mr. Hatcher!'

" 'Get off!' sez I, for I was mad as a bull pecked with Camanche lances fur his disturbin' me, 'Get off? I have been trying to, ever sence I came in this infernal hole.'

" 'You can do so now. Be quick, for the company is waitin',' sez he, piert-like.

"They all stopped talkin' an' were lookin' rite at me. I felt riled. 'Darn your company. I've got to lose my scalp anyhow, an' no difference to me how soon—but to obleege ye'—so I slid off as easy as ef I'd never been stuck.

"A hunchback boy, with little gray eyes in his head, took old Blue away. I might never see her agin, an' I shouted—'Poor Blue! Good-bye Blue!'

"The young devil snickered; I turned around mity starn —'Stop your laffin' you hellcat—ef I am alone, I can take you,' an' I grabs fur my knife to wade into his liver; but it was gone—gun, bullet pouch, an' pistol—like mules in a stampede.

"I stepped forrad with a big feller, with har frizzled out like an old buffler's just afore sheddin' time; an' the people jawin' worse 'an a cavyard of parokeets, stopped, while Frizzly shouted—

" 'Mr. Hatcher, formerly of Wapakonnetta, latterly of the Rocky Mountains!'

"*Well*, thar I stood. Things was mity strange, an' every darned niggur on 'em looked so pleased like. To show 'em manners, I said—'How are ye!' an' I went to bow, but chaw my last 'bacca ef I could, my breeches was so tight—the heat way back in the kanyon had shrunk them. They were too polite to notice it, an' I felt fur my knife to rip the doggone things, but recollecting the scalp taker was stolen, I straightens up an' bows my head. A kind-lookin' smallish old gentleman, with a black coat and briches, an' a bright, cute face, an' gold spectacles, walks up an' pressed my hand softly—

" 'How do you do, my dear friend? I have long expected you. You cannot imagine the pleasure it gives me to meet you at home. I have watched your peregrinations in the busy, tiresome world with much interest. Sit down, sit down; take a chair,' an' he handed me one."

"I squared myself on it, but a ten-pronged buck[4] wasn't done sucking when I last sot on a cheer, an' I squirmed awhile, oneasy as a gut-shot coyote. I jumps up, an' tells the old gentleman them sort of 'state fixins,' didn't suit this beaver, an' he prefers the floor. I sets cross-legged like in camp as easy as eatin' *boudin*. I reached for my pipe—a feller's so used to it—but the devils in the kanyon had cached *it* too."

" 'You wish to smoke, Mr. Hatcher?—we will have cigars. Here!' he called to an imp near him, 'some cigars.'

"They was brought on a waiter, size of my bullet bag. I empties 'em in my hat, for good cigars ain't to be picked up on the peraira every day, but lookin' at the old man, I saw somethin' was wrong. To be polite, I ought to have taken but one.

" 'I beg pardon,' says I, scratchin' my old scalp, 'this hos didn't think—he's been so long in the mountains, he forgets civilized doins,' an' I shoves the hat to him.

" 'Never mind,' says he, wavin' his hand an' smilin' faintly, 'get others,' speakin' to the boy aside him.

"The old gentleman took one, and touched his finger to the end of my cigar—it smoked as ef fire had been sot to it.

" 'Wagh! the devil!' screams I, drawin' back.

" 'The same!' chimed in he, biting off the little end of his'n, an' bowin' an' spittin' it out—'the same, sir.'

" 'The same! what?'

" 'Why—the Devil.'

---

[4] A deer adds a prong to each succeeding year of his existence—hence a ten-pronged buck is ten years old.

" 'H——! this ain't the holler tree for this coon—I'll be makin' "medicine" '; so I offers my cigar to the sky, an' to the earth, like Injun.

" 'You must not do that *here*—out upon such superstition,' says he, sharp-like.

" 'Why?'

" 'Don't ask so many questions—come with me,' risin' to his feet, an' walkin' off slow, a blowin' his cigar smoke over his shoulder in a long line, an' I gets alongside of him, 'I want to show you my establishment—did not expect to find this down here, eh?'

"My briches was stiff with the all-fired heat in the kanyon, an' my friend seein' it, said, 'Your breeches are tight; allow me to place my hand on them.'

"He rubbed his fingers up an' down once, an' by beaver, they got as soft as when I traded them from the Pi Yutes on the Heely. (You mind, Louy, my Yute squaw; old Cutlips, her bos, came with us far as Sangry Christy gold mine. *She's* the squaw that dressed them skins.)

"I now felt as brave as a buffler in spring. The old man was so clever, an' I walked 'longside like a 'quaintance. We stopped afore a stone door, an' it opened without touchin'.

" 'Hyar's damp powder an' no fire to dry it,' shouts I, stoppin'.

" 'What's the matter—do you not wish to perambulate through my possessions?'

" 'This hos doesn't savvy what the "human" for perambulate is; but I'll walk plum to the hottest fire in your settlement, if that's all you mean.'

"The place was hot, an' smelt bad of brimstone; but the darned screechin' *took* me. I walks up to t'other eend of the 'lodge,' an' steal my mule if thar wasn't Jake Beloo, as trapped with me to Brown's Hole! A lot of hellcats was a pullin' at his ears, an' a jumpin' on his shoulders, a swingin' themselves to the ground by his long har. Some was runnin' hot irons in him, but when we came up, they went off in a corner a laffin' and talkin' like wildcats' gibberish on a cold night.

"Poor Jake! he came to the bar, lookin' like a sick buffler in the eye. The bones stuck through the skin, an' his har was matted an' long—all over jest like a blind bull, an' white blisters spotted him, with water runnin' out of 'em. 'Hatch, old feller! *you* here, too?—how are ye?' says he, in a faint-like voice, staggerin' an' catchin' on to the bar fur support—'I'm sorry to see you *here*, what did you'—he raised his eyes to the old man standin' ahind me, who gave him *such* a look: he went howlin' an' foamin' at the mouth to the fur eend of the den, an' fell down, rollin' over the damp stones. The devils, who was chucklin' by a furnis, whar was irons a heatin', approached easy, an' run one into his back. I jumped at 'em and hollered, 'You owdacious little hellpups, let him alone; ef my skulp taker was hyar, I'd make buzzard feed of your meat, an' *par flêche* of your dogskins,' but they squeaked out to 'go to the devil.' "

" 'Wagh!' says I, 'ef I *ain't* pretty close to his lodge, I'm a niggur!'

"The old gentleman speaks up, 'Take care of yourself, Mr. Hatcher,' in a mity soft, kind voice; an' he smiled so calm an' devilish—it nigh on froze me. I thought ef the ground would open with a yairthquake an' take me in, I'd be much obleeged any how. Thinks I—you saint-forsaken, infernal hell-chief, how I'd like to stick my knife in your withered old breadbasket.

" 'Ah! my dear fellow, no use in tryin'—that is a *de-*

cided impossibility'—I jumped ten feet. I swar, a 'medicine' man couldn't a heerd me, for my lips didn't move; an' how *he* knew is moren this hos *kin* tell.

" 'Evil communications corrupt good manners. But I see your nervous equilibrium is destroyed—come with me.'

"At t'other side, the old gentleman told me to reach down for a brass knob. I thought a trick was goin' to be played on me, an' I dodged.

" 'Do not be afraid; turn it when you pull—steady there —that's it'—it came, an' a door, too. He walked in. I followed while the door shut of itself.

" 'Mity good hinges!' sez I, 'Don't make a noise, an' go shut without slammin' an' cussen' 'em.'

" 'Yes—yes! Some of my own importation; no! they were made here.'

"It was dark at first, but when the other door opened, thar was *too* much light. In another room was a table in the middle, with two bottles an' little glasses like them to the Saint Louy drink houses, only prettier. A soft, thick carpet was on the floor—an' a square glass lamp hung from the ceiling. I sat cross-legged on the floor, an' he on a sofy, his feet cocked on a cheer an' his tail quoiled under him, cumfortable as traders in a lodge. He hollered somethin' I couldn't make out, an' in comes two, black, crooked-shank devils, with a round bench on one leg an' a glass with cigars in it. They *vamosed*, an' the old coon, inviting me to take a cigar, helps himself, an' rared his head back, while I sorter lays on the floor, an' we smoked an' talked.

"We was speakin' of the size of the apple Eve ate, an' I said thar were none but crabapples until we grafted them, but he replied, thar *was* good fruit until the flood. Then Noah was so hurried to git the yelaphants, pinchin bugs, an' sich varment aboard, he furgot good appleseed, until

218

the water got knee-deep; so he jumps out, gathers a lot of sour crabs, crams 'em in his pockets, an' Shem pulled him with a ropy in the ark agin.

"I got ahead of him several times, an' he sez—'Do you *really* believe the preachers, with their smooth faces, upturned eyes, and whining cant?'

" 'Sartainly I do! cause they're mity kind and good to the poor.'

" 'Why I had no idea you were so ignorant—I assuredly expected more from so sensible a man as you.'

" 'Now, look'ee hyar, this child isn't used to be abused to his own face—I—I tell 'ee it's mity hard to choke down —ef it ain't, skulp me!'

" 'Keep quiet, my young friend, suffer not your temper to gain the mastery; let patience have its perfect work. I beg your pardon sincerely—and so you believe the Bible, and permit the benighted preachers to gull you unsparingly. Come, now! What is the reason you imagine faith in the Bible is the work to take you to Heaven?'

" 'Well, don't *crowd* me an' I'll think a little—why, it's the oldest history anyhow: so they told me at home. I used to read it myself, old hos—this child did. It tells how the first man an' his squaw got hyar, an' the buffler, an' antelope, an' beaver, an' hosses, too. An' when I see it on the table, somethin' ahind my ribs thumps out: "Look, John, thar's a book you must be mighty respectful to," an' *somehow* I believe it's moren human, an' I tell 'ee, it's agin natur to believe otherwise, wagh!'

"Another thing the old gentleman mentioned, I thought was pretty much the fact. When he said he fooled Eve an' *walked* about, I said it was a *snake* what deceived the ole 'oman.

" 'Nonsense! snake indeed! I can satisfactorily account for that—but why think you so?'

" 'Because the big Bibles, with picters, has a snake quoiled in an apple tree, pokin' out his tongue at Adam's squaw.'

" 'P'shaw! the early inhabitants were so angry to think that Satan could deceive their first mother and entail so much misery on them that, at a meeting to which the principal men attended, they agreed to call me a serpent, because a serpent can insinuate himself so easily. When Moses compiled the different narratives of the earlier times in his five books, he wrote it so, too. It is typical, merely, of the wiles of the devil—my humble self'—an' the old coon bowed, 'and an error, it seems, into which the whole world, since Moses, have irretrievably fallen. But have we not been sitting long enough? Take a fresh cigar, an' we will walk. That's Purgatory[5] where your quondam friend, Jake Beloo, is. He will remain there a while longer, and, if you desire it, can go, though it cost much exertion to entice him here, and then only after he drank hard.'

" 'I wish you would, sir. Jake's as good a companyero as ever trapped beaver or gnawed poor bull in spring, an' he treated his squaw as ef she was a white woman.'

" 'For your sake, I will; we may see others of your acquaintance before leaving this,' sez he, sorter queer-like, as if to say—'no doubt of it.'

"The door of the room we had been talkin' in shut of its own accord. We stopped, an' he touchin' a spring in the wall, a trapdoor flew open, showin' a flight of steps. He went first, cautioning me not to slip on the dark sta'ars; but I shouted 'not to mind me, but thankee for tellin' it though.'

[5] Hatcher was no Roman Catholic, but if he saw Purgatory, surely I should mention it.

220

"We went down, an' down, an' down, till I 'gan to think the old cuss was goin' to get *me* safe, too, so I sung out—'Hello! which way; we must be mity nigh under Wah-to-yah, we've been goin' on so long?'

" 'Yes!' sez he, much astonished, 'We're just under the twins. Why, turn and twist you ever so much, you loose not your reckoning.'

" 'Not by a long chalk! This child had his bringin' up to Wapakonnetta, an' that's a fact.'

"From the bottom we went on in a dampish, dark sort of a passage, gloomingly lit up with one candle. The grease was runnin' down the block as had an auger hole bored in it for a candlestick, an' the long snuff to the eend was red, an' the blaze clung to it, as ef it hated to part company, an' turned black, an' smoked at the p'int in mournin'. The cold chills shook me, an' the old gentleman kept so still, the echo of my feet rolled back so hollow an' solemn. I wanted liquor mity bad—mity bad.

"Thar was noise smothered-like, an' some poor feller would cry out worse 'an Camanches chargin'. A door opened, and the old gentleman touchin' me on the back, I went in, an' he followed. It flew to, an' though I turned rite round, to look fur 'sign' to 'scape, ef the place got too hot, I couldn't find it.

" 'Wa-agh!' sez I.

" 'What now, are you dissatisfied?'

" 'Oh, no! I was just lookin' to see what sort of a lodge you have.'

" 'I understand you perfectly, sir—be not afraid.'

"My eyes were blinded in the light, but rubbin' 'em, I saw two big snakes comin' at me, thar yaller an' blood-shot eyes shinin' awfully, an' thar big red tongues dartin' back an' forad, like a painter's paw when he slaps it on a deer, an' thar wide jaws open, showin' long, slim, white fangs. On my right, four ugly animals jumped at me, an' rattled ther chains—I *swar*, ther heads were bigger an' a buffler's in summer.[6] The snakes hissed an' showed thar teeth, an' lashed thar tails, an' the dogs howled, an' growled, an' charged, an' the light from the furnis flashed out brighter an' brighter; an' above me, an' around me, a hundred devils yelled, an' laffed, an' swore, an' spit, an' snapped ther bony fingers in my face, an' leaped up to the ceiling into the black, long spiderwebs, an' rode on the spiders bigger an' a powderhorn, an' jumped off onter my head. Then they all formed in line, an' marched, an' hooted, an' yelled; an' when the snakes jined the percession, the devils leaped on thar backs an' rode. Then some smaller ones rocked up an' down on springin' boards, an' when the snakes kem opposite, darted way up in the room an' dived down in their mouths, screechin' like so many Pawnees for sculps. When the snakes was in front of us, the little devils came to the eend of the snakes' tongues, laffin, an' dancin', an' singin' like eediuts. Then the big dogs jumped clean over us, growlin' louder 'an a cavyard of grisly b'ar, an' the devils holdin' on to thar tails flopped over my head, screamin'—"We've got you—we've got you at last!'

"I couldn't stand it no longer, an' shuttin' my eyes, I yelled rite out, an' groaned.

" 'Be not alarmed,' and my friend drew his fingers along my head an' back, an' pulled a little narrow black flask from his pocket with—'Take some of this.'

"I swallered a few drops. It tasted sweetish an' bitterish —I don't exactly *savvy* how, but soon as it *was* down, I

[6] A buffalo being divested of hair in the hot season, his head looks larger at that period.

jumped up five times an' yelled—'Out of the way, you little ones, an' let me ride'; an' after runnin' longside, and climbin' up his slimy scales, I got straddle of a big snake, who turned his head around, blowin' his hot, sickenin' breath in my face. I waved my old wool hat, an' kickin' him in a fast run, sung out to the little devils to git up behind, an' off we all started, screechin' 'Hooraw fur Hell!' The old gentleman rolled over an' bent himself double with laffin', till he putty nigh choked. We kept goin' faster an' faster till I got on to my feet (though the scales were mity slippery) an' danced Injun, an' whooped louder than 'em all.

"All at once, the old gentleman stoped laffin', pulled his spectacles down on his nose an' said—'Mr. Hatcher, we had better go now,' an' then he spoke somethin' I couldn't make out, an' the animals all stood still; I slid off, an' the little hellcats a pinchin' my ears, an' pullin' my beard, went off squeakin'. Then they all formed in a half-moon afore us—the snakes on ther tails, with heads way up to the black cobwebby roof; the dogs rared on thar hind feet, an' the little devils hangin' everywhar. Then they all roared, an' hissed, an' screeched seven times, an' wheelin' off, disappeared, just as the light went out, leaving us in the dark.

" 'Mr. Hatcher,' sez the old gentleman agin, movin' off, 'you will please amuse yourself until I return'; but seein' me look wild, 'You have seen too much of me to feel alarmed for your own safety. Take this imp fur a guide, an' if he is impertinent, *put him through*; and, for fear the exhibitions may overcome your nerves, imbibe a portion of this cordial,' which I did, an' everything danced afore my eyes, an' I wasn't a bit scairt.

"I started fur a red light as came through the crack of a door, a stumblin' over a three-legged stool, an' pitchin' my last cigar stump to one of the dogs chained to the wall, who ketched it in his mouth. When the door was opened by my guide, I saw a big blaze like a peraira on fire—red **and gloomy**; an' big black smoke was curlin', an' twistin', an' shootin', an' spreadin', and the flames a licking the walls, goin' up to a pint, and breakin' into a wide blaze, with white an' green ends. Thar was bells a tollin', an' chains a clinkin', an' mad howls an' screams; but the old gentleman's 'medicine' made me feel as independent as a trapper with his animals feedin' round him, two pack of beaver in camp, with traps sot fur more.

"Close to the hot place was a lot of merry devils laffin' an' shoutin' with an' old pack of greasy cards—it minded me of them we played with to rendezvoo—shufflin' 'em to 'Devil's Dream,' an' 'Money Musk'; then they 'ud deal in slow time, with 'Dead March in Saul,' whistlin' as solemn as medicine men. Then they broke out of a suddent with 'Paddy O'Rafferty,' which made this hos move about in his moccasins so lively, one of them as was playin' looked up an' sed—'Mr. Hatcher, won't you take a hand—make way, boys, fur the gentleman.'

"Down I sot amongst 'em, but stepped on the little feller's tail, who had been leadin' the Irish jig. He hollered till I got off it—'Owch! but it's on my tail ye are!'

" 'Pardon,' sez I, 'but you're an Irishman!'

" 'No, indeed! I'm a hellimp, he! he! who-oop! I'm a hellimp,' an' he laffed an' pulled my beard, an' screeched till the rest threatened to choke him ef he didn't stop.'

" 'What's trumps?' sez I, 'an' whose deal?'

" 'Here is my place,' sez one, 'I'm tired playin'; take a horn,' handin' me a black bottle, 'the game's poker, an' it's your deal next—there's a bigger game of poker on hand,' an' pickin' up an iron rod heatin' in the fire, he pinched a miserable burnin' feller ahind the bars, who cussed him an' run way in the blaze outen reach.'

"I thought I was *great* at poker by the way I took the plews an' traps from the boys to rendezvoo, but hyar the slick devils beat me without half tryin'. When they slapped down a bully pair, they 'ud screech an' laff worse 'an fellers on a spree. Sez one—'Mr. Hatcher, I recon you're a hos at poker away to your country, but you can't shine down here—you are nowhar'. That feller lookin' at us through the bars was a preacher up to the world. When we first got him, he was *all-fired* hot and thirsty. We would dip our fingers in water an' let it run in his mouth to get him to teach us the best tricks—he'a trump—he would stand an' stamp the hot coals, and dance up and down, while he told us his experience. Whoopee! how we would laugh! He has delivered two long sermons of a Sunday and played poker at night on fip antes with the deacons for the money bagged that day; and, when he was in debt, he exhorted the congregation to give more fur the poor heathen in a foreign land, a dying and losing their souls for the want of a little money to send 'em a gospel preacher— that the poor heathen 'ud be damned to eternal fire ef they *didn't* make up the dough. The gentleman as showed you around—Old Sate, we call him—had his eye on the preach- er for a long time. When we got him, we had a barrel of liquor and carried him around on our shoulders until tired of the fun, and then threw him in the furnace yonder. We call him "Poke," for that was his favorite game. Oh, Poke!' shouted my friend, 'come here; thar's a gentleman wishes you—we'll give you five drops of water, an' that's more than your old skin's worth.'

"He came close, an' though his face was poor an' all scratched, an' his har swinged mity nigh off, 'make meat' of this child if it wasn't old Cormon as used to preach to the Wapakonnetta settlement! Many a time this coon's har's stood on eend when he preached about t'other world. He came close, an' I could see the chains tied on his wrists, whar they had worn to the bone, showin' the raw meat an' dried and runnin' blood. He looked a darn sight worse an' ef Camanches had skulped him.

" 'Hello! old coon,' sez I, 'we're both in that awful place you talked so much about, but I ain't so bad off as you, yet. This young gentleman,' pointin' to the devil who told me of his doins—'this young gentleman has been tellin' me how you took the money you made us throw in on Sunday.'

" 'Yes,' sez he, 'ef I had only acted as I told others to do, I would not have been here scorching for ever and ever —water! water! John, my son, fur my sake, a little water.'

"Just then a little rascal stuck a hot iron in him, an' off he ran in the flames, caching on the cool side of a big chunk of fire, a lookin' at us fur water; but I cared no more fur him than the Pawnee whose topknot was tucked in my belt fur stealin' my cavyard to the Coon Creeks; an' I sez—

" 'This hos doesn't give a *cuss* fur you; you're a sneakin' hypercrite; you deserve all you've got an' more too—an', lookee hyar, old boy, it's me as says so.'

"I strayed off a piece, pretendin' to get cool; but this coon 'gan to git *scairt*, an' that's a fact, fur the devils carried Cormon till they got tired of *him*; 'an',' sez I to myself, 'an' *hain't* they been doin' me the same way? I'll *cache*—I will —fur I'm not overly good, specially since I came to the mountains. Wagh! but this beaver must be movin' fur deep water, if that's the way your stick floats' [a floating stick attached to the chain marks the spot of the submerged beaver trap].

"Well now, this child felt sorter queer, so he santers 'long slowly, till he saw an' open place in the rock; not mindin' the imps who was drinkin' away like trappers on a bust. It was so dark thar, I felt my way mity still (fur I was afraid they 'ud be after me); I got almost to a streak of light, when thar was sich a rumpus back in the cave as give me the trimbles. Doors was slammin', dogs growlin' an' rattlin' thar chains, an' the devils a screamin'. They come a chargin'. The snakes was hissin' sharp an' wiry; the beasts howled out long an' mournful; an' thunder rolled up overhead, an' the imps was yellin' an' screechin' like mad.

"'It's time to break fur timber, sure,' and I run as ef a wounded buffler was raisin' my shirt with his horns. The place was damp, an' in the narrow rock, lizards an' vipers an' copperheads jumped out at me, an' clum on my legs, but I stompt an' shook 'em off. Owls, too, flopped thar wings in my face, an' hooted at me, an' fire blazed out an' lit the place up, an' brimstone smoke came nigh on chokin' me. Lookin' back, the whole cavyard of hell was comin', an' devils on devils, nothin' but devils, filled the hole.

"I threw down my hat to run faster, an' then jerked off my old blanket, but still they was gainin'. I made one jump clean out of my moccasins. The big snake in front was closer an' closer, with his head drawed back to strike; then a helldog raked up nearly 'long side, pantin' an' blowin' with the slobber runnin' outen his mouth, an' a lot of devils hangin' on to him, was cussin' me an' screechin'. I strained every jint, but no use, they still gained—not fast—but gainin' they was. I jumped an' swore, an' leaned down, an' flung out my hands, but the dogs was nearer every time, an' the horrid yellin' an' hissin' way back, grew louder an' louder. At last, a prayer mother used to make me say, I hadn't thought of fur twenty year or more, came rite afore me clear as a powderhorn. I kept runnin' an' sayin' it, an' the niggurs held back a little. I gained some on them—Wagh! I stopped repeatin', to get breath, an' the foremost dog made such a lunge at me, I forgot it. Turnin' up my eyes, thar was the old gentleman lookin' at me, an' keepin' alongside without walkin'. His face wasn't more than two feet off, an' his eyes was fixed steady, an' calm an' devilish. I screamed rite out. I shut my eyes, but he was thar, too. I howled an' spit an' hit at it, but couldn't git the darned face away. A dog ketched hold of my shirt with his fangs, an' two devils, jumpin' on me, caught me by the throat, a tryin' to choke me. While I was pullin' 'em off, I fell down, with about thirty-five of the infernal things, an' the dogs an' the slimy snakes a top of me, a mashin' an' taren' me. I bit big pieces out of them, an' bit an' bit again, an' scratched an' gouged. When I was most give out, I heerd the Pawnee skulp yell, an' use my rifle fur a pokin' stick, ef in didn't charge a party of the best boys in the mountains. *They* slayed the devils right an' left, an' sot 'em runnin' like goats, but this hos was so weak fightin', he fainted away. When I come to, we was on the Purgatoire, just whar I found the liquor, an' my companyeros was slappin' thar wet hats in my face to bring me to. Round whar I was layin', the grass was pulled up an' the ground dug with my knife, and the bottle, cached when I traded with the Yutes, was smashed to flinders 'gainst a tree.

" 'Why, what on airth, Hatcher, have ye bin doin' hyar? You was a kickin' an' taren' up the grass, an' yellin' as ef yer 'har' was taken. Why, old hos, this coon don't *savvy* them hifelutin' notions, he doesn't!'

" 'The devils from hell was after me,' sez I mity gruff, 'This hos has seen moren ever he wants to agin.'

"They tried to git me outen the notion, but I swar, an' I'll stick to it, this child saw a heap more of the all-fired place than he wants to agin; an' ef it ain't fact, he doesn't know 'fat cow' from 'poor bull'—Wagh!"

So ended Hatcher's tale of Wah-to-yah, or what the mountaineer saw when he had the *mania potu*.

CHAPTER XX

THE FARM

Our route in the morning was the same trail by which we entered Taos. Long hills gave hard work to our mules, who, panting and in single file—a miniature caravan—patiently toiled; and we, slowly following, cheered them with snatches of merry song. In a mountainous country such as this, the absence of mules would be a serious drawback to trade; for the Indian horses, though of compact build and inured to a scanty subsistence of grass, cannot bear up under the severe fatigue attendant on such journeys.

Once more on the prairie we experienced a feeling of relief, for the jostling on the uneven pathway and the cold and snow gave place to rapid and easy travel. The weather was more genial, and hares, starting from the sage bushes, enlivened our progress. We made camp before nightfall, on El Rayada, a half-mile above a party of men whom we did not go near; they, supposing us Indians, corralled their animals in haste.

Succeeding a refreshing night's rest by the rippling Rayada, we saddled and packed; a tin cup of coffee and *biscoche* served to break our fast; and, ere the distant Raton had gleamed with the dawning light, we were far on our way. Two hours' ride brought us to the bluff, at whose base, a hundred feet below, trickled *El Agua Vaca*.

The Farm

The same chain on which we stood, converging above and below, so shut out the chill winds that, this early, the tree-dotted streamlet margins upbore the joyous mantle of green, blending so harmoniously with the more tardy growth of the swelling hills beyond. A soft cloud of mist, gently overshadowing and gradually retreating, chidingly clung to the topmost tree branches in seeming unwillingness to depart. Through the rugged gorge at the entrance of this spot tumbled the foamy brook in rapid descent; then whirled impetuously; it soberly meandered in glassy pools away from the eye in the intricate windings of the rock. By the still, purling waters, sleek, contented cows pulled the sweet verdure or quietly reposed; while, hid from them by a jutting point in front, many calves frisked about or basked in the sheltered sunbeams. Embowered in a thicket of dogwood and cedar at our feet, with huge detached masses of upreared rock, guardian-spirit-like surrounding it, was the humble and romantic abode of Antonio, the *vaquero*.

Descending the sliding point, with mules reined back on their haunches, we stopped in the crystal-brown waters, which, murmuring a laughing farewell to the Dryads of the fountain, sped away merrily in the heedless race for the distant plain. Antonio's house was composed of a few logs, merely—altogether not seven feet in height or length; in front was a miniature court, while numerous goats, browsing among the rocks, enhanced the domestic air of *El Agua Vaca*.

In the corner of the hut we found a bucket of milk; so, *sans cerémonie*, it was hung over the fire with crumbled *biscoche*. While discussing its merits, an object enveloped in a blanket and topped with a tall-peaked, rusty-looking *sombréro* rode up on a sorry bay horse. He was armed with

huge spurs, lasso, and bow and sword—his *tout ensemble*
cutting such a ridiculous figure we laughed outright. *Don
Quixote de la Mancha*, thought I, how came he here? But
it was only Antonio. He was a good Mexican, if any of the
nation deserve that prefixing adjective. He asked us con-
cerning his *esposa, mujer*—his wife.

An hour more brought us to the Cimarone *ranchero*,
where our old *compañeros* welcomed us. They were much
pleased with our recital of adventures in El Valle de Taos.

Hatcher and William Bent had made preparations for
farming in the Purgatoire valley, below the crossing of the
Santa Fé Trail. Hatcher was to take the company's mules,
horses, and cows to the farm. For two days we were busied
in separating the United States stock from ours; and in the
afternoon of the third, with Tibeau for wagon driver and
Louy Simonds, Antonio, and myself, Hatcher turned his
face to the Raton. Staying on the Cimarone that night,
we passed the following *jornada* in monotonous cattle
driving. The weather was warm, and calves, worn down
with walking, were hauled in the wagon; but considerable
chasing and final lassoing were necessary to capture the
young brutes ere they submitted to the unceremonious
hoisting. At night the Verméjo afforded water, and a grove
of willows, hard by, shelter and fuel. With milk, *biscoche*,
beef, and coffee, we enjoyed ourselves; for when mountaineers have plenty to eat, they are cheerful; but, in starving times, wagh!—an old bear is better company.

The succeeding morning, a calf preferring the shade of
the willows to the hot sun and evading all attempts at capture, Hatcher sent a ball through it. His was a short, heavy
rifle, the stock unvarnished; and, when he brought it to his
face, the game most always came. He was the best shot
within my knowledge.

The Farm

The rifle I brought from the States proving too light for this windy country, I exchanged it with Garmon for a long, heavy one, whole-stocked, and the barrel fastened to its place with two wooden and one iron pegs. At the guard the stock had been accidentally broken short off, and was secured again with a strip of skin, warm from a buffalo's flank, sewed on with sinew and awl. Seven years before it came into my possession, Louy Simonds, while trapping on the northern lakes, in a hand-to-hand conflict with a black bear, shattered the old stock. An ingenious Dutchman made a new one, with a hatchet, drawing, and pocket knife, of a piece of curled maple which had been riven by lightning. The same stock still remained; and the associations connected with it, together with its qualities as a shooting iron and its antiquated appearance, made it a favorite with me.

The sun was setting as we turned from the trail and unsaddled in a horseshoe bend of *El Río Canadiano*, near a grove of cottonwoods. The oxen were unyoked, the droves directed to water, and the cows milked. When night overshadowed the scene, we sat on outspread blankets close to the fire, with "a heap" inside and pipe in mouth, enjoying our ease with dignity.

This section of country I have often heard spoken of as uninteresting; but to me there were many attractions. Here, with mule and gun and a few faithful friends, one experiences such a grand sensation of liberty and a total absence of fear; no one to say what he shall do; costumed as fancy, or comfort, dictates; his blanket his house, the prairie his home. Money he needs not, except to buy coffee, ammunition, and "Touse." No conventional rules of society restrict him to any particular form of dress, manner, or speech—he can swear a blue streak or pray; it is his own affair entirely. Here, too, one soon learns to say nothing, and do less, but for himself; and the greenhorn is often reminded, amid showers of maledictions, to confine his philanthropic deeds and conversations to his own dear self. I was quite amused by the kindly-intentioned remarks of an old mountaineer to me, shortly after my appearance in the country. "If you see a man's mule running off, don't stop it—let it go to the devil; it isn't yourn. If his possible sack falls off, don't tell him of it; he'll find it out. At camp, help cook—get wood an' water—make yourself active—get your pipe, an' smoke it—don't ask too many questions, an' you'll pass!"

The cattle were too fat to travel fast, and their heated tongues lolled out as they pantingly walked along. We were in motion the entire day, for water was not to be procured; and, when the sun's intense rays were diverted by a range of isolated hills, we joyfully hailed the approach of evening. The mountain which we were nearing was rough; its pine-clad sides grew black with the shades of night. To the south the chain was continued till lost in the uncertain twilight. Hatcher, who had been reconnoitering for water in a canyon two miles to the east, returned unsuccessful. Scarcely before dark we stopped on a grateful rivulet. The cattle—a hundred in number—scenting the water, ran bellowing and goring one another in the struggle; the *caballada* galloped up the bed of the stream, making the water unfit for our own throats. The cows lowed for their calves, who, in turn, bleated most lustily; the mules squealed and kicked, while we shouted and clubbed them off our camp and saddles. It was a grand concert, each one playing his own tune. But soon the uneasy juveniles were industriously nudging at swelling teats in silence, and the mules ranging the hillsides.

234

Building a fire near the brook, we were quietly seated by the blazing logs—the meat cooking and the mouth of the *biscoche* bag convenient. The *biscoche* occupied the center of the circle when we ate, and, in the total absence of plates, the leg doubled up served, except when the meat was too hot; then a rock, chip, or anything handy, interposed. Indeed, we *have* used dry buffalo chips on the plain, instead of the more agreeable delft.

That night parched coffee gave out. We had nothing in which to burn more; but, as necessity is, ever, the mother of invention, we selected two flat stones from the channel at hand, twenty-five to thirty inches in diameter, which we placed on the fire till heated; then one was taken off, the coffee poured on, and stirred with a stick. The stones served alternately as they became cool. When the coffee was sufficiently burned, a piece of skin was laid on the ground, and a clean stone, a foot in diameter, rested on the knees of the grinder, with one edge on the skin. A smaller stone, held in the hand, reduced the grains between it and the larger one to powder by a rotary motion.

The cattle were in better plight on resuming the journey. Further up the pass we found a camp of United States teamsters, their wagons and position in unison with their character—strung along the road for two hundred yards. A half-dozen Apaches could have scalped the men and robbed the wagons with impunity.

We passed without stopping, and at a steep hill near, we dismounted, to put our shoulders to the wagon wheel. Returning to the train, I galloped up to our party again, with a piece of mess pork, for which I gave one dollar. A little salt meat, with an abundance of fresh, was palatable. The continued use of the "salt" too plainly showed in the teamsters' sallow countenances. Their Purgatoire encampment had quite a large graveyard attached—comrades of the survivors in the Raton.

A mile beyond, we came upon a group of three men cooking, the leader of whom was a man known from the Yellowstone to *El Río Bravo*, from Salt Lake to Sangre Cristo, from Santa Fé to Missouri—the shrewd, independent Jim Beckwith [Beckwourth]. He claimed parentage on the maternal side from one who, in childhood, played 'neath the palm trees in the golden sands displaced by "Afric's sunny fountains"—and, on the paternal, from a slip reared among the vine-clad hills of La Belle France and transplanted in reluctant haste on the western shore of the great Mississippi.

While yet a boy, Beckwith ran from St. Louis with a trapping party, who, with dollars and beaver galore, stalked the thoroughfares of the then frontier town in pardonable pride and consequence. After much buffeting to the head-waters of the Yellowstone, he took a wife with the Crow Indians, and to that nation attached himself—joining their war parties with alacrity, dancing around the scalp trophies, and making trades of his squaw's well-dressed robes to the fur companies.

But what white man was ever long constant to his Indian nymph, or Mexican *muchacha?* And Jim Beckwith, ere many moons, found himself traversing the prairie-skirted Black, Sweetwater, Wet, and other noted mountains; now trapping beaver on Bijou; now "fetching" the "goats" from Pike's toppling crags; and now again at Greenhorn settlement, "raking" the "plews" from the less fortunate "euker" and "poker" players, who after solitary sojourns of months in their favorite haunts emerge and "make" for rendezvous, to revel in the pleasures of intoxicating forgetfulness, and to dance, in a rude but genuine way, with the laughing squaws and thoughtless *señoritas*.

In Santa Fé last winter, Beckwith kept the best-furnished saloon in the place—the grand resort for liquor-imbibing, monte-playing, and *fandango*-disposed American officers and men.

He was a large, good-humored fellow; and, while listening to the characteristic colloquy, I almost forgot that he was of a race who, in the much-boasted land of liberty, are an inferior, degraded people. With their *caballada*, we found a horse of Mr. St. Vrain, which we drove to our own band, without a previous by'r leave or a single compliment to Jim's honesty. Hatcher thought that the party was upon a horse-stealing expedition, to which propensity, however, in the mountains, small blame should be imputed.

By noon we stood on the dividing ridge of the Raton. On reaching the Purgatoire valley, an object like a buffalo was descried beyond the stream. Louy went over; an ox, attenuated by hunger and hard work, looked mournfully up to him as he rode in front. "Poor buffler!" said he, as he joined us again, leaving the solitary vagrant to pick, unmolestedly, the scanty herbage.

It was a beautiful April afternoon in which we journeyed down the Purgatoire and halted by a snow-supplied rill, whose springing waters invited us to rest our wearied limbs by its side. The *caballada* crowding forward, and slaking their thirst, betook themselves to the crispy hill grass. A few sticks were gathered, flint and steel produced; and, as the smoke curled languidly upward from the Indian-fashioned fire, we partook of the same insouciant feeling, and reclined on the warm ground with eyes half-closed, solacing ourselves with the blessed pipe.

The sun was yet above the Raton, which, with its escarpment of gray, time-worn rock, frowned upon us. Hatcher, who had been talking of grizzly bear, proposed to take a hunt, "for," said he, "this child savvy's a heap 'bout them. It's more nor ten year sence I've drawed 'bead' on antelope and 'black-tail,' and ef *some* meat as *is* meat hasn't 'come'—wagh! Away to the buttes, yonder, b'ar gangs plenty, an' this hos is fur some afore *'veheo esevone'*— 'white man's buffalo'—goes in his meatbag agin"—and so soliloquizing, he picked up his "bullthrower," as he fondly termed his rifle, with—"Hyar's for them buttes," pointing to some isolated hills, two miles to the south from camp, "b'ar's out playin' like Shian *ki kun* [children]."

Louy Simonds, jumping up with his ever-ready gun, knocked the ashes from his pipe; and, depositing it in a small leather pouch strung from his neck, black and greasy with time and perspiration, exclaimed—"This child never stuck around camp when work's on hand—hosguard, meat huntin', it's all the same to him; this 'mudhook,' holding out his foot, "hasn't a moccasin on for nothin', an' that's a fact!"

"Say! my young Shian trader, you's the chap what stayed with John Smith last winter; ef *you're* for b'ar, grab your lightnin'-stock [my rifle] and make 'Pimo' tracks for yon butte [I had a pair of Pimo Indian moccasins on, a present from Hatcher, who was then talking to me]. Away down to the Pimo country, nigh about the Heely [Gila], they make the best Injun shoe this coon ever put his foot in—well, hyar's for meat"; and off he started, Louy and myself in his wake.

The plain was covered with a low, spreading growth of cactus, and we continually had to cast an eye to our feet to avoid trampling on the bristling spines.

"Keep your eye skinned," said Hatcher, in a tone of warning, "them prickly pear is worse by a long chalk than nettles I used to see to Wapakonnetta settlement. When I was no higher 'an old 'bullthrower' here," touching his gun with his free hand, "I sometimes went out hunting with my old man—he was a keener at squirrels an' woodpeckers, an' so tall I had to rare back to look in his face, as tall as the cedars of Lebanon old Cormon talked about."

Within some hundred feet of the buttes, toward which, with elastic step, we had been advancing while listening to one of Hatcher's yarns, a band of nine deer sprung from a hollow, bounding along with heads high in air. Simultaneously our rifle reports rang out in the still afternoon; the graceful animals, frightened into greater speed, disappeared behind the rise. We now commenced the ascent of the hill, catching hold of bushes and rocks to assist us up its rugged front. Bending forward and cautiously proceeding, we walked under the trees, searching for fresh "sign" among the huge beartracks. Caching ourselves behind some detached fragments of coarse sandstone, we, in a low tone, conversed, while scanning the outstretched plain for the anticipated game.

Beneath us lay a gently undulating valley, destitute of trees, and which, swelling and receding, blended itself into handsome slopes beyond, covered with scrubby pine. At one side, removed a short distance, rose an easy eminence carpeted with grass and studded with groves of cedar and piñon, seemingly tended by other hands than those of Nature.

With eyes half-closed, I fancied myself in the shady orchards far away to the East, among venerable trees, never again to be reposed under with the same boyish pleasure. Interspersed in groups among the low clumps were bands of deer and antelope; some lying down, others cropping the tender blades of spring grass, and others skipping about, unconscious of danger. The waning sun shooting streams of mellow light through the dark-green foliage formed a constant change of scenery and tinged the valley with a sea of golden light, subduing the rougher features and harmonizing the whole.

In silence we enjoyed the delectable picture of peace and innocence, unwilling to fright the graceful herds with deadly rifle, or even with rude, but harmless, shout. To the north rose *Las Cumbres Españolas,* whose snow-wreathed crests glittering, the brightest gem of Nature's tiara in the Sierra Blanca, seemed to touch the sky. To the west, somber-hued Raton loomed up as the orb of day disappeared beyond. Rousing from the reverie, we retraced our steps with yet another look.

While at supper, a party of men rode up, the foremost of whom shook hands with Hatcher. It was the renowned *Kit Carson,* so celebrated as the companion and guide of Colonel Frémont. Without a desire to detract from Carson's well-earned fame, I can say, in genuine good feeling and full belief, that there are numbers of mountain men as fearless and as expert as he, though to the reading world little known, whose prowess in scalp taking and beaver trapping is the theme of many campfires, and the highest admiration of younger mountaineers.

Lieutenant Beale, United States Navy, Lieutenant Talbot, California Battalion, and several men dressed in California costume composed the rest of Carson's party. The high-pommeled saddles, large live-oak stirrups, and huge iron spurs, a few inlaid with silver, the rowels four and five inches in diameter, formed a unique appearance.

In the morning we gathered the stock and lassoed the

riding animals. My large beast, Diabolique (for never mule gave more trouble), was refractory, owing, in some degree, to the unusual quantity of good grass the preceding night. After repeated vexatious trials, I succeeded in "roping" her. Holding the lasso in one hand and two other mules by their bridles, I led them toward camp, jumping over an intervening mud hole, expecting them to follow. But no such thing! and, instead, astern flew their heads, and flat went I in the puddle. I then endeavored to drive them over, but they backed their ears preparatory to kicking the hind-sights off the first man that struck them. With a running noose over Diabolique's nose and a "heave-yo," I pulled lustily, but she held stiff her elongated neck and head, planted firmly her feet in front, and with strained eyeballs stood provokingly patient. How exquisitely malignant does one feel the "mounting devil in his heart" in such a position, and but for the want of her as a riding animal, a bullet would have been the reward of her stubbornness. Nor is this uncharitable feeling peculiar to myself; for there is yet the first amiable mule rider to be seen, as the best mule, at times, will become refractory, and from clubs and curses to refrain is a moral impossibility.

We stopped not the next day until four o'clock, when turning to the left, we encamped in a thick growth of underbrush. After helping unyoke, gather wood, etc., I went in quest of turkeys, piping hard by in the bushes, but a storm drove me to camp after an unsuccessful half hour's dripping bush skulking.

The rain falling fast, we sheltered ourselves, as we were able, until sunset; when, the weather clearing, we shot at targets until darkness consigned us to the miseries of a soaking-wet night. By twelve o'clock the next day, William Bent's camp was discernible in a bottom on the east bank of the Purgatoire, which we reached with some difficulty through the luxuriant growth of weeds, young timber, and across a deep ford. We pulled the saddles from the impatient mules a few feet of the conical Indian lodge, in which, at the back part, sat the host himself, cross-legged, on an outspread buffalo robe.

The spot selected for cultivation was in a handsome, level bottom, a mile in length, and from fifty to two hundred yards in width. The gentle curving of the shallow "River of Souls," its banks fringed with the graceful willow and thorny plum, on which were affectionately entwined the curling tendrils of the grape and hop; the grouping of the slender locust and the outspreading umbrageous cottonwoods, with the clustering currants, dotting the green sward, gave a sweet, cultivated aspect to the place; while the surrounding hills, within their sheltering embrace, seemed to protect the new enterprise. The *caballada*, half-hid in the luxuriant thickets, and the cows, standing idly over the running waters in the quiet shade, with whisking tail, and others in the secluded vistas, reposing in sheer plenitude, served much to increase the domestic countenance of the first farm on the Purgatoire.

William Bent's party consisted of himself, Long Lade, and two others. They had plows, and the *acequia*, by which the land would be irrigated, was nearly finished; the dam to elevate the water in this was yet to be constructed, so the following morning we went hard to work. For two days we labored as though the embryo crop depended upon our finishing within a specified time. When the water flowed in the *acequia*, we watched the bits of wood and scum floating with the first tide with intense interest and satisfaction.

In the course of my wanderings I met with men whose

strongest argument against farming in New Mexico was that the soil required irrigation, which mode I upheld as a certain means of insuring a good crop. But the valleys are the only portions thus capable of cultivation, and they bear a small proportion to the many thousand leagues of land too rough and too sterile for agricultural purposes. Years hence, sheep and cattle grazing may be profitably engaged in on the upland; now there is no market for the beef, and the depredatory character of the nomadic Indian tribes, deter men from certain tillage or herding.[1]

Frank De Lisle, with his wagons, from the Cimarone, joined us, he having left Bransford and the herders two days after our departure. His men were soon helping us with hearty good will; their garrulity and fun gave new life to our exertions, and their ox teams did most worthy service in hauling logs and brushwood to the dam.

[1] Bent and Hatcher's farm, of which I have just been speaking, was attacked by Indians, and the enterprising projectors forced to abandon their scheme, two months after I left the *Río Purgatorio*.

CHAPTER XXI

THE ARKANSAS

F<small>RANK STARTED</small> for Bent's Fort three days after his arrival, and I accompanied him. The morning the teams stretched up the gently rising hill, in commendable order, from the valley of *El Río de las Animas,* was one of the loveliest of balmy April. Our party was all animation and bustle; the shouts and songs of the ever-joyous teamsters were in consonance with the universal gaiety of Nature; the *"enfans," "diables," "sacrés"* had more than their usual music. Bands of bewildered antelope, dashing in all directions, afforded excitement, and rifles rung out sharply in no slow succession.

Our intention, when starting, was to make a near cut across the prairie, to the "Hole in the Rock," instead of the circuitous route up the Purgatoire, to regain the Bent's Fort trace. This near cut was destitute of water or shade, and by twelve o'clock the sun shone depressingly upon our heads, and the oxen worked slowly. Patches of verdure, in hollows, invited us from afar to search, though uselessly, for water, and the oft-seen optical delusion—*mirage*—showed that the glassy lakes on that prairie were a "vain and fleeting show." Though the spring was far advanced, the new grass was not in sufficient quantities for pasturage. A root (*Psorlea esculenta,* of the botanists) of good flavor, was found in hard, dry ground during the day's travel, and we dug with our butcher knives enough to but illy satisfy our own appetites.

Journeying until sunset, we dismounted to light a pipe. When the sun disappeared behind the snow hills to the west of *Las Cumbres Españolas,* we rode on. Night over-took us, still in the saddle; for yet two mortal hours we stumbled over the sidelong hills amid the fragments of sandstone. Right glad were we to reach the "Hole in the Rock," and we rushed to the puddle of lukewarm water, burying our burning faces in it and striking back the im-patient mules from intruding their dry, ugly mugs along-side of their masters'. Both man and beast drank nigh unto bursting, as they well might, after fourteen hours' ab-stinence in a sweltering sun. Hobbling the mules in a grassy spot and selecting a camp, we struck a blaze to direct the tired teamsters, whose urgings to the jaded yokes rolled up to us from the valley in the rear. Partaking of a hearty sup-per, I listened to their talking and singing—Edmond and Petout interpreting the burthen of their lays.

We found our mules at dawn *in statu quo,* otherwise, as hungry as when we left them the preceding night.

Sleeping, as we always did, without shelter overhead, the day-spring did not find us between the blankets; so, by the time the slanting sunbeams had ceased to peer under our hatbrims, we "rolled" along the elastic turf, with "Bent's Fort, ho!" as the watchword, for it was part of the way home—so gushing-full of melodious thought—so touching and so peaceful!

The route was long and dreary; no water by the way-side; and, at dusk, brackish, diminutive Timpa gave small comfort to our parched throats. This section of country, on the maps, is written as "desert"; if the total want of wood, the scanty presence of brackish water, much burning, sand-reflected heat during the day, and chill winds at night, would justify the topographers in marking such as desert, the lands on either side the Taos Trail, from the Hole in the Rock to the Arkansas, most certainly deserve the title.

While in motion the next morning, a party of men was descried coming. It proved to be Captain Jackson and his company of mounted men, en route for Santa Fé. Volunteer-like, they were in the rear, at the side, and in advance of their commander; they disregarding military deference, he military control. For a mile and a half, others were strung along the trace, in irregular squads, riding, sauntering carelessly, some without arms, and a few with muskets, beating the sage bushes for hares.

On passing the three baggage wagons, the first lieutenant—the same who helped the sheriff at the Taos execution—poked his head under the wagon sheet. He was in his shirt sleeves, his hair uncombed, and altogether he was a rare specimen of that peculiar genus known as a Missouri volunteer officer. He shouted as I passed—

"How are ye—would ye like to hang any more Mexicans? Now wasn't that a tall time down to Touse!"

Judging from all appearances, discipline had been drummed out of the service some time previous to our meeting with the company; for they seemed to have no knowledge of anything relative to their position, except that they were entitled every day to three-fourths of a pound of mess pork or "Ned," a pound of superfine flour, and as much coffee as could conveniently be stowed away 'neath their dingy blue jacket. Despite their seeming want of the attributes of soldiers, they astonish the braggadocio New Mexicans in battle or *fandango* amazingly.

It is an irresistible inference to draw from the premises our volunteer service affords that Americans born were never intended to fight under the strict discipline of the regular service. Deference and subordination they learn neither as children nor as men—and an army of invasion is a poor school to remedy the defect in education.

We stopped for noon camp on the trail, without water, as the grass was good and the oxen tired. A keg half-full from the salty Timpa served to make a decoction of coffee, and, with unbolted Mexican flour and bacon grease, a thick mush was manufactured. We ate from the pan in which it was cooked, each one replenishing the point of his well-licked butcher knife from the *one* dish, until the greasy mass had vanished. We then stopped and looked at each other with that hungry, ill-satisfied stare which, had there been but *human* about, might, by the timid, have been mistaken for the glare of cannabalism.

After dinner, De Lisle, Ed ——, and myself pushed on for the river, leaving the wagons to follow as they could. It was oppressively warm (hot), and we wilted in the heat as weeds. Coming in sight of the low bluffs beyond the Arkansas, we met one of Captain Jackson's company, trudging on foot. He had stopped at Bent's Fort while the company preceded him, and when we met him, he was *solus*, afoot in the broiling sun, and his mouth so dry his articulation was quite indistinct. A canteen, filled with molasses costing two dollars, he was willing to give for one drink of water, but we, unfortunately, had none, and the poor fellow trudged on again, carrying with him our pity, at least.

In the Arkansas we gulped again and again of the warm stream, returning to it a half-dozen times. By dusk, we entered the heavy-browed far gateway, glad, in truth, to rest in security. Captain Enos, Doctor Hempstead, Messrs. Drinker, Holt, and others extended to me the hand of friendship; books were plenty, and my rifle once more quietly occupied its corner. Buchanan, of winter-bathing memory, was to start to the States in a few days with a return train. He invited me to share his comforts. In the large corral outside the fort were a hundred wild and foolish mules starving into tractability.

Putting my "possibles" in a wagon, I received my account of coffee, sugar, etc., from the affable Doctor Hempstead. There was much bustle the day we started; the mules brayed impatiently through hunger, thirst, and confinement; the teamsters shouted, and whined, and cursed the foolish teams who appeared to have forgotten, during the winter's grazing on the wild hills, that there were such words in the ox, mule, and teamster vocabulary as "wo-ha" and "gee." By the time the train was fairly in motion, my little Bonita, decked with a blue blanket, and firmly-strapped saddle, pranced before the gate in impatient glee.

I bade my friends "good-bye" with feelings of regret, but the idea of turning my face to the States much alleviated the pain of parting; and thus, a shade of melancholy mingled with recollections of home produced an equilibrium, sometimes upturned by the recurrence of a good story, jovial campfire, or image of a clever *compañero* to my memory, but again restored, by thought equally fascinating, far more pure, of a tranquil home, where could be relaxation from the responsibility of self-preservation and cares, vexations, and burdening. When the somber bastions faded at last from view, I felt as can none but those alike circumstanced. There were a few men for whom I acknowledged an attachment. One of them was Hatcher. To manifest my regard for him as was in my power, I left, in a box securely nailed, some hundreds of waterproof caps, my backgammon board, and a few useful volumes to while away with profit a spare hour on his Purgatoire farm.

The rude American teamster in place of the polite Canadian, coarse jokes instead of *voyageur* yarns, and other changes for the worse made me sadly experience the parting from mountain joys. The charm of my backwoods life was broken, though nearly seven hundred miles intervened between me and civilization; and notwithstanding the toil, hardship, and danger commingled with the loved scenes I was quitting, many a backward glance did I cast on the homeward trail.

We made camp in a bottom opposite the mouth of the Purgatoire. Captain Enos, Mr. Drinker, and others composed one mess, with Rosalie for cook. She was Ben Raymond's wife, a half-breed French and Indian—bye-the-bye, a most diabolical compound—the woman he enticed from Ed—the inconsolable carpenter at Bent's Fort. Ours was a jolly mess, and composed of the best men in camp, viz: Buck, or Buchanan, Tom Sloan, Rhodes, Knowles, and Sam Caldwell. We progressed admirably—every man helping. We lived better than the other messes, except the captain's, for at the Fort we purchased pepper, pepper sauce, and other rarities. Tin plates—one degree of civilization above my past five months' experience—were used at supper.

In the morning, I made a detour of two hours' fast riding, through a large bottom, while the wagons, going across, were hid by bluffs. I was alone, on the *qui vive* for game; when the road was regained, I saw, by looking at the track, that the party had not passed; selecting a good spot of grass, I undid the trail rope from the saddle pack, and let Bonita feed until the train came up.

Ours was a motley party, having for its composition Captain Enos, A.Q.M.U.S.A., commanding; the rest were wagon masters, teamsters, and amateurs. George F. Ruxton, the English traveler, with two men, here joined our party. Mr. R. was a quiet, good-looking man, with a handsome moustache. He conversed well, but sparingly, speaking little of himself. He has passed over the burning sands of Africa, penetrated the jungles of India, jogged on patient mule through the *Tierra Caliente* of Mexico, and laid down amid the snowdrifts of the Rocky Mountains. The same day Mr. Ruxton joined us, Davis, Brackenridge, Step, and a California Indian, members of Kit Carson's escort from California, added somewhat to our numerical, and incalculably to our fighting, strength; for they have stood the shock of more than one Indian skirmish, and have led the van, at a sweeping gallop, through many a dangerous mountain pass, with rifles cocked and unconfined hair streaming—the mountaineer's pennon. With Brackenridge and party were left the broken-down mules, to recruit by rest and grass.

While in advance of the train with Mr. Ruxton and the Californians, a large, gaunt, white wolf, leaping from his lair in the long bottom weeds, scudded across the prairie for the distant hills. Davis and I raised the view halloo, and gave chase. Together with our yelling and spurring, it made quite an exciting run. I was first in, but as Davis ought to have had, by right of seniority, the first shot, I yielded the honor; he declined, and I, bringing up my rifle, crashed a ball through the wolf's head.

The following afternoon, we passed the spot where had been the Cheyenne village—the scene of so much novelty and interest to me the preceding winter.

Three of the mule teams made handsome runaways,

streaking it over the level ground at a great rate, with the light wagons rattling at their heels; but the skillfulness of the drivers prevented any accident.

"Pretty Encampment," the loveliest on the river, with its glossy-leaved cottonwoods, was that evening early our home. Half a mile above was the Cheyenne village. Many of the savages who thronged the camp uttered the well-known *"Hook-ah-hay, Numwhit,"* as they took my hand. A party coming in from a buffalo hunt—the veritable John Smith at their head—stopped; we had a cordial embrace. His lodge, pitched with the rest, his squaw, son, and other "sign," proclaimed him an Indian—almost. On returning to camp from a visit to the village, I found that *Buck* had traded my best blanket to a squaw for a robe worked with porcupine quills and beads.

When the train straightened out in the trail after sunrise, I was surprised to find Smith, his family, lodge dray, and *caballada* bringing up the rear. He was engaged the evening previous by Captain Enos to take charge of the fort now in progress of erection on the Santa Fé Trail, twenty miles below the Cimarone crossing, and for which the six-pounder, mounted on light wagon wheels and drawn in front of the train, was intended to deal death to the presumptuous Camanche. A long frontier residence and knowledge of Indian character would seem to qualify Smith particularly for the station of commander of a fort in this country.

Buffalo were in sight, and one was killed by Mr. Ruxton. A man who had for some weeks been sick with the scurvy died while the train was in motion—the hot sun and want of proper attention hastened his death. Our mess was detailed to bury him, and on a knoll overlooking camp, we dug a grave, not quite three feet in depth, the sun broiling us the meanwhile. Taking hold of the blanket in which he died, we laid him on the ground, searched his clothing for papers and money, and, rolling him up as we found him and without ceremony, deposited him in his last home on earth. The burial was mere form, for the wolves scratch up the bodies again, and often before we were out of sight, the prairie ghouls were at their horrid work.

Another man died, and while the teams were being yoked up before starting the next morning, a grave was dug. A man, after hitching up his team, pulled off his coat to put it in his wagon; in there he found a man stiff in death. The poor fellow alone and without a groan had passed away. The corpse was quickly taken out, another hole, scarce deep enough to hide him, scraped, the earth rudely shoveled back, the cry "drive on" given by the captain, and the two men were left on the desolate, wind-swept prairie, without even a simple board to mark the spot where lay their wasted, pain-released frames. Dolefully howling wolves, loping around camp, waited impatiently for our departure, to scatter with ravenous jaws the tattered blanket shrouds of the unfortunates.

Step and I were out for buffalo. We "crawled," unsuccessfully, for a band of cows on our knees, and returned to the train, which was corralling. Repairs being necessary, camp remained stationary the rest of the excessively warm day; Mr. Ruxton, Brackenridge, and myself, wanting "fat cow," started on foot for the numerous bands to the eastward literally blackening the hazy river bottom. As we drew nigh, old bulls, with tufted tails high in air in token of defiance, pawed the ground in impotent rage; discretion getting the better part of valor, they lumbered heavily before us, starting, to our vexation, other valorous knights of the "juicy hump" from quiet grazing, and driving in the picket guards of frequent bands of fleet-footed cows. Three miles fast walking brought us to a favorable position for crawling; under cover of weeds, we sent, simultaneously, our bullets into the unconscious band. Fatigued by walking in the hot sun, our aim was not steady, though two of the running herd halted often in their flight. We followed fast; again we fired, not altogether without effect, and, but for our impolitic presence, one would have stopped. He limped on slowly, we too tired to pursue.

We retraced our steps, our eyes aching with the intense heat and pained by the sun's glimmering reflection from the saline efflorescence whitening the cracked and parched ground. The mirage, reducing objects animate and inanimate to a state of uncertainty, afforded no relief. Mr. R. told us of his sufferings on the African deserts and of the unhospitable character of the natives. But contrast with worse sufferings brought us no succor. We longed to stop in some sylvan grove and, amid the murmur of tinkling waterfalls, to be lulled to refreshing slumbers; but no such joys awaited us. All was reduced to hateful reality. We saw no relief but by slow and patient toiling. I bore up under the combined influence of the sun and thirst, until sinking to the ground scarcely able to move; but through the persuasion of my friends, I slowly walked to the river, they very kindly stopping with me every little while, where we buried our faces in the lukewarm water. That afternoon's tramp almost finished me.

Davis and I crossed the river for the favorite game when the train left camp. We crawled in the hot sand, stuck our knees and fingers with burrs, but no buffalo could be induced to stay and be shot at. We kept the same side until the wagons "nooned." Opposite we were fortunate in finding the decaying fragments of an Indian bulwark. Loading ourselves with pieces of wood, we rode across; the teamsters, unyoking hastily, hurried over for the remaining fuel. The river was not knee-deep; in places the sand was washed out, leaving holes, into which the hunger-impelled teamsters stumbled in reckless haste, getting themselves and burdens soaked, much to the amusement of the lookers on.

When anything relative to eating was concerned, the United States employees were active enough; when performing work—'t would make one's head ache to see their slow motions.

Many employees were afflicted with the scurvy—a disease brought on by great change from their usual diet to superfine flour and fat mess pork. First the tendons under the knee contract, the leg mortifies; the patient lays and limps around camp, at the same time possessing a morbid, ravenous appetite for strong food; a dysentery reduces him to mere skin and bones, and he dies. His body, revolting to the sight, is rolled in blankets, and the unclean mass thrust hastily in a mere hole, only to be disinterred and gnawed by wolves. Dependent on themselves for medicine, they suffer much. Several poor fellows were far gone in the disease; an anodyne which I had, relieved them.

We became more circumspect in our wanderings, and the wagons loitered not behind; for the dreaded Camanche and his savage competitor, the Pawnee, claim the region over which we were journeying as their own, to be preserved inviolate from the track-leaving, wood-wasting, and game-scaring white man. We passed the Cimarone crossing; and, by noon of the 15th of May, we were at Mann's Fort, on the Arkansas.

CHAPTER XXII

SERVICE

The fort was simply four log houses connected by angles of timber framework, in which were cut loopholes for the cannon and small arms. In diameter the fort was about sixty feet. The walls were twenty in height.

Outside, forty men were making adobes for chimneys. They supposed our advance party Indians, but discovering us to be "true men," they testified their delight by repeated glad cheers at the prospect of being relieved and returning home.

First, I should say who these men were, and for what purpose they were here sent. A station, equidistant from Fort Leavenworth and Santa Fé, was needed by the government, at which to repair the wagons and recruit the animals, by rest, in safety. In accordance with this want, Captain Enos sent Mr. Mann, a wagon master, with forty teamsters and several yoke of oxen, to build, in an eligible site below the crossing of the Cimarone, a log fort and blacksmith shop.

Six days before our arrival, a small party of Camanches shot and lanced a man fishing in the river, not three hundred yards from the fort, in sight of the forty armed men; then, waving the reeking scalp aloft with yells of triumph and derision, they retreated to the plain unharmed.

Two days subsequent to the above, fifteen yoke of oxen

and forty mules—these latter staked within seventy yards around the fort—were carried off by the Indians, who, driving a loose band of their own animals before them, with startling yells created a stampede, in which those of the fort joined, jerking up their picket pins in the furor.

But the whites were not altogether idle. Flying shots were exchanged; one savage fell, but was borne off between two fellow warriors, at a fast gallop.

In consequence of the above forays, timidity became a second nature to the teamsters, and they ventured not to show their uncomfortable countenances outside the gate. All were determined to go to the "States," and Captain Enos found much difficulty in persuading enough to remain to guard the fort. "We don't care to stay here on fat pork and be scalped by the Injuns," was their usual reply to the Captain. After two days' persuasion, he induced nine men to stop by offering ten dollars in addition to their present wages, making thirty dollars per month and rations. As I had never been in an Indian fight, nor had ever seen service, and as Smith, my old friend, was to be in command, I concluded, for excitement's sake, to join them.

On presenting myself to Captain Enos, he raised his eyes in surprise; for my trip to the country was one of pleasure, and to voluntarily enter into such dangerous service astonished him. Drinker, Davis, Brackenridge, and others endeavored to dissuade me from my purpose; but, thanking them for their solicitude, I refused to leave.

The next day Captain Enos left. Drinker[1] shook hands with me at the fort entrance. He and I had traveled more than eight hundred miles in company—chilled through by the same blasts—wet by the same rains; and, part of the time, covered by the same blankets. Davis and Bracken-

[1] He is now dead.

ridge[2] were fine, gentlemanly fellows. Their manners and conversation were most acceptable on the route down. Though Mr. Ruxton[3] and I were not well acquainted and although he partook somewhat of his national reserve, we parted as became fellow-travelers.

A guard was mounted on one of the houses as soon as the train was in motion. As they receded in the distance, a slight feeling of fear and loneliness ran through me, decreased not a whit by the sight of our own few numbers. The large gates—two ponderous wooden puncheon concerns, a foot in thickness, were to be swung on wooden hinges, which operation, together with relieving the guard, occupied us until night.

We were now alone, that is, ten well men and three sick ones; these last doomed to many a weary hour of unheeded pain, not within our power to alleviate by healing medicine or nourishing food. Our fighting force was as follows:

[2] They were with Frémont in his disastrous trip across a Rocky Mountain pass in 1849, in which several men and all the animals perished with hunger and cold.

[3] Mr. Ruxton published, after his return, a highly entertaining work, entitled *Adventures in Mexico and the Rocky Mountains*—a book well deserving popularity. When at Buffalo, in August, 1848, I saw in the throng awaiting admission to the dining room a moustache which struck me as familiar. After dinner, advancing to the wearer, I said—"How do you do, Mr. Ruxton?" He did not recognize me; my greasy buckskins, old wool hat, hickory shirt, and moccasins having been exchanged for more civilized habiliments; and, to aid his memory, I said—"Don't you recollect the wolf chase near Tharpe's bottom; the little sorrel mule, Bonita, and its owner stopping at Mann's Fort?" He then immediately called me by name. Retiring to one side, we had a talk of old scenes, his book, and other matters. Of the Blackwood series of *Life in the Far West*, then in course of publication, he acknowledged the authorship. He was then on his way to the mountains—that afternoon he left, but the poor fellow died in St. Louis. He was a true gentleman, and his loss is much to be deplored.

CAPTAIN
John Simpson Smith

MEN

Thomas Sloan	James Strickler	Ben Raymond
—— Johnson	Samuel Caldwell	Andrew ——
—— Roy	L. H. Garrard	William Taylor

— ALSO —
One six-pound cannon
Forty rounds of grape and canister
Forty cannon cartridges
Six rifles and seven muskets

In addition, Smith had his squaw and two children; Raymond his half-breed Rosalie, which, with Smith's seven mules and horses, Raymond's one, my two, three old government scarecrows, and five broken-down United States steers, was the sum total of all the objects—animate and inanimate, offensive and inoffensive, with the exception of Rosalie's diminutive fiïst and an Indian cur, scarce half made up—left to vegetate in the "Prairie Prison," aptly so called; for even a visit to the river for water, a hundred yards distant, required the bucket in one hand—the rifle in the other.

We felt this to be a small band to guard a fort in the Pawnee and Camanche range—both tribes noted for their dexterity and willingness to take the white man's "hair" or his *caballada*.

Being possessed of writing materials, I was made clerk to keep account of rations issued and chronicler of events, such as passing trains. In addition, the office of orderly sergeant devolved upon me, the duties of which consisted in arranging the night sentries. There were ten men, including Smith, and *calling* from twilight to dawn ten hours, we made five watches of two hours' duration each—two men on duty at once; the first standing until the evening star sank beneath the horizon, which, though more than the allotted period, made not much difference, as it was in the fore part of the night. When the first watch "guessed" his time had expired, they awoke the next on duty, who repeated the process, and so on through. Smith and I were on first watch; and to avoid contention or dissatisfaction, the first guard was second the next night, third the next, and so on through—those behind filling up the vacancy.

Two were appointed as day sentries—a permanent office, they doing nothing else. At his own request, seconded by our wishes, Strickler was *promoted* to the office of cook; and he so exerted his culinary skill as to make the monotonous rations quite palatable. Smith's squaw cooked for him; Rosalie for Raymond and Taylor.

On the 18th May, we built of adobes, on the northwest house and its corresponding diagonal, a breastwork, for a defense against the wind as well as arrows. The waterproof roofs were flat, being made of small poles, laid parallel, with six inches of mud piled on and an inclination of one and a half inches to the yard. Standing guard was anything but pleasant, and, at night, exceedingly dreary. Smith would mount post on the roof for a while, and I, down below, would creep from port to port, now listening for the foe—now seated on the cannon, holding my breath at the least sigh of the winds. In pacing my lonely walk, I was filled with gloomy forebodings. The wind whistled a mournful tune—the damp, fitful gusts nearly overturned me in their suddenness. Scarce fifteen yards distant, brutal wolves fought over the grave of the murdered man. A large white one, whose faint outline I could see below me, gave a most unearthly howl, which going out in the stillness, sent back its lonely echo from the distant hills, and which met a response from others afar, who, with fiend-like screams, congregated under the walls, growling and bristling in fearful wrath, or continuously loped around the fort in hungry expectation. When relieved from watch, I nestled in my warm blankets, and, after sending, mentally, the Pawnees and accursed wolves *a los diablos*, I dropped into an inappreciable state of blessed forgetfulness, to be waked at sunrise with the cry of "Turn out!"

Rain and wind were our uninterrupted visitations for two days. The animals had to be picketed close—the sentry meanwhile keeping vigilant lookout. At night we brought them inside the fort.

Callahan, a trader, passed on the 20th of May, to the States. He was from Chihuahua, and short of provision. Smith, empowered to hire men for the "fort service," induced one young man to stay who was journeying with the train without leave, license, or provender. Sloan, in his fondness for nicknames, called him *Rasamus Cowhorn*, a cognomen which clung so tenaciously to the young gentleman we never knew his right one.

Sam Caldwell and I were now on the same guard. Smith reposed undisturbed through the night. One of the guard fell asleep on his post, for which he received a reprimand, interlarded with expressive terms from Smith, and no gentle *hint* from all, that a repetition of the same would subject him to a tying across the cannon with the accompanying jerking!

In the afternoon succeeding the above transaction, Roy, a heedless fellow, on one of Smith's animals and two in

lead, and I on Bonita, with Diabolique in tow at the end
of a rawhide lariat, crossed the river for grass. We were
barebacked, our guns in hand, and the slippery mules rendered the possession of our seats uncertain. A gun fired
from the fort was to be the signal of danger. We were a
mile off, lying down talking, the mules quietly grazing,
when the full heavy sound of the gun was heard. Snatching
my blanket with one hand, and with Diabolique's lead
rope and my gun in the other, I started after Roy. The
animals, as if interpreting our wishes, went in a full run
from the start. With rifles ready to fire, we came within a
hundred yards of the river, where Diabolique broke from
me, galloping up the river bank, head and tail high, neighing and frantic. "There goes eighty dollars," thought I, but
no time for calculation when probably the whole tribe of
yellowskins were at our heels. Off flew my hat to the breeze;
now we plunged into the water, jamming against each
other; when halfway across, Diabolique, with streaming
tail, widespread nostrils, and wild eye, charged in among us.

Our excited friends met us at the entrance; the sentry
shouted to hurry. We barred the gate, drew tightly our
belts, and fixed on guncaps anew, when the party bearing
down on us proved to be a band of wild horses, scudding
northward some two miles to the east. After a talk and
recovery from the fluttering effects of the false alarm,
Johnson and I waded the river, where we picked up my
hat and baited a wolf trap.

With the forewheels of the cannon wagon, we carried
adobes and stiff mud for mortar, to build chimneys to the
blacksmith shop and the messroom. Luckily, Captain
Mann's party made enough adobes to last some time, for
small fun was it to mold brick. On the evening of the 23d,
a train of wagons came in sight and encamped above the

Caches, much to our disappointment, as we wished to meet with them. The next morning they stopped in the road opposite the fort, and the men came to see us.

It was Bent & St. Vrain's company. William Tharpe, an Indian trader, had joined them with his wagons for safety. Mr. Holt, the fort storekeeper, Ed, the Frenchman, whose squaw was enticed away by Raymond, and Frank De Lisle, the wagon master, were all in the train on the way home. Charlotte, the cook (who, with her husband was set free, by the company, for the valor evinced by the latter, Dick, at the Pueblo de Taos), also grinningly showed her ivory as I extended my hand. After greeting warmingly Edmond Paul and Petout, my two Canadian friends, I gave them the thirty days' rations of flour and coffee I had purchased at Bent's Fort, for which they kindly thanked me. Traders do not provision themselves well, and these clever fellows were "feasting" on "poor bull."

Smith, who had been showing, in private conversation with me, a fear of losing his hair, gave notice of leaving with this train, which stopped while he collected his possibles. While on guard together, he often told me the utter folly, the downright madness, of staying in the fort at the mercy of the Indians, and that his pay would be nothing in comparison to the loss of his animals and the risk of life. To the men his reasons were plausible enough; his animals, picketed around the fort, were starving, and that he would go with this train, and let them feed on good grass every night until he would meet a train to return to us. Knowing this to be his intention, I sent Bonita and Diabolique along with the band, for the risk in keeping them was greater, in fact, than letting them go. It was a trial to part with Bonita; indeed I felt nearer to him than to any of my friends. When I tied the lariat about his neck, and gave him a good-bye pat with my hand, he broke away, kicking and shaking his long ears joyously, and with head to the ground, joined, neighing in delight, the *cabellada*.

It was difficult to withstand the solicitations of my friends to leave, but my promise to stay had to be complied with, however earnestly I wished to be with them. Our brave commander, squaw, and Jack were pleased with the change. Little Jack had contributed much to my happiness; for, although he could not talk American, the sight to me was as an oasis in the desert. Among rough men, and no kind words, Jack, at least, was not void of childish affection, and to amuse and talk to him recalled home and cheerful retrospections.

CHAPTER XXIII

A WELCOME ARRIVAL

THE LOSS of Smith we all felt, for he was of an agreeable temperament. Sloan was now in command, though from Roy's turbulent disposition we anticipated difficulty. I retained my position, and Sloan was pleased to be lenient in his requisitions on my time for labor, thus giving me opportunity for enlarging the small journal noted elsewhere. He wished me, however, not to incur the ill will of the rest by abusing the privilege.

The morning following the departure of Smith, we carried charcoal from the pit to the intended "shop." With coffee sacks on our shoulders, we lifted until our appearance would have well vied with that of a city charbonnier. Dirty work it was to be sure, but necessity overcame any scruples on the subject, and we began to think our thirty dollars and rations rather a poor compensation for so small a sprinkling of adventure and so much hard work.

The morning of the 26th, there being a cessation of hostilities on the mud brick and coal pit, I improved the time by lying full length on a plank in a cool corner of the messroom, my rifle within reach (for our guns and selves were "one and inseparable"), when the cry of "Indians! Indians!" from Taylor, the sentry, set me miraculously quick on my feet. I rushed into the sleeping apartment and back again before finding my gun, so bewildered was I by the startling announcement. Seizing it, I helped the men run the cannon to the gate. Near were some eight or ten mounted Indians, striving to take our little band of animals. Andrew, with lumbering musket, blazed harmlessly away. A party dashed furiously up from the plain, and others rode back and forth with glistening lance and spotless shield; while in the narrow strip of wood fringing the river, some hundred yards distant, the dusky forms of the foe could be seen gliding hastily toward us. Caldwell, understanding more of gunnery than the rest, pointed the piece at the nearest squad, Sloan adjusted the burning match, and I primed the touchhole.

There was a scene. Sam Caldwell, a six-foot, three-inch man, encased in a flaming red-flannel shirt and in a stooping position, moved the piece carefully, sighting with his fine eye, and waiting for the command from Sloan—a little to one side, Sloan himself, with fiery beard and moustache of no small pretensions, intently watching the maneuvers of the savages—there Bill Taylor, with his mouth thoughtlessly open, leaning against the portal, a long government blunderbuss at rest in the bend of his arm, and nearer the gateway, in attitudes of indecision, stood Rasamus Cowhorn, Cain, and Andrew, not more interesting than usual, except their perturbed countenances were robbed of the bloom of health at other times apparent. Close to Sam was myself, feeling first rate, as I thought at the time—but perhaps an egotistical description had better be omitted. Imagine this in a flat bottom, wearing away undulatingly to the low hills in the background, and along whose base, in the glimmering distance, irregular bands of horsemen fast clattered toward us; on the other hand, the placid Arkansas, winding its tortuous course between lonely and barren banks, with straggling cottonwoods to mark the course, then a small log fort, discernible at no great distance through its insignificancy, and at the gate of which scarce ten men, grouped around a six-pounder, waited in stern silence for greater demonstration of war from the foe ere the commencement of bloodshed.

The Indians were close to our horses, three hundred yards from us, and attempting to drive them away. They then charged toward us, and we fell back from the cannon, while the match descended; they, seeing the piece, beat a hasty retreat. One presumptuous warrior, on a fine black horse, dashed at Sloan's picketed mule in desperation; he left again with several balls whistling about his ears. We could have easily killed several of the foe, but warfare once commenced, we might have fared badly in the end; so we were amicably disposed. One old fellow, seeing that we had decidedly the advantage, dismounted, and, coming within two hundred yards, took the robe from his shoulders, sat down, rose and shook the buffalo again, to show that he was unarmed, and with other signs, meant, as I judged, *peace*.

Roy, placing confidence in my knowledge of Indian signs, met the warrior under range of the cannon, telling us, "If the Indian jumped on him, to blaze away and kill both!" They shook hands but could effect nothing, so Roy called for me; with the aid of signs and the Cheyenne tongue, they proved to be Arapahoes. Two others came up, and then two of our men. I told them their warriors must go away; the first man arose, and by some fancy manipulations, dispersed them. The spokesman then commenced an excuse for their presence by professing great friendship for the whites, saying that his object in calling was to inform us—"That the Camanches were in great numbers at a small stream, a day's ride to the east, and were to make

a descent upon us [that we doubted not], and that had it
not been for the Arapaho chiefs, our fort would have been
taken."

This, with a lot of other stuff, he told, which wound up
with a request for tobacco. We set before them coffee and
bread, and my long pipe, Roy and I smoking with them
on the prairie, peace and good will—our men the while
keeping vigilant watch from the fort to prevent surprise.
As we wished them not to spy out the nakedness of the
land, the guests were not allowed to approach nearer than
fifty yards of the fort. In a short while they left. Though
the Indians came undoubtedly with hostile intention, so
soon as they found our power superior to theirs, they, having confidence in us (or any other white man), sent a messenger to confer with us. Reverse the matter, wagh! the
white scalp would be off in a hurry.

The next day a buffalo, breasting the breeze, hove in
sight on the hill back—a good sign of the presence of Indians, as they never travel adverse to the wind, or come to
the river but for water, of which there was abundance
everywhere on the prairie by reason of the recent rains—
and Roy, with his usual heedlessness, started in pursuit,
killing it. He came to the fort, saddled a horse to get the
meat, but had scarcely reached it, when we, who had been
watching, saw him urging his horse in a full run on the
backtrack, with three yelling Camanches at his heels. We
greeted him with a shout of glee as he cut around to the
gate.

Supper was at sundown; and after which we generally
congregated on the sentry's house, to smoke and talk, with
guns in repose on the arm, to make shots at the skulking
coyotes, who not infrequently took ugly balls with them
in the ignominious flight. The sun in setting cast flickering

beams far up on the meandering, broad-sheeted Arkansas, and shone on the numerous verdure-teeming islands. The slow winging of a forsaken-looking crane, or the more merry flight of smaller birds up the stream, darting into the glittering spot, to disappear as if by magic, often excited our attentive admiration. But it was our favorite pastime, after a day's work, with plenty within and a pipe without, to stretch out on the flat roof and listen to the yarns spun by the different fellows.

Sam Caldwell had been on shipboard much of his life, and amused us in his style and broadly-pronounced "a's." Sloan was a blacksmith, with stories of a prosy, every-day nature. He joined a company of horse-soldiers for the war and Santa Fé, but it was rejected by reason of the requisition being filled before the tender of its services, and so he started out as extra teamster "to see the country anyhow." He received, at Mann's Fort, sixty dollars per month and rations.

Cain Strickler was a schoolmaster, nineteen years of age (he and I the youngest), and somewhat green; his teaching was a good exemplification of "the blind leading the blind." He was from Virginia ("of the first families," of course), and, being on a tour to Missouri at the commencement of the Mexican War excitement, was seized with a desire to see the oft-vaunted "elephant," so he started out as teamster. He was, however, apt, and though he never learned cards before this trip, the way he went ahead of the fellows playing poker put him at once in that class called "hopeful."

Roy was rather mysterious, and from circumstantial evidence we found that he had been in a penitentiary. He was heedless of danger and hardened in feelings; to his former state's imprisonment we attributed his recklessness.

When his acquaintance of Captain Enos's company bade him good-bye, they said—

"Roy, we never expect to see you again, you are so foolhardy—the Indians will have your hair yet." This proved but too true.

Andrew, whose last name I have forgotten, was from the Platte purchase, in Missouri. He was principal witness in a murder case; and, being of a malleable temperament, was bribed with a horse and considerable money to perjure himself, and then to leave the country. We ascertained a few leading facts, and, by Sloan's skillful queries, we learned the whole state of the case. He swore not to return to Missouri.

Rasamus Cowhorn was another genius. He left the States a year before, as teamster to a trader's train—went to Chihuahua—was at the battle of Sacramento, and told great tales of bombshells, cannon balls, valorous Mexicans, and smoke; and was now on his way home sans the needful. He remained at our fort some days on trial, helping us eat our rations. The wolf-like appetite manifested for a week was alarming; when his gastronomic demands slackened in a degree, Smith hired him.

On the 28th of May, we noticed an approaching body of men, and finding them Indians, we stopped work, shut the gates, and lounged with guns freshly capped.

Two riding up to the wall, I saluted them in the Cheyenne tongue. They were Arapahoes and wished to come in, but that was against orders. I asked for Warratoria (the most peaceable and renowned of their chiefs), and was told he soon would arrive. They then wanted *veheo mah-pe* (whiskey). Being negatively answered, they, much dissatisfied, rode off. The sight of the lodge drays, squaws, children, and dogs recalled many thoughts most gratifying.

The Indian encampment was three hundred yards above us on the river bank.

When Warratoria came, he was admitted, though Sloan much distrusted him. I made his acquaintance in the Cheyenne village, and knew his friendly disposition toward the whites and the good effect it would have to treat him with confidence. Shaking hands as old friends and inviting him into the messroom, we set before him coffee, bread, and the long pipe. The chief wished "Beardy's" presence, which after a while was granted. He is so called from a tuft of hair growing on the point of his chin, which gave him an odd appearance. His features were coarse, inclining to sensuality. Warratoria's face, on the contrary, wore a benign expression, and the slight furrows of age were so tempered as to give his countenance a cast of deep thought; his expansive brow, slightly receding, was worthy of a statesman. I was filled with reverence for the old man, though he was but an ignorant savage. He spoke in short sentences only, so different from the volubility of most savages, though many persons give them the character for taciturnity, as if conscious of the lasting impression he was making on me.

In an hour, the pyramidal lodges dotted the ground at irregular distances; before the larger ones, the stainless shield and *medicine bag*, with blue-enrolled pipe stems, were supported on the three whitened wands. Where, a short while before, lay a bare spot of turf, was now the site of eighty lodges, nearly three hundred human beings, and eleven hundred horses capering, rolling, and cropping the sweet bottom grass. The girls, from twelve years up to womanhood, waded the river for fuel; some crossing, a few returning laden with sticks, others carrying water, and all laughing, talking, and splashing. Boys played their favorite game of arrows, or astride of ponies, ran races over the smooth prairie. This commingled scene of comfort, youth, and hilarity brought back, with yearnings for a repetition, last winter's experience.

Sam Caldwell and I visited them without other weapon than butcher knives, for we felt little danger while the cannon ranged the village and the two principal chiefs were in the fort. A guard was at the gate to admit or shoo out the few savages having the "freedom" of the place, but we were impolitic in discovering our weak force to them. A queer-looking case begged of Sam and me powder and ball, with a load or two of which we satisfied him. He had an old English carbine, with "George" and a crown on the barrel—the property, most likely, of a *pelado*, whose scalp was now the decoration of some coup-loving Arapaho.

We noticed great commotion on reaching the fort again. The villagers hurried in the direction whence they that morning came—soon returning, triumphantly, with a young man who had been taken prisoner by a trading party in a skirmish two days before. We now found out that the braves of this village were leagued with the Camanches in attacking trains. To the surprise and great joy of the Indians, the prisoner was set at liberty—a different fate from that a captive experiences at their hands. The traders had given the young man a new blanket and ornaments; but, as the Indians had outraged the expected wagons, they struck their lodges, pitching them a half mile from the fort.

A train from Santa Fé, in command of Captain Fowler, arrived during the day, corralling a few steps from the gate. A Mexican *ranchero* was in company—like his brothers, with national peculiarity in features and expression.[1]

[1] This same Mexican, with one of Fowler's men, was scalped by the Comanches three days after leaving the fort. The poor *pelado* had the skin stript from just above the scalp, leaving a rim of hair by the ears and on the neck; yet, strange to say, he lived for a month after.

Sloan employed a young man, John Nagle by name, for the "fort service." His mule he sold to a teamster for forty dollars. We shut the gate at the usual hour, mounted guard as if alone, being more apprehensive of the light-fingered teamsters, after a winter's sojourn in Santa Fé, than of the Indians.

We hauled wood while there was a large numerical force by the fort, not daring to venture while alone. We fastened the gates, and leaving two on guard, crossed the river astride the coupling pole of a wagon, holding on with one hand and clenching our rifles in the other. Sloan sat on the fore standard, examining the edge of an ax; Bill Taylor, with bawling voice and an ox whip, kept up "steam." Johnson, who was an adept in the wood line, during the rest intervals told of his questionable feats in cording steamboat wood on the Missouri River. Cain Strickler and I did our best at loading. We threw the wood from the wagon into the fort yard, not caring to give the teamsters a chance to supply their fires at our expense.

The Indians, striving to trade with the wagoners, became quite troublesome; they would endeavor to drive the Arapahoes away by cries of *"bamouse, bamouse,"* calling over the Spanish-Mexican term, *"vamos,"* which they used for "leave, get out, go," and a half-dozen similar exclamations. These same fellows had enjoyed the privilege, in New Mexico, of keeping the "great unwashed" at a respectful distance from the provision trains; they thought the same ejecting appellation would serve for the Arapaho.

Among the Indian boys splashing and riding across the river on the empty wood wagon was one of thirteen years, whose features wore such a mild and manly air, and whose eyes were turned on me so intelligently, I took him to my baggage, put on him a clean, bright blue shirt, and then tied a colored handkerchief around his neck. His hair was neatly combed, and the deerskin moccasins fitted nicely. When I sent him away with some brown sugar, he looked the happiest boy in the country.

The traders with whom these Indians had been fighting arrived about three o'clock. Not a savage was visible. For three consecutive days, they fought these Indians, who, charging, hamstrung the oxen and annoyed them much. This outrageous conduct was the principal theme of conversation, which the sight of the distant lodges increased to such a degree that one well-proportioned six-footer proposed, with the cannon, to "rake the village." Now, we were opposed to this decisive measure for two good reasons. First was the indiscriminate slaughter of women and children that would have ensued. The second was that on our own heads and weak fort would have fallen the speedy vengeance of the tribe. Not choosing to remain the scapegoats of their iniquities, we at once refused the use of our gun—and told them they should take it by force alone.

Nagle, the recruit, and others came in from the hunt, their animals loaded with buffalo. The men were out of available funds, and to accommodate them, as well as ourselves, Sloan and I, from the traders, bought a box of chewing tobacco. I was to open an account with each man and supply them, and receive in return drafts on the quartermaster.

Cowhorn borrowed fifty cents, bought tobacco, traded it for moccasins, which selling to the teamsters, gave him three dollars' gain. Sloan purchased six gallons of whiskey; and, out of the "mess fund," our untiring cook, Cain, laid in a store of saleratus and pepper sauce, thereby contributing much to the relish for government rations.

The next morning the traders left for Santa Fé, and the

United States train, homeward bound, "rolled on," with many an agonizing shriek from the rickety, sun-cracked wagon wheels. I drew up a paper for Sloan to sign, showing what had become of the man received into service, so that the captain of the train, on arriving at Fort Leavenworth, could satisfactorily account for the nonappearant. With the train, our invalids left. Poor fellows! They no doubt had a wretched time jolting over the road in springless wagons, and little probability was there of their ever reaching the States. We shut the gates and cautioned anew the guard. How different the scene within two short hours! Of a busy crowd of 120 men and 60 wagons, none save our little force remained.

Toward noon the next day, the sentry shouted—"Train in sight!" Soon a wagon and horsemen appeared. Turning from the trail, they passed the fort in a long trot and encamped three hundred yards distant. I was glad to see Messrs. St. Vrain, Folger, and Chadwick—old friends; also, F. P. Blair, Jr., Estis (the Taos tavernkeeper), and Fitzgerald, the dragoon. Tibeau, the Canadian driver, and Blas, the Mexican herder, were along, too. A goodly company, indeed! They had twenty-five horses and mules, in prime order. That morning, thinking the Arapaho village to be Camanche lodges, they moved to an island in the Arkansas and threw up a temporary fortification. They stopped two hours, and then concluded to run the risk.

Mr. St. Vrain urged me to go with him, offering me a horse to ride. He said it was foolish to stay with so weak a force and that I would assuredly lose my scalp. I became scared when such mountain men feared danger, but feeling bound to Captain Enos, we parted, and sorry enough was I.

One night Sam and I were on guard. The rain poured

in torrents, the air was damp and chilly; and, as we knew bowstrings and flintlocks would not avail the foe much in an encounter, we merely leaned in the doorway and listened by turns and, at intervals, floundered in the mud from porthole to gate. Some spoiled buffalo meat, thrown over the wall, attracted many wolves. I watched, not five feet distant, through a port, where, in the dim light, the coarse gray hairs of the back could be seen bristling with rage. At daylight, one large fellow remained, slowly retreating and returning. I put the government musket (not caring to use my rifle in the rain) through a loophole, and, aiming at the animal twenty-five steps distant, fired, killing him immediately. When the gates were opened, Sloan and I dragging him in, took off the hide, and stretched it with pegs to dry.

We again worked, this time making our own brick. Some dug earth, others, with the fore wheels (tongue and hounds attached) of the cannon wagon and a half-barrel, brought water from the river, playing "hossey," as our fat commander facetiously observed. We had two yoke of oxen to tramp the mud; and I, being the least strong of the company, with a long stick punched up "Ball and Bright," when their movements grew tardy.

The 7th of June, according to our reckoning, was Sunday—no work in consequence. The "Three Guardsmen" and my pocket Testament amused us (can't vouchsafe a great amount of edification) for a while, and, in the evening, we shot at a target across the fort yard.

The painful necessity of making brick was forced upon us at last, with all its muddy unpleasantness. The molds were sixteen inches long by eight in width and four in depth—the facsimile of brick molds on a larger scale. These were filled with stiff mud and turned out on the smooth ground—the molds brought back, dipped in a barrel of water to free them of earthy particles, filled again, and so on *ad infinitum*. Johnson and I, the carriers, had two molds each; the wet adobes grew heavier as the work progressed. Three hundred and twenty-six were the result of the day's labor.

Mr. Coolidge, with four wagons and five men from the Arkansas Pueblo and the Platte, arrived during the day. He concluded to remain here for a further reinforcement, ere proceeding through the suspicious "Coon Creeks."

We made 210 adobes on the 12th, and then employed ourselves in digging a ditch beyond the fort walls to carry off the accumulated rain water, which might engender sickness the coming summer.

Roy, Nagle, Rasamus, and one of Coolidge's men went for buffalo. Being absent the entire day, we felt much anxiety for their safety. It was late at night. We gave up all hope of seeing them and were moodily cogitating what to do in regard to fortifying ourselves more securely, when a rifle report and a shout not to fire were heard. Rushing up the ladder, the men whom we had scalped in our imaginations answered to their names.

"What's the matter? What kept you so long?" asked we, impatient to know.

"Oh! had to go a long ways for meat; then a chase of five miles; hottest kind—were way out on Coon Creeks."

"See any Indians?"

"Yes! darn 'em, sixteen. They gave chase for a mile; but, after a few shots, one was wounded by Roy, and they hauled off. Rasamus was pretty bad scared—thought his hair was gone; he began to talk about Franklin."[2]

Sam and I were waked up at midnight to stand post—

2 Cowhorn's home, in Missouri.

the rain pouring. We did not leave the messroom. Thinking the foe would not attack in such weather, we sipped at the hot, lye-like coffee, and smoked until off of duty.

No work on the 14th, by reason of the incessant rain. We had two packs of cards, and as the specie circulation was limited, rations of beans served as legal tenders; the way they changed hands was a caution to hungry men.

In the Indian attack on the trading party, a colt was captured by the latter, which was given to Sloan. In commemoration of the event, he named it Camanche. One night, hearing a strange moaning, we collected to inquire. Seizing our rifles, we found poor Camanche outstretched, with a half-dozen wolves at work on him. We drove the brutes away, and carrying the victim into the fort, saw that he was too badly eaten to live; he was shot with a pistol. In the morning a few well-picked bones and strips of sinew were all that remained.

No work on June the 15th, by reason of the sullen rains. This was my eighteenth birthday. Quite a different one from the last—then at home and nothing particular to do but to cast enervated glances at dull books—here, in government service and surrounded by the most hostile Indians on the continent, my scalp in danger of sudden hoisting on some yelling Camanche's lance point—my body drenched by frequent night rains. Well! there is something refreshing in variety, and the comforts of civilization will be better appreciated when regained.

The afternoon was sunshiny and warm; the swollen Arkansas received our nude bodies in its swift current, after a half mile's run up the bank; while the sentry on the fort and another on the river's edge looked sharp for the foe.

In the middle of the day a train hove in sight, and camped near the "Caches." Roy started for it, though he might have been killed before going halfway. He soon returned with several men. To my surprise Charley M'Carty, with whom I parted in the spring on the Poinel, in New Mexico, shouted—"Why old fellow, you here! what have you been doing since I left you? St. Vrain told me you was in Taos, on guard, when the old palous were hung, and that you cut a 'big swath' generally."

"In government service," rejoined I. "I wanted to see an Indian fight, though my curiosity is not yet gratified. We have come quite near it, however."

"If they'd see you in the settlements with those buckskins and old wool hat, you'd pass for one of the mountain boys—be da-arned if you wouldn't! Do they feed you on 'Old Ned,' as Hatcher called the pork?"

"Where are you going, and what's your party—government or traders?" asked I.

"I'm bound for old Fayette County, where white people live—where you can get cornbread and sleep sound at night without having screeching yellow devils skulking around ye; and, old feller, there's a girl that wants to see me, and I'd give my mule to see her—be da-arned if I wouldn't—you know I told you about her last winter; she's the greatest—"

"Never mind now, Charley—we'll talk of your girl after a while. Nobody here cares for her but yourself. I want to know who is in the train yonder—maybe I have friends—a scarce genus in this region."

"That's a great old way to bluff a feller off, when he's half-froze to see his girl, but if you *want* to know, Colonel Russell from California, secretary of state, under Frémont, is in that crowd, with sixteen of the greatest 'boys' you ever came across. They are of the California Battalion. The Colonel is bearer of dispatches to Washington, from Stockton—"

A Welcome Arrival

"Who are the rest? There are at least thirty wagons."

"A train of 'Neds,' under command of Captain Bell, of the *wagon masters*' department. Any danger of Pawnees here?"

"Yes, there are a few about, but walk in."

The fort soon filled with the hard-looking teamsters, and before long, Colonel Russell himself appeared, dressed in California buckskin pantaloons, open from the knee downward, a light summer coat, white wool hat, and yellow California *zapotes*. Charles introduced me. On hearing my name, he asked that of my father. He then grasped my hand warmly, saying they were classmates in college. We went to the provision room, and sitting on some flour sacks, talked of friends far away.

"What brought you out here, my boy; your mother, of course, gave you leave, and how long have you been in the country?"

Seeing the drift of that and other questions of like import, I replied—"Do not think, Colonel, I came here in an improper manner, for I have letters with me to show to the contrary—this is a trip for fun and health, though I must say it's rather rough fun."

"I am indeed pleased to hear it, for at first I feared that you had committed some misdemeanor, as many youths do, and run away in consequence, but, my dear boy," said he, laying his hand affectionately on my shoulder, "you are in a most dangerous place; I wonder you have not been killed before this. I never heard of such a thing before. Ten men in a fort in the Camanche range, and you are *hardly* a man yet, you know!"

"Oh! 'our hearts are big,' and we are all center shots."

"You must go along with me, only ten men in the fort! it is sheer madness to be here," soliloquized he.

"I have promised Captain Enos to stay until relieved by troops from the States."

"Ah! but we must waive all such rash promises. Had I a son here, no greater kindness could be done me by a friend than to take him away—you must go—you must go."

"Smith has my mules."

"You can take the best one in my *caballada*. Were you to be killed here, I would never cease to blame myself."

Through the Colonel's solicitation, Sloan gave me a discharge, entitling me to pay on reaching Fort Leaven-worth and showing that I left with his consent. I made a hasty settlement with him of the fort accounts, tobacco, &c., put my small kit in the Colonel's wagon, my saddle on one of his best mules, shook hands with my tried friends, and with light heart, bade farewell to the "Prairie Prison." Cain Strickler, Sam Caldwell, and others, coming in with a load of wood, met me a short distance out. Sam shouted: "What's up now, that you are going to leave—not showing the white feather—if you are, may the cursed Camanches get your scalp"—

"Hold on, old fellow, take breath and I'll tell you; Colonel Russell, here, is an old friend of the family; and, when he found me out, he would not let me stay. Well, good-bye; Sloan will tell you more; the train's gone on, and for the sake of my 'hair' I must keep with them."

"Give us your hand, my hearty," and a warm grasp was our parting salutation.

The party with which I was now associated numbered eighty-five men, sixteen of whom composed Colonel Russell's guard, in command of Lieutenant Brown. The Colonel and his party, for thirty-five days of their route in to Santa Fé, were compelled to live on the meat of their broken-down mules. I at once made Brown's acquaintance.

A Welcome Arrival

He was attired in Apache-Indian costume—a graceful dress. Two years before this, he went from the Missouri frontier with a company of emigrants to California—thence to the Sandwich Islands. He returned to find affairs in a turbulent state, and received an appointment as second lieutenant in the California Battalion. Soon after, he was detached in command of this escort. He was, at the time of our meeting, not twenty years of age.

We went about three miles to camp. The Colonel's tent was pitched. He and I became its inmates, where we talked until his sable cook announced supper. Camp presented a lively scene. Charley McCarty, holding in his hand the wolf skin I had given him, was telling a group of teamsters, full of supper, stretched at length on the grass, how the musket had skinned my nose when the wolf was killed. Some of the men were cooking, others corralling the mules and oxen, and all, with joke and laugh, making themselves merry.

My own spirits, not less from the contagion of this gaiety than from the great change that had just taken place in my circumstances, felt a corresponding elevation. I cannot be too grateful to Colonel Russell for his genuine kindness to me. He is an honor to his native state, Kentucky, and a valuable acquisition to that of his adoption—California.

CHAPTER XXIV

THE BRUSH

W E WERE started early. The wagons traveled in double file, so that in case of an attack from the leagued Camanches and Arapahoes, whose propinquity was as well known as dreaded, they would not be strung along too great a space. The *caballada* was driven and kept between these two lines of the train.

Late in the afternoon, when the sun was fast sinking to its golden-hued, silver-flecked bed and the drooping ears of the flagging mules betokened weariness, objects were seen directly before us in the trace. Keen-eyed Barton, in calling our attention to them, uttered his opinion in the single significant word, "INJUNS!"

"Indians, say you, Barton?" inquired the Colonel, looking in the direction pointed, "Indians? Upon my word I believe so. Come on, we'll reconnoiter and say nothing to the train until the fact is ascertained—indeed, I hope not" —and, striking spurs into his large brown California mule, he loped forward, followed by some eight or ten of us. We soon ascertained, beyond a doubt, enough danger to lessen our party to five—the Colonel, Barton, Brown, McCarty, and myself, who kept on until within less than a quarter of a mile of the large party of mounted warriors. That portion of our men who had put back with all possible speed set the train in a ferment by their prodigious narrations.

The Brush

In front, on the opposite rise of ground, was a sight to make the stoutest heart among us quail; for the Indian force, displayed within long rifle shot, numbered, according to our unanimous estimate, four hundred strong, glittering with gay pennons, bright lance heads, and savage ornaments. Young braves rode their plunging barbs restlessly to and fro. The shrill and startling notes of preparation reached us but too plainly; and we hurried back to await for the expected charge. The train was in almost inextricable confusion, but the Colonel soon restored order. The wagons, mules, and men advanced to the brow of the hill and made a corral; that is, the two front wagons came together, and the inside fore wheels of those following were made to touch the outside hind wheel of the one immediately in front. In this manner, a secure but irregular oval pen was formed, into which were driven the oxen, the *caballada*, and the riding animals, thus leaving the men free to devote their whole attention to the enemy. There was little noise, but much alacrity and considerable trepidation among the poor teamsters, thirty of whom were without firearms. We had scarcely finished our preparations for defense, when the Indians, with poised lances, furiously charged upon us. For some time they circled around our corral with guns unslung and white shields continually shifted to protect their bodies. At last they drew rein, and, on each side of our party, commenced a lively demonstration, sending their balls singing through the air, some overhead, some perforating the wagon sheets, and some knocking the fur from our hide-bound oxen.

We were drawn up in line outside, fronting the main body, two hundred and fifty yards distant. We gave them several rounds, one-half of us reserving fire until the discharged arms were reloaded. The Indians scattered after

283

our rather ineffectual volleys, and their position became more menacing, their war whoops more dissonant and savage than before. We posted ourselves about the wagons, each man to his liking. Lieutenant Brown with five men took a position on a knoll fifty yards from us, and kept up an incessant firing, which was warmly reciprocated by the foe. It became exciting; the warriors galloping furiously, bent down, now on this side, now on that, until nothing of their person could be seen but the heel and part of the leg thrown across the cantle of the saddle. From under the horse's neck would issue a smoke cloud, as we heard the sighing of the ball as it cut its way overhead or knocked the dust from the dry plain. Sharply-sighted rifles gave ready answer; cheers rang out from our exhilarated party, and unfortunate oxen, stung by furrowing bullets from lumbering *escopetas*, plunged and horned each other from side to side of the crowded corral.

A California Indian belonging to Colonel Russell, ran, with gun in hand, far out toward the foiled enemy, making the Indian sign of insult and derision and, in Spanish, abusing them most scandalously. He came back before long, in no small hurry, with three of the outraged foe at his heels, who were in turn repelled at fullest speed by us. A ball overhead causes even the coolest man to dodge involuntarily, however surely he may know that the whistling bullet has already missed him. This is especially the case in a desultory scattered fire. Many a hearty laugh was had at the ludicrous positions into which we found ourselves thrown by these badly-aimed missiles.

The Indians detained us an hour, and then, relinquishing their *coup* attempts, moved off toward the west, to our extreme gratification. Had the charge been made before the corral was formed, they would have scalped the whole party, for our force was small and composed for the most part of green teamsters. Yoking up, we reached camp by the river's side, hot, thirsty, and irritated at our meager "satisfaction."

June 19th. The train proceeded with much caution. Indian spies watched us in the distance, hanging like wolves on our rear; the gleam of their lances was often seen among the sand buttes beyond the river. They were evidently intending to make another descent on the first fair opportunity. Our flank guards were on the alert, and the day ended without a conflict. The country was sparsely wooded with cottonwod and box elder, and *bois de vâche* supersedes substantial fuel for several days' travel through the region of the "Coon Creeks."

Our animals were saddled, hitched, and the train in motion after an early cup of coffee. The air brisk and cool, and the sky clear, gave promise of a fair day's travel; and even uneasy fears of Camanche attack were not sufficient to check our joyous feelings. It was the duty of the horsemen to push forward at mealtime, select a camp, and wait for the arrival of the train. Near noon, we entered a large "bottom," horseshoe-shaped, around which the river made a circuit of three miles or more. The wagons kept the trace across the neck, and a party, composed of Colonel Russell, Mr. Coolidge, and myself, on mules, and three others, on horses, followed the course of the stream to gather fuel. This I laid across the pommel of the Colonel's saddle as I collected it, and he was already loaded with sufficient to boil our cup of coffee and fry the slice of pork for which we were well prepared by several hours' fasting, when, all at once, the three horsemen strung out in a straight shoot for the wagons, without a word to us. "Hallo!" shouted we, "What's your hurry?" The fast-receding men said nothing, but pointed to the southwest, in which direction there approached, at full speed, a war party of about forty, endeavoring to cut us off from the wagons which were then corralling in great confusion. Dusky figures and light puffs of smoke showed faintly in the distance, the attack on the straggling train. No time was to be lost in rejoining our company, and back we spurred, to the tune of Camanche take the hindmost. The lines of the Indian attack and our return were convergent, and it was a mere question of speed whether we lost our topknots or gained the corral. The pursuers already had the advantage. The Colonel threw down his wood, and I replaced the old cap on my rifle with a fresh one, determined that one should "go under" before my "hair was lifted." I led the retreat, mounted on a small iron-gray mule—a native of the California savannas—who bounded most gallantly—for a mule —over the prairie. Colonel Russell followed in my wake, but Coolidge was still behind. Our pace seemed snail-like, and we jammed our rifle butts into the flanks of the poor beasts most unmercifully.

"Come on, Coolidge," shouted the Colonel to the frightened trader, "come on, we'll soon be safe."

"Yes, yes! but this fool animal isn't worth a cuss for running," and, with that, he gave the poor mule another "*chug*" with his sharp rifle stock. No exertion was spared, no incentive was neglected, to urge our dull beasts along; and though there was but small chance for escaping a lance thrust, we answered loudly their yells. When within three hundred yards of the wagons, I looked back and saw Coolidge far behind, with several Indians close upon him, the foremost brandishing his lance. I shouted to the Colonel that Coolidge was gone, and immediately we jerked our animals around. The colonel aimed hastily, fired, and galloped back to the corral. I spurred on to cover Coolidge's retreat, who came lumbering with the *"Owgh-owgh-he-a"* of his pursuers close to his ear. When I drew rein and placed it between my teeth, my mule, contrary to all precedent and custom, stood stock still, while I took steady aim at the nearest savage, who, flying along with eager look and harsh yell, was striving to make a sure blow. His band followed on his track, at distances various as their horses' speed. Coolidge, with eyes staring with fright, bent close down to his mule's neck. When I first drew bead on the Camanche's painted hide, he was approaching in a quartering direction to my right; as the gentleman was rather fleshy about the umbilical region, and tender withal, to make a sure shot, I kept the silver bead at my rifle point at that particular spot until he had passed to the left. With the report, the yellow devil's leg twitched in pain (I was so close to him that I could see even his features with disagreeable distinctness), and throwing up his horse's head, he galloped off to the river. Those who watched say that he did not come back.

Reloading at full speed, Coolidge and I hurried into the corral, which was just being closed. We dismounted, merely giving each other a look of congratulation; for the rattling of the guns and the war whoops and yells of the men drowned our voices, and left us nothing to do but fight. For that work, with a good will and quite systematically, we prepared ourselves. The Colonel's party were firing with much earnestness. A short distance of the place we were gathering wood, a large force was descending the sand buttes, glittering with bright gun barrels, swords, and lances—a well-armed band. They crossed the river in a trot, which was quickened into a charge as they reached the bank, and, at 150 yards distance, they opened their fire.

For a few minutes, rifles, war whoops, *escopetas*, hurrahs, contended in discordant strife—a tumult of wild sounds. But they could not stand our well-directed fire, and fell back. They left no dead on the field. This is never done, and the only token of the effect of our balls was by the wounded precipitately leaving the immediate scene of action. To give straight-out evidence of injury, by show of pain or otherwise, is a breach of their code of honor—an infringement severely rebuked by the taunts of the tribe— a weakness not soon forgotten or forgiven by the old chiefs, whose duty and care it is to sustain, by precept and example, the national bravery and hardihood. They consider not the death, merely, of an enemy, a victory—a *coup* must be counted. On a horse-stealing expedition, this is a horse; in battle, a scalp; and the trophies must be shown at home, before the warrior is allowed to decorate his robe with the black hand.[1] When an Indian falls too far gone to rescue himself, his friends rush up and bear him off between their fleet steeds.

They rallied and again circled around us, with their white shields protecting their bodies, tossing their spears and showing off their beautiful horses and their own graceful persons to the best advantage. Their intention was to make a charge on the first vulnerable point, but we, being too well guarded, they, after many feints, fell back. I sat flat on the ground, my rifle resting on the spoke of a wagon wheel—firing as often as an Indian came within range— and, when the painted, war-whooping target *vamosed* for safer quarter at the crack of the gun, certainly no other than a smile of satisfaction lit up my face. If none fell outright, it was not that any qualms of conscience prevented my tak-

[1] The warrior who counts a *coup* is allowed the distinction of wearing a black hand, painted on the flesh side of his robe.

ing cool and sure aim at those who, after chasing a mile and nearly scaring the life out of us, were then keeping us penned in the hot sun without water.

One Indian, who, from his distinguished, though scanty, dress, was a "brave" of the first order, came close into our lines, throwing himself behind the body of his horse, so as to show nothing but a hand and foot; but, as he raised himself, one of the Colonel's men cut, with his rifle ball, a neatly-dressed skin, that hung at his neck, which we picked up after the fight, as our only trophy. They now tossed their balls into us from a long distance, by elevating their pieces, being convinced that our corral could not be broken without great loss of life. Two teamsters, about this time getting scared at the whistling missiles, crept, for security, into an empty wagon. They had scarcely made themselves comfortable when a ball, crashing through both sides of their defense, buried itself in the side of a poor steer. The terrified Neds tumbled out, greeted by the roars of the men around.

"That's what you get for your cussed cowardice," drawled out one of the fellows.

"Well, I'll be darned, if that wasn't a grazer," ejaculated Charley McCarty. "Feel if you haven't got a hole in your dogskin—I'd hate to be as bad scared as you, by thunder!"

We were detained upward of two hours. Our fatigued and heated oxen were nearly dropping with thirst. The savages filed slowly up the sand buttes on the other side of the river, and we proceeded to camp, each man talking of his own shots.

June 22. We expected to reach the Pawnee Fork during the morning's march, and as there were bluffs near the camp and several streams intervening, thick-set with tim-

ber, favorable for ambuscade, the advance guard preceded
the train a quarter of a mile. We were on the alert, our
eyes searching every object, our guns ready to fire, as with
bridle rein firmly grasped, we galloped along in the bright
summer morning. Our exposed position and the continual
expectation of the Camanche yell kept us excited wildly
enough, although no foe delayed our march. By noontide,
the saddles were off—the wagons corralled, and the tent
pitched once more. Among the remains of the old camps,
I found the skull and skeleton of an Indian. The sinews,
well gnawed by the wolves, were not yet dry, and the skin
and hair still graced the head, which, passed from hand to
hand by the curious, was, at last, tossed into the turbulent
waters of the flooded Pawnee Fork. The Camanche whose
head this was had been killed a few days previous in an
encounter with traders. One or two others "went under"
at the same time, but their bodies had been rescued.

On the opposite side of the creek, a train from the
States was stopped like ourselves by the risen waters. I
accompanied some of our men over to it. We swam across,
holding our shirts and buckskins in one hand. At the camp
we found a government train, some traders' wagons, any
quantity of gaping men, and a *white woman*—a real white
woman! and we gazed upon her with great satisfaction and
curiosity. After gleaning the "news," we returned in a full
run to the creek and, crossing as before, retailed our scanty
information.

The next day was beautiful, and we waited impatiently
for the slowly-receding stream to become fordable. The
men scattered on both banks, the grazing cattle and *caballadas*, with the white wagon tops of the three camps, made
a serene and lovely scene. About ten o'clock an immense
drove of buffalo was seen running in the prairie to the

southwest. Some of our party set off in pursuit on their horses, while twenty or thirty of us ran down to intercept them as they crossed the creek. A faint cry of "Indians! Indains! Indians!" from the camp reached those nearest the mule guard, and by them it was repeated and wafted on to us, who, hardly knowing whether to cache in the undergrowth or to run for camp, stood for a moment undecided, and then "streaked it" for the wagons. Turning our eyes to the furthest train on the hill, we perceived it in great commotion. Fifty Indians were charging among them with their lances, recoiling from the light volumes of smoke at times, and again swallowing up the little force with their numbers and shutting them in from our sight. Others were stampeding the oxen. After a conflict of several minutes they retreated, bearing with them a dead warrior, behind the bluff hill which jutted boldly from the opposite shore.

Our teamsters, during the fight, looked on with mouth and eyes open in wonderment, regardless of their own cattle, still feeding in a deeply-fringed savanna. Tall cottonwood timber, overgrown with the luxuriant vine and thickset underbrush, impervious to the eye, confined our stock to this secluded spot. The creek, half encircling it with a grand sweep, added its protection. A light guard of three men watched the grazing herd. We were still congratulating ourselves on our escape, when from the guard we heard the cry that the Indians were swimming the creek and driving off the oxen. More than half the camp started in full run to protect them. As we rounded the angle of the stream, yells were heard, then the dusky forms of a few Indians were seen; and, by the time we were within long gunshot, some sixty were among the luckless herd, goading them into a lumbering gallop. The Colonel's party led the van, and would have saved the cattle had the teamsters supported them. But, they hanging back, we told them their oxen might go to ——. Hurrying back to camp, Colonel Russell mounted his force and went in pursuit; but in vain we tried to repair the loss that negligence and cowardice had effected. Our ride only rescued thirty oxen and gave us a view of the retreating savages thrusting their lances into the remainder. In that unfortunate half hour, the train lost 160 steers; which, at the purchase price—one-half less than they were worth on the prairie—was a damage of four thousand dollars, together with a total loss from five to seven thousand more in the necessary abandonment of the wagons—the natural result of sending on the plains a set of green men, commanded by as raw a director, poorly and scantily armed with government blunderbusses, and meagerly furnished with from eight to fifteen rounds of cartridges each, which were often wasted on game or targets long before reaching the Indian country. And this was not the only instance of miserable economy, as the official reports show.

Our train was in a sad condition; half a yoke to each wagon. Mr. Coolidge was really to be pitied—nearly four hundred miles from the States, with but two oxen to haul four large wagons, heavily loaded with robes and peltries. The Colonel carried a few packs (as many as he was able); he bargained with one of the outward-bound trains to take some back to Mann's Fort, and the rest he cached. The government people crowded their "kits" and provision in three wagons; and, toward evening of the next day, we crossed the creek, which had now subsided, leaving twenty-six wagons and any amount of extras, to the Indians and the wolves. Toward sundown, as we were hitching up to travel in the night, a party of dragoons, filing down the hill, made camp near. Lieutenant J. Love, commanding, was informed of the outrage and promised satisfaction. We stopped a moment at the train with which the first fight had occurred. One poor fellow, named Smith, from Van Buren County, Missouri, had been lanced seven times through the neck and breast. He killed the Indian that fell, while on his back and already wounded.

CHAPTER XXV

FAREWELL!

As we approached the States, running water and heavy timber became more frequent. The advance guard had a grand time the first night after abandoning the wagons, keeping far ahead of the now slim train, which the dim starlight, cut off by fleeting clouds, failed to keep in view. On approaching wooded streams, plainly marked by their blackness, our pace quickened into a gallop, and through it we spurred at a break-neck pace, uncertain whether a deadly blaze from northwest fusils or big-mouthed *escopetas* would welcome us. This we did that our speed might render an enemy's aim uncertain. It is a well-recognized rule of prairie warfare when darkness or thick cover gives concealment to the foe. We awaited the arrival of the train on the further bank; then, traveling on, we encamped about midnight near Pawnee Rock. The dew fell heavily, and by the time the mules were picketed, we, worn out with watching and riding, wet, cold, and hungry, retired to our blankets. In the morning, early, preparation was made by the mounted men for leaving the slow train; and, by seven o'clock, twenty-five of us, with one light wagon and a train of four mules, took our departure. We went to Walnut Creek to dinner (twenty-six miles). Taking the heavy Spanish bits from the mules' mouths to let them drink, we pitched our tent on the north bank. Here were the graves of Tharpe and McGuire, both killed by the Camanches.

Tharpe I have mentioned as being in the train with which John Smith left Mann's Fort. They proceeded thus far without molestation, and encamped as usual. Tharpe had left the wagons but two hundred yards, "approaching" a band of buffalo grazing near, when four parties of Indians, from as many points, charged in and threw all into confusion. Five of them fell; and Tharpe, after keeping his pursuers for a long time at bay, was killed and scalped. Repulsed, they retreated, carrying with them sixty head of mules and horses and forty yoke of oxen. Smith, to whom I had entrusted my two mules, Bonita and Diabolique, lost both of them and his seven.

Our exhausted party sank to sleep, until the Colonel's cook aroused us to our meal. A short nap, after eating, refreshed us still more, and we proceeded. Toward sundown we saw our last buffalo, rolling his unwieldly bulk out of rifle shot. We stopped, in the twilight, on the banks of the Arkansas, and, as a final farewell, I bathed my weary limbs in its tepid waters. After a laborious march through loose sand buttes, we wrapped in our blankets at ten o'clock, without keeping guard. During the next day we felt comparatively safe, though still maintaining caution. The country was flooded, and the water stood in pools over the soaked prairie; and, on a heavy, rainy morning, we breakfasted on Cottonwood Fork, eating our sobby food from a reeking saddle cover for a tablecloth.

On the first day of July, we met an encampment a few miles from Council Grove, and rode to it.

"Only a green teamster train," said one of the Californians returning, "a green lot for sure, but they've got arwerdenty, and that's a fact. Hurra for whiskey on a rainy day, any how!"

With the aid of a few bottles of the liquor, our crowd soon became uproarious. With lassoes whirling, they spurred their jaded mules, and in drunken merriment "roped" and hauled each other from the saddle. Wiping-sticks, hats, and even rifles fell unheeded to the ground, to be gathered by the two sober ones of the party, and the mad ride was ended by the whole party raising the war whoop and charging on a lot of greenhorns at Council Grove. The Colonel made camp a quarter of a mile from the grove and ordered his men to it, but they, ridiculously elated with their first spree, set all commands at defiance. The outward-bound train looked in astonishment at these leather-clad, weather-beaten Bacchanalians, and stood clear of their rifle stocks and lariats.

The next morning, Colonel Russell, Charley McCarty, Henry Murphy, the Colonel's Indian, and I left in advance of the train, with two pack mules, for the "States," hoping to reach the nearest frontier town, about two hundred miles distant, in three days. We jogged over the trail, moistened just enough by the late rains to be good traveling. We were grateful for the sweet prairie flowers and the green sward, for we were again in the long-grass country. Lively brooks with crystal waters danced past, over pebbly beds. The whirring grouse and the antlered deer attracted our attention as we crossed the open plain or entered the exalted forest.

But it was in the economy of nature to provide a set-off to the joyous contentment of our party. Myriads of biting flies attacked our poor beasts with such fury that speedy progress was impeded. Gouts of blood spotted their hides, and their efforts, although assisted by us with half-covered boughs, gave no relief. In a gnat-infested, fly-ridden, miserable-hot, and uncomfortable hollow, we made noon camp. That night we slept securely, without a guard.

Late at the close of another hot day, a neat log house stood in our path. It belonged to the nephew of the renowned Indian chief, Logan. We again sat at a table and enjoyed the kind hospitalities of this family, but preferred our blankets in the open air to the proffered bed. Bidding farewell to our kind entertainers in the morning, who would accept no remuneration, we rode through fields of waving corn, and pastures, whose fences and careful culture denoted the white man's civilizing hand. This was the domain of the Shawnees and Delawares, who farm extensively and are prosperous.

The shady banks of Blue River made our ride a short one, and, at sunset, we rode into the town of Westport, where, giving our mules to the hostler and pledging each other in *aguardiente* with the mountain toast of "luck," we sat down to supper in the United States, after an absence of many months. Our hands unconsciously found their way to the scalp knife at the waistband, and we laughed more than once at ourselves for using the left-hand fingers in lieu of the awkward two-tined fork. A nephew of the Pioneer Boone, with the old man's love for a frontier life, has here a store, at which I put myself into civilized garments. The old blue blanket, which had been my house and my pillow for a twelvemonth, I gave to a grinning Negro boy; the sorrow in parting with it being lessened by the idea, that with him, it would still be near the much-loved prairie.

Colonel Russell and his party went to Independence by land, and I rode four miles to Kansas on the coupling pole of our ox wagon, where I embarked on a steamer for Fort Leavenworth, to get my pay for services rendered. I dined with Lieutenant Prince, to whom I had a letter.

Captain Enos was absent, but I met him the next morning, gave him the state of affairs in the Territory, and at Mann's Fort, and he handed me my hard-earned dollars.

Our company was now broken up. Some went to St. Louis by land. I reached there by water, and from that point a speedy steamboat trip restored me to home and friends.